George Buchanan gives us a provocative and compelling portrait of Jesus we hardly know: a master diplomat, organizer, chief executive, and statesman. This is a story that will open our eyes to new possibilities in understanding the life of the Good Shepherd. Buchanan's Jesus is someone that every lay person will want to meet anew.

Mike McCurry, White House Press
Secretary 1995-98.

Professor George Wesley Buchanan has succeeded in tracking the historical Jesus, where others have failed. He has persisted like a bloodhound on the trail of a fugitive in flight. He tracks Jesus through the Holy Land and the greater Roman Empire using several forms and modes of analysis. He makes a good case. This book should prove ideal for Sunday School discussion groups. It opens new vistas for laymen and scholars alike. Professional scholars and historians ignore it at their peril.

Dr. Charles Shields, Esq.
Attorney at law.

Many know George Wesley Buchanan as a scholar who probes areas that other scholars dare not touch, but many will not know George Wesley Buchanan the pastor intent on addressing issues of relevance to the Church. In vintage Buchanan style, he draws on his extensive knowledge of the ancient world and its literatures, archaeology, and legal studies to prove the words and actions of the historical Jesus. The result is a provocative book that forces the reader to look at old data through new lenses–with surprisingly fresh, challenging, and insightful results.

Stanley E. Porter PhD
President, Dean, and Professor of New Testament
McMaster Divinity College,
Hamilton, Ontario, Canada

to our good friend,
Eddie McWilliams
for his honor

Jesus The Statesman

of becoming an

Without Default Settings

Eagle Scout

with many blessings

∽

George Wesley Buchanan

GEORGE WESLEY BUCHANAN,
PH.D., LITT.D., D.S.L.

TO MY SON

George Wesley Buchanan, Jr.

Contents

PREFACE

Most of the church members who asked me the questions that motivated me to spend nearly sixty years in research are no longer living. I am grateful, however, to the United Methodist Church for providing me with intelligent parishioners who were able to ask the thought provoking questions that I was unable to answer at the time. Those questions prompted me to spend the rest of my life finding answers that I did not know at the time they were asked. I am now publishing these discoveries so that other questioners may find answers that they also are asking. I also appreciate the good librarians who have assisted me in research in Hebrew Union College, The Institute for Antiquities and Christianity at Claremont, California, Indiana University, Cornell University, The government university at Göttingen, Germany, Hebrew University, Jerusalem, Catholic University, the Library of Congress, and especially Wesley Theological Seminary, where I still enjoy the benefits of the capable and kind librarians, Ms. Howertine Farrell Duncan, MLS, MDiv, Head of Public Services, and the librarian, Prof. D. William Faupel, Ph.D.

My former student, Rev. Tom Will Gregory has taught me almost everything I know about computer software and hardware that is required to write books such as this. Two of my friends, who are famous for their communication skills, Mike McCurry and Dr. Gregory Seckman, have both read this manuscript more than once and made important contributions to its clarity. My good friend and neighbor, the artist, Duane A. McKenna, designed and painted the book cover. I have learned much from three of my friends, Col. Edgar Martin Esq., Hon. Roberta Lamb Swartzendruber Esq., and Dr. Charles Shields III Esq., in my search for legal meanings of concepts used by Jesus. Dr. Richard Cleave, Rohr Productions, provided the aerial photograph included in this manuscript. My wonderful wife, Harlene, has proofread all of my books and almost all of the sermons, church school materials, and articles I have written for academic journals. I am thankful for all of these. I am especially grateful to have George Wesley Buchanan, Jr. for my son. He was a good Greek and history student early in life and wanted to get a Ph.D. in history, but when he graduated from the university, there were 3,000 unemployed people in the United States with Ph.D.s in history, so he became a successful accountant, but he has never lost his interest in languages and history. I am proud of his many achievements and gladly dedicate this book to him.

INTRODUCTION

PERSONAL EXPERIENCES

Pastoral Ministry. This little book represents the central insights that have come from fifty years of serious study about the historical Jesus. My professional Christian ministry began when I was appointed to my first church at the age of 22. The answers for which I searched ever since then have been mostly those that church members asked. Members of the congregations learned that I did not have all of the answers, but I was willing to listen to their questions, think about them, look for answers, and tell them as much as I knew and as much as I did not know. There was no question that anyone had that was too personal, threatening, or controversial for discussion. I had no religious, philosophical, or academic default settings that excluded questions. It seemed to me that there should be answers to these questions. If we knew the meanings of the biblical words and concepts, these terms would all make sense. Questions that were important to them were not to be dismissed. They became important to me, and I have spent the rest of my life finding answers to their questions. I have found most of them. There are reasonable answers to their questions, indicating that their questions were reasonable. I spent fourteen very happy years, vocationally as a pastor, while involved in continuously discussing questions raised by laymen and women of the United Methodist Church. The next 31 years were spent with students in a university and in a theological seminary. The questions students asked were the same questions church members had asked, and this book deals with those questions that are related to the historical Jesus.

Academic Development. I began believing that all of the things reported in the gospels that Jesus said were true. After more than half a century of study, I still think that it is mostly true. The difference is that now I know the academic basis for this belief. Academic study of the gospels, however, let me know that scholars had many questions about the validity of these reports. They reminded me that the church had preserved all the reports. They asked, "How could anyone know that the church did not only preserve them but also created them in the first place for their own defensive needs?" By the time I had finished my professional Master's degree, required for ordination, I still did not have all the answers. I needed more information, so I enrolled in an academic Masters Degree program, but I did not face the problem directly. Instead I took a sidetrack. I wrote my thesis on the theology of Paul. That seemed safer. Scholars did not challenge the existence of Paul, so I could concentrate on his theology without worrying about the historical problems.

I intended to continue in Ph.D. studies on Paul, but when I observed how far removed Jesus was from New Testament (NT) interests among scholars, I renewed my interest in the historical Jesus. Scholars seemed to think there was really nothing secure about the historical Jesus. You could not even be sure that he ever existed. In their judgment, it was the theology and psychology of the NT that was important. The question was not, "Did Jesus really say that, and if so what did he mean?" Instead it was, "What does this mean to you?" "How does it make you feel?" "When you read it, what does it make you think?" "It doesn't matter whether or not Jesus said these things and what they meant to him." "The important thing is what they mean to you, today." Jesus was only a stimulus to your thinking.

That was not satisfactory to me. As a Christian I should know about Jesus himself. How could you learn what Jesus really said? How could you test the data? It was not enough to learn what the German, English, French, and American scholars had conjectured 2,000 years after Jesus lived. I needed to learn as much as I could about the age in which Jesus lived, the historical circumstances in which he taught, the thought forms of the people of his country and generation, and his reason for teaching. I needed to study the historical Jesus the way I would study any other human being in history. This had to be done objectively, fairly, and without importing my own preferences and convictions into the picture. This is not easy for a Christian who has been reared and taught in the United States during the twentieth century, where Jesus had been reincarnated to match American individualism. Here we have been taught about Jesus, following the heroism of Abraham Lincoln, Saint Francis of Assisi, and Mahatma Ghandi. I was convinced that the search for the historical Jesus could not begin in any of the western countries. Jesus did not live in Germany, England, or the U.S.A. He lived in Palestine two thousand years ago. To learn about Jesus I would have to learn about the history, languages, and political situations, customs, and thought forms of the people in that geographical area and at that particular time.

During this time the Dead Sea Scrolls appeared, and they immediately attracted my attention. These were Jewish documents that had not been preserved, edited, or altered by the later church or the later synagogue. They were genuine, contemporary, Jewish writings. No one could accuse them of being the composition of later authors who attributed them falsely to Jews of an earlier day. They were not forgeries. They were roughly contemporary to the age of Jesus, and they reflected the political and religious situation of his day. I did not expect them to mention the name of Jesus or tell anything about him, but they would reveal something valid about the world in which Jesus had lived. Like Jesus, they were Jewish, so they could reveal customs and teachings that were similar to his.

After I had finished the academic requirements for a Ph.D., before writing my dissertation, I was invited to participate in an archaeological excavation at Shechem, near Nablus, Jordan. I went a couple of weeks early so that I could visit the actual caves and ruins at Qumran where the scrolls were found and where the community resided when they preserved them. In preparation for this, I learned a small amount of conversational Arabic from Victorola records used to train employees for the oil industry in Saudi Arabia. It was enough to allow me to converse with local Arabs, so every day, while the other members of the archaeological team were taking naps, I walked around the area and visited with Arabs in their tents, ate with them, drank water out of their goat skin bags, and had dysentery all summer long. In the process I learned a lot about customs the Arabs had preserved for thousands of years that reflected customs reported in the Bible. That was in 1957 before the Near East had been westernized. Since Jesus was a Jew who lived in this area, he probably practiced these customs, and taught people who understood them. That was important for me to know.

With the aid of an interfaith fellowship, I spent the next very important three years at Hebrew Union College, studying Hebrew intensively – biblical Hebrew, Rabbinic Hebrew, and modern Hebrew. This enabled me to read the Dead Scrolls easily from photographs of the scrolls themselves. While I was there I also enrolled in the graduate school of classics at the University of Cincinnati and became competent in classical Greek as well as New Testament Greek.

By the end of three years I could readily read the Bible in Hebrew just as Jesus would have done, and I had become familiar with rabbinic literature, some of which was similar to the scrolls and to the reported teachings of Jesus. I also understood rabbinic rhetoric. Since I was also studying Aristotle and Quintilian, the classical Greek and Latin scholars of rhetoric, I noticed the similarity between the logic of the rabbis and that of the Greek and Latin teachers of rhetoric. In the process I became familiar with a Greek literary form known as the chreia (*khráy-ah*), which became very important for testing the validity of Jesus' teachings. These will be introduced in the next chapter.

Prior to the discovery of the Dead Sea Scrolls the earliest documents of the First Testament (FT), which is often called the Old Testament, belonged to the tenth century after the life of Jesus. Scholars assumed that the numerous scribes that had copied these texts for hundreds of years had made many changes and had introduced scribal errors, but when the same documents were found that had been written more than a thousand years earlier they were so similar to the biblical texts that the skepticism almost vanished. Scribes had been faithful. I wrote my Ph.D. thesis on the Dead Sea Scrolls and continued studying Greek and Syriac New Testament (NT) and Hebrew and Aramaic FT while teaching at a theological seminary. With the aid of a Claremont-Society of Biblical Literature fellowship and an Association of Theological Schools fellowship, I spent a sabbatical year using the excellent classical library at Claremont, CA. I also spent most of two sabbatical years and a few summers in Israel, Jordan, Lebanon, and Syria, learning the geography and topography of the land, engaging in boundary research, and translating many medieval Jewish documents.

An important unplanned area of research was in modern civil law. Because I needed legal support in response to injuries, and I could not afford lawyers, I found it necessary to study modern law and be able to defend myself in court. Fortunately, I had a student, Col. Edgar Martin, who was a retired attorney who spent about an hour teaching me how to use a law library. I adapted to the situation very quickly, and I have continued to learn from other attorney friends. I learned that much of the same kind of logic, the same arguments, the same practices, and the same trial techniques used today in modern courts were used three thousand years ago. The kinds of satisfactions that are provided by courts today are often the very same judgments made in biblical courts and Roman courts, years ago. Learning these from modern books and journals of law clarifies concepts in the Bible that are also legal. Legal insights are helpful in defining the meaning of practices and teachings of Jesus. Jesus was well trained in the field of law.

It was from legal insights that I learned the validity of some church confessions and New Testament claims about Jesus. Chapter six will show how Jesus could be both human and divine, what it meant to be born of the spirit, and what it meant to be born of a virgin.

Application of Academic Insights. Throughout this entire period of discovery, I was relating the insights I learned to the historical Jesus. I never moved away from the church. I continue to preach, teach, and sing in the church. My research was directed in two ways:

1) I needed to know about reliability of the literature that preserved the teaching of Jesus, and
2) I needed to know what these teachings meant at the time Jesus lived. Therefore, I continued to study the geography of the land where Jesus lived, the Jewish customs and teachings of his day, and the political significance of Jesus' titles of Messiah, King, Son of God, and Son of man.

I first published the results of my research for scholars in *Jesus: the King and his Kingdom* (Macon: Mercer U. Press, 1984). I have learned more since then but that book contains much of the documentation necessary to support the claims made in this little book. The difference is that I have had more time to clarify my insights and offer them to a different reading public, so I have omitted all of the technical footnotes and detailed arguments, but I also updated this book to reflect new insights. Anyone who reads this book and wants documentation may turn to the earlier book.

While I was engaged in the research necessary for the book, I did not follow the methods of study designed by anyone else. I moved from one institution to another – not just to get more academic degrees – but primarily to learn what I needed to know about the historical Jesus. I do not belong to any of the recognized schools of research. I began this research when no one else was interested in the subject. I was the one who chose where I would go, and what I would do to find out what I wanted to learn. I had good teachers, good libraries, and good archaeological opportunities, but they were in different places related to different institutions, and I learned different things from them. Consequently the results of my research are different from all other books on the historical Jesus that are on the market today.

The Hound Dog Researcher. Hound dogs are different from Collie dogs. Collie dogs are useful on the farm. They go out by themselves, on command, into the pasture and gently bring all of the cows or sheep in to the barn. Once this is done their days are over. They never notice any wild beasts and are not capable of smelling a trail to start looking for a beast that is not in sight. Instead of calling me a Collie dog, people have sometimes called me a "hound dog researcher." I spend a lot of time sniffing out trails that others do not realize exist. The image is that of a hound dog trailing a wild beast. The animal comes to a fence with a sign, saying NO TRESPASSING, but the beast finds a hole in the fence and goes right on through. When the hound comes to that fence and sign, what does the hound do? It goes right on through, if possible. If not, it digs under the fence or jumps over it, but it is not deterred either by the fence or the sign. If the beast escapes into a hole, the hound starts digging. If the beast goes up a tree, the hound has a special howl, hunters understand, and it barks "treed." That means to the hunter that the hound has the beast isolated up a tree. It continues with its goal of catching that beast. I do the same. The NT signs of prohibitions do not specifically say, "No Trespassing." They come in the form of nineteenth century hypotheses, following the consensus, and being politically "practical." Here are some of the signs.

1) It is forbidden to think there is any literature about Jesus earlier than the Gospel of Mark.
2) It is forbidden to look in the Gospel of Matthew, Luke, or John for any quotations of Jesus.

3) It is prohibited even to think of suggesting that consensus scholars are ever wrong.

I also have come to many "fences" and read many "warning signs," but I have not allowed them to limit me. The primary reason that I have made some wonderful discoveries that I have found is that I did not follow the standard, consensus strengthening practices. Here I am sharing some of the insights.

This book is not just for devoted Christians; it is planned for people who should be interested in the historical Jesus, just the way they are interested in Julius Caesar, Alexander the Great, or Napoleon, just because he was a very important leader in world history who deserves the interest of all those who came after him. It is also intended to be useful to church schoolteachers and other interested Christians. It will be a useful textbook for college or theological seminary students.

The following terms are some that are repeated many times in the book. They are here defined so that the reader will easily and readily understand the way they are used in the rest of the book.

GLOSSARY OF TERMS

Corporation. The word "corporation" comes from the Latin word, which means "body." A corporation, however, is not a physical body of flesh and blood. It is a legal body that has only legal existence, but that is very important. A corporation has all the legal rights and responsibilities of a human being. It can be defended in court; it can be taxed; it can be legally punished. It differs in that it never dies. All the members of the corporation can be changed, but the corporation continues.

There can be a corporation of one member, "a corporation sole." This consists of a physical human being who holds a legal office, such as a king. A king has two bodies,

1) a physical body that is born from a woman, grows, gets ill, and dies.

2) a legal body or corporation that never dies. This is the king's political or legal office, his corporation. When the physical king dies, the legal king continues and is matched up with another physical body. So the people say, "The king is dead. Long live the king!"

3) When Paul said that there was both a "natural body" and a "spiritual body" (1Cor 15:44) he meant there is a physical body and also a legal corporation. Most corporations consist of more than one member.

Today most Americans associate corporations with huge business institutions. That was also true in antiquity, but it was a normal part of everyday life as well. Most groups, large or small, had legal bases that most people understood. Today in western civilization many groups can be formed and discontinued easily and frequently. That was not so in antiquity. In antiquity almost everyone belonged to some group, but not to many groups. There were accepted ways by which people could join groups, but it was not done casually. It was a serious matter to become a member of a group, and once a person joined a group he or she was expected to continue as a member of that group for the rest of his or her life. The laws that defined the way people lived in those days provided them the security and stability they needed to belong to something greater than themselves. The group to which a person belonged provided the chief means by which each person was recognized.

Whether large or small, all of these organizations were legally organized and were understood to be corporations. Belonging to a group or family was an important part of life. American individualism was unknown. The ancients did not sing, "Don't fence me in." They wanted to be fenced into some stable organization. They wanted to be predestined to remain a member – "once in grace, always in grace," was the kind of security a corporation provided. No one wanted to be left out. Westerners today, who want to know anything about ancient human existence, need to know about the corporations to which people belonged.

The oldest corporations are family corporations, of which the oldest male member was the chieftain or "father of the family" (*pater familias*). The chieftain had understood authority, but his physical death did not fatally damage the corporation. His office would be filled with another member of the family, and the corporation would continue. At his death it was understood which member of the family would succeed him in office and what would happen to his possessions, debts, and credits. Well known laws governed the way all of this would happen. There were traditional ways of doing this, and almost everyone knew the laws by which they functioned.

Almost everyone belonged to one or more of these corporations. The family, legal body, or corporation to which a person belonged was more important than the individual. Loyalty to the corporation was a basic quality of existence. People were willing to die for the good of the group to which they belonged. A Spartan mother, for example, went out to meet the returning soldiers after a battle. The soldiers told her that her five sons had been killed. She then asked, "Did we win?" They said, "Yes." Then she responded, "May the gods be praised!" With all of the American individualism, there is still inherent in our culture the importance of belonging to something greater than ourselves, and we still have corporations. We know what it is to be loyal and patriotic, but we have not always associated all of this to being parts of corporations.

For example there is a corporation that began with the family of Abraham. Initially it began with only Abraham, his wife, and his son, Isaac. Later legal members were added by marriage or adoption. These became "in law" members of the family, but they had the same legal rights as those with Abraham's blood in their veins. Once they joined the family, they became the children of Abraham. Today all Jews, Samaritans, Christians, and Muslims claim Abraham as their father, even though there is probably not a single one who has Abraham's blood in his or her veins. The legal ties of corporation hold us together.

At the Last Supper Jesus performed a legal ceremony through which he established a new corporation of which he was the chieftain. It was called the "body of Christ" or the church. At first the apostles were the only members who belonged to that corporation, but the membership grew quickly and now numbers in the millions.

Monasteries existed centuries before the time of Christ. A monastery consisted of a legal corporation. No single member was physically born into the monastic family. All members left some other family and joined this family corporation by legal adoption. They were all celibate males who were legal brothers that had been legally born again. They were held together by their intense religious devotion and religious beliefs, which every monk professed. The monasteries were the first to organize groups beyond the genetic families with the equivalent of a president, secretary, and treasurer. All of the large corporations that exist today owe their organization structure to the early monasteries.

Legal Agency. Prophets, apostles, attorneys, and ambassadors are all legal agents. They are people who act and speak for others, rather than for themselves. The people for whom they act and speak are principals. A principal can be a king, a CEO in business, or a political officer, like a president. In the Bible, the prophets spoke and acted in behalf of God; and the New Testament apostles spoke and acted for Jesus.

If a king sent an ambassador to another country to negotiate with another king in behalf of the king who sent him, then the ambassador's word was as valid as if the king who sent him were physically present and speaking. The ambassador was the word of the king made flesh, or, said differently, the incarnate word of the king. Within the limits of his assignment, the ambassador was legally the king, and when the ambassador was present, the king was legally present. The Gospel of John begins with the word of God. When this word became flesh and was physically present, that meant that God had sent Jesus as his legal agent to speak and act in God's behalf, in his name, and at his responsibility (John 1:1, 14). Jesus was not God made flesh, but God's word made flesh. The one who had seen Jesus had legally seen the Father, but the

Father, as the principal, was greater (John 14:9, 28). Jesus claimed his status as God's legal agent 40 times in the Gospel of John.

Legal Birth. Physically, there was only one time and one way in which a person could be born. That was from his or her mother, but legally, there was a way by which a person could be born again. That was being born legally or spiritually. A person who belonged to one country, religion, or family could be born again through legal adoption into another country, religion, or family. This required some legal liturgy, such as baptism, the laying on of hands, anointing, marriage, naturalization, provision of new clothing, or coronation. Only women can bear human children, physically, but a male can bear a child – even an adult "child" – legally. For example Yehowah, a male deity, declared to an adult male, "You are my son. Today I have given you birth" (Ps 2:7). At the same time that some king was being crowned as an adult prepared to rule, he was also legally born again as a king – without an extensive gestation period. It was the male deity who appointed him to be the Messiah and gave him birth. No female was involved. By some legal ceremony a citizen could be born again as a king. A Roman citizen could be born again as a citizen of Egypt. The Pharisee, Nicodemus, could have been born again when he was old as a member of Jesus' legal family. This would require the liturgy of water (baptism), and the spirit (laying on of hands or putting on new Christian clothing) (John 3:1-5).

Coherence. The term "coherence" is used in this book in association with two or more literary units that are joined by some principle. They fit together like parts of a jigsaw puzzle. They are stuck together as if by glue. They are connected by some interrelatedness. They belong together in some basic way. In relationship to teachings, they are coherent if they have the same basic message and style. They reflect the same attitude, vocabulary; opinion, and point of view; they belong to the same geographical origin and the same period in history. For example, Jesus was shown by many teachings to be in conflict with the Pharisees. A teaching that was pro-Pharisaic would not fit the normal pattern of Jesus' teachings. Therefore it would not be coherent with the teachings of Jesus.

TEACHING METHODS

In western thought today, the teaching method of Socrates is well known. It is called the Socratic teaching method. Diogenes was a contemporary of Socrates, and in Jesus' day the teaching method of Diogenes was at least as well known as that of Socrates. The literary forms he used were popular with church fathers and secular writers at least until the time of Doxapatres (tenth century A.D.). Jesus used the same literary forms as Diogenes competently, so they will be introduced in the next chapter.

CHAPTER ONE

THE TECHNIQUES OF DIOGENES AND

THE TEACHING OF JESUS

(Anyone interested in the works of other scholars of the historical Jesus may stop at this point and read the appendix at the end of the book.)

The problem the biblical world is facing today is one for which I found the solution more than thirty years ago from the ancient philosopher, Diogenes, and the Greek rhetoricians. Once the rhetorical techniques of the ancient Greeks are known, it does not seem difficult at all to distinguish the teachings of Jesus from the additions of the later church, and it certainly is a worthwhile insight into knowledge about Jesus. It recovers the trustworthiness of the gospels that Kümmel thought was lost and that Johnson argued had not been found. A Christology without knowledge of Jesus is based only on a movement and a philosophical or psychological attribution. The Jesus recognized in all of his historical reality is much better than all of the fabrications and hypotheses that have been unrealistically attributed to him.

The amount of data for learning about the historical Jesus is extensive and historically sound. This chapter will only open the door so that we can begin to see the marvelous character revealed, but it will go further and show how it is possible to evaluate the text to begin such a research. This chapter begins by uncovering an important literary form that was popular in Jesus' day. It is not possible from the teachings of Jesus to provide a total biography of Jesus from his cradle to the grave, but they will provide significant information about the adult Jesus during the years of his ministry that are the most important to Christians. This study will show how the teachings of Jesus can be separated from the teachings of the later church, but it will not assume at the outset that the church was not a reliable agent for preserving these teachings. There is more basis for giving respect to the gospels than has been normally recognized.

THE CHREIA

The important form for Jesus study is the chreia. This literary form was not conjectured more than two millennia later by western scholars. It was popularized, and possibly invented by the philosopher Diogenes. I translated 194 chreias in which Diogenes was the character. They are impressively coherent. Anyone who wants to know about Diogenes should begin by reading all of these chreias. The techniques of Diogenes' teaching methods were more popular than those of Socrates at least until the tenth century A.D. Diogenes taught his students to use chreias in their learning process.

Diogenes and Jesus. Diogenes was one of the most interesting and important characters in antiquity. I learned about him while learning about Jesus. Before I became acquainted with Diogenes I had spent many years studying ancient history, philosophy, poetry, Scripture, and rabbinic literature in an effort to learn more about the people who lived in the Near East, either a few centuries before Jesus or a few centuries after Jesus. I wanted to know their customs and beliefs. All of this was useful, but it was not until I met Diogenes that I finally discovered something that I could test.

I wanted to know whether or not the things Jesus was reported to have said were reliable, or whether they were just handed down through the oral tradition. Then I was fortunate enough to learn about Diogenes. Kümmel was not the only scholar who thought that the gospels could not be trusted to have reported material about Jesus that was reliable. Many scholars think that later church members intentionally wrote the gospels to give false authority to their own arguments, rather than valid contemporary reports about Jesus. Therefore the gospel reports are not reliable. People who are not scholars have also heard about all of this skepticism and are asking if that is really so.

While I was confronting these questions I found an ancient three volume work in classical Greek that was designed as text books to train ancient lawyers and other public speakers in debate. Part of this instruction involved teaching students the kinds of literary forms that they had at their disposal, such as illustrations, fables, historical narratives, and poetry. One of these forms was the Chreia.

The Chreia as a literary form. A chreia was defined as something that was remembered so that it could be told. It was succinct and told about a person whom it credited. The person was identified and the entire unit was very brief. Chreias were familiar and used by Diogenes nearly 2,500 years ago. Diogenes was an ancient Greek philosopher and teacher. He may have designed chreias, himself. He certainly taught his students to use them, and the earliest record we have of chreias were those of Diogenes, and these continued to be very popular for more than a thousand years. For that reason the first chapter of this book about Jesus will introduce the readers to Diogenes. Although Diogenes seems at first glance to be off the subject, you will find that Diogenes was an interesting character and that Jesus learned some of his teaching skills from Diogenes.

Diogenes required his students to memorize important passages from the writings of great people, including his own.

He taught students short cuts in memory, which probably meant selecting sharp lines from Diogenes' writings and putting them into chreia form, so that a much larger report could be remembered. Memorization was an important part of education in those days, but that does not mean that it took the place of writing. Students learned to read and write, and they memorized important documents that had been written. Memorization was not an indication that no writing was involved. People did not memorize materials just because there were no textbooks. It was from an ancient three volume Greek text for teaching that I learned about the chreia. These volumes were written for the use of ancient students who could read. The existence of such textbooks as these makes it more difficult for scholars, like James Dunn, to continue claiming that there were no textbooks in antiquity. The existence of the Bar Mitzwah tradition also provides an obstacle to Dunn's affirmation. Jewish males were required to be able to read the written Scriptures by the time they were twelve or thirteen in order to pass their exams. It was this tradition that is reflected in the report of Jesus' early wisdom (Luke 2:40-49). Paul was speaking of the Bar Mitzwah liturgy when he told of his own experience "when the commandment came" (Rom 7:9), but Dunn holds that it is unlikely that either Jesus or Paul could read or write.

The learning went from the writing of Diogenes to writing of his students. They were used in a way that is similar to the use public speakers make of "triggers," today. Chreias were also created from the spoken word. When students heard important things that Diogenes said they did not just remember and tell them to later generations. They wrote them down at once in chreia form and collected them, so that they would be remembered. Whether they copied the quotations from the writings of Diogenes or wrote them down immediately after they heard them, it is likely that Diogenes actually checked the work and approved the writings that have survived. Quotations copied into chreia units were not lost in many years of oral tradition.

Most of these units are only one sentence long and were introduced by a grammatical form that was called a genitive absolute. A genitive absolute was an introductory phrase in a Greek sentence in which two things happened at chronologically different times. When that was the case, the Greek normally put the first event into an introductory phrase and the second into a declaratory clause. The introductory phrase included a participle, and every word that did not have to be placed in a different case because of its position in the phrase was put into the genitive case. Because the genitive absolute dealt with the first thing that happened, the phrase would be translated into English by some term like, "Having done or said thus and so" or "After he did or said thus and so" or "after this took place," then the following happened. That was a perfect form for a chreia. The person that was identified and the event that prompted the speaker or actor to speak or act were all put in the introductory phrase. That was followed by the quotation of the speaker. There were two kinds of chreias:

Kinds of Chreias.

1) The declaratory chreia: This told about something the speaker said many times, the writer would simply report, " . . . used to say . . . ." For example, "Plato used to say that his best students were children of the gods." That implied that Plato said that many times.

2) The responsive chreia was the one used most frequently: The student recorded

   a) the identity of the speaker or actor,
   b) the situation that prompted him or her to act or speak, and
   c) that which was said or done.

Diogenes often taught in the open market place, and at one time he evidently taught the children of some man named Xeniades. He taught them everything from good manners to philosophy. Like other ancient philosophers and rabbis who were teachers,

Diogenes taught his students all things they needed for life. This involved academic subjects, but also diet, athletics, proper etiquette, and ethical principles. Students were expected to imitate their teachers. Diogenes taught his students to memorize many passages from historians and poets, *as well as the writings of Diogenes himself.* An ancient historian, Diogenes Laertius, said Diogenes drilled his students and taught them how to record short cuts in memory (Diogenes Laertius 6:31). That may have involved using the literary form that became very important to later rhetoricians and historians

Instead of writing down all of the details of an event or a saying of some important person, Diogenes taught students how to select choice sentences from a text or a discussion and to summarize. In one sentence, in most cases, they could record enough to remind them of all the rest. This may have been the way this literary form originated. Rhetoricians later provided a label for these units, calling them chreias (*cráy-ah*). Although there are more chreias preserved in which Diogenes was the character than anyone else on record, other philosophers and leaders were subjects of chreias as well.

I have found and translated 194 chreias that have survived in which Diogenes was the principal character. These are amazingly coherent. Although Diogenes obviously wrote down his ideas, the only ones that have been preserved are in the chreias that have survived.

Someone, other than the character quoted, always composes chreias, but the character provided the quotation, either in speech or in writing. His students, for example, probably composed chreias about Diogenes. They may have selected the quotations from things they heard him say, or they may have selected them from his writings, which they were expected to memorize, encasing the quotations into a chreia form. In any event, the quotations were taken from Diogenes, but written into chreia form by others who were his contemporaries. Nobody conjectured them years later and attributed them to Diogenes. They did not develop out of discussion groups about Diogenes. The method of teaching employed by Diogenes, which resulted in many quotations from him in chreia form, may have been similar to the methods of other teachers about whom chreias have survived. They were understood by later rhetoricians and historians to have been validly composed at the time the statements were made by the characters about whom the chreias were attributed. Some responsive chreias, with their adjectives in genitive absolute grammatical forms italicized, are as follows:

Illustrations

Having seen an undisciplined youth, Diogenes chided the instructor, saying, "Why are you teaching such things?"

Having been advised by his friends to build up resources, Alexander, king of the Macedonians, said, "But these things did not help even Croesus."

Having heard that her son had claimed to be [the son] of Zeus, Olympias, the mother of Alexander, said, "Will that boy never stop accusing me to Hera?"

Having been asked where the muses dwell, Plato said, "in the souls of those who have been educated."

Having been asked where the boundaries of Sparta were, a Lacedaemonian pointed to his spear.

Having been asked if anyone who does anything wrong escapes the notice of the gods, Pittacus of Mitylene replied, "Not even one contemplating [doing wrong]."

One of his pupils, Apolodorus, *having said* to him, "The Athenians have unjustly condemned you to death." Socrates, the philosopher, laughed and said, "But would you prefer [that they condemned me] justly?"

His sandals *having been stolen,* Damon, the lame gymnasium teacher, said, "May they fit the thief."

These chreias were all attributed to recognized teachers, scholars, or kings, with two exceptions – Olympias, the mother of a king, and an unspecified Spartan. Olympias was the only feminine character I have seen mentioned in a chreia. The Spartan answered with an action that carried a sharp message. By pointing to his spear he indicated that the borders of Sparta were limited only by Spartan military strength. Except for the Spartan, the individual identity of the speaker or actor was given in all cases. In that case the identity of the individual was not as important as the identity of his country. In some of the chreias that are recorded in lists, the context of the collection shows that all of these chreias are about the same character. In that case, the identification is given with only a pronoun, with the identity of the character understood.

Chreias could be used as texts for sermons and arguments in court. They were designed to do that, but the resulting form was a sermon or an argument rather than a chreia. They were intended to be helpful for rhetoricians in their court arguments or public speaking, but they were also considered valid sources for early historians. Early historians employed collections of chreias as basic sources for their work, obviously trusting their reliability. Those historians had many collections of chreias at their disposal. The famous Zeno of Citium published one of the early collections (333-261 B.C.).

In one of my seminars on Luke, I presented to the class a folder prepared by Art Linkletter, entitled, "Kids Say the Darndest Things." This was a contest offering parents an opportunity to enter. I asked my students if their children ever said really bright things. Of course, they had. We took class time to have them told in detail. Then I asked every student to return to class as if he or she were entering the contest, and bring the same report, following Linkletter's requirements – in 35 words or less. They all returned with chreias. This technique that Diogenes popularized was very practical and useful.

Twentieth Century Form Critics. Dibelius, Bultmann, and Taylor were famous form critics in the twentieth century. They all conjectured that Jesus used brief literary forms, but they did not prove that this was true. Neither did they agree on the definitions, the names of the units, or their identification. They did not gain a huge following. What was different about the chreias was that they were defined, identified, and used in antiquity by Greek rhetoricians, church fathers, and the apostles of Jesus. Westerners who were inadequately acquainted with Greek rhetoric did not deduce them 2,300 years later. They were well known and used in composition in Jesus' day. I was excited to learn about them, because I recognized them in the gospels, associated with Jesus. I was then like a hound dog that had just picked up a hot trail. I knew I had grasped the important data necessary for learning accurate information about the historical Jesus. I was moving far ahead of the consensus scholars who were guided by NO TRESPASSING signs and resting comfortably in 19th century hypotheses. I was clearly on the right track.

The chreia was very popular. It was widely known and used before, after, and during the lifetime of Jesus. Rabbis also recorded chreias, but not extensively. One of the reasons for this is the purpose for which Rabbis wrote and the nature of their literature. Rabbis were primarily court judges who recorded the decisions of earlier courts for the benefit of later jurists. Today their works would be recorded in law journals. Their work was not biographical, first of all. Rabbinic chreias do not fit the exact form that Greek chreias do. Introductory phrases in Greek were cast in grammatical forms, called genitive absolutes. These included participles and were put in the genitive case. Because there is no genitive absolute grammatical form in Hebrew, Hebrew chreias follow different grammatical principles. The following are examples recorded about the character Rabban Gamaliel:

It happened with Rabban Gamaliel when he recited [the Shema] the first night of his marriage that his disciples asked him, "Did you not teach us, our Rabbi, that the bridegroom is exempt from reciting the Shema the first night?" He said to them, "I will not listen to you to cast off from me the Kingdom of Heaven, even for one hour" (mBer 2:5).

If that had originated in Greek, it would have begun with a genitive absolute, like this:

After Rabban Gamaliel had recited the Shema on the first night of his marriage, his disciples asked him . . ." The same is true of the next chreia: *He washed himself on the first night after his wife died.* His disciples said to him, "Did you not teach us, our Rabbi, that a mourner is not permitted to wash?" He said to them, "I am not like all [other] men. I am weak" (mBer 2:6).

When Tabi, his servant died, he accepted condolences over him. His disciples said to him, "Did you not teach us, our Rabbi, that there is no acceptance of condolences for servants?" He said to them, "My servant, Tabi, was not like all other servants. He was *Kah-sháyr*" (mBer 2:7).

All three of these units required two statements to tell who the character was who spoke and what the situation was that prompted Rabban Gamaliel to speak. There were no participles used to accomplish this function, but the speaker was identified and the situation was given in preparation to the quotation of Rabban Gamaliel that was given. The purpose of a unit was given without the genitive absolute. Therefore these were all chreias, without the exact Greek form. Also when Rabban Gamaliel's name was given in the first chreia in the list, it was understood in all of the rest. That was normal with lists.

The importance of all of this to Jesus research is that there are 25 chreias in the gospels in which Jesus was the character involved. Because of their Semitic origin, however, gospel parallels are not confined to the exact grammatical form that was standard for Diogenes. Nevertheless, they are always brief and easy to identify. Not all of the chreias in which Jesus was the character mention Jesus' name, but because the disciples had kept these in lists, the name of Jesus was understood.

SUMMARY

In Jesus' day Diogenes' teaching methods were probably at least as popular as those of Socrates. Jesus seems to have employed some of the same teaching techniques Diogenes popularized. Like Diogenes, Jesus probably also had materials he had written himself to share with his disciples. His disciples were probably the ones who wrote the chreias in which Jesus was the character, just as the students of Diogenes probably wrote the chreias in which he was the character. They were also probably composed on the basis of statements the disciples heard Jesus say or read from his written compositions. Like Diogenes, Jesus probably checked the writings of his students for accuracy. We have no documents Diogenes wrote but we know that he wrote literature. There are reports that he taught his students to read his writings, and they were compelled to memorize them.

It is normally assumed that we also have no documents Jesus wrote, but some of the chreias may have been taken from Jesus' manuscripts with which his disciples were acquainted. Jesus had students that were probably trained in literary skills before he recruited them. They would have been familiar with popular literary forms, such as the chreia. The fact that Jesus was able to use their talents and skills in producing the literature now preserved in the NT refutes the accusation of some scholars that Jesus and all of his disciples were illiterate. The claim that they could talk but not read or write does not make sense, considering all of the written data we have preserved. Although some Christian scholars still claim that Jesus was illiterate, the Jewish NT scholar, David Flusser, concluded that Jesus' Jewish education was superior to that of Paul.[1] Dunn, however, having read all of Paul's letters, still assumes that Paul, also, was illiterate. Only his secretaries were able to write. Are all people who have secretaries illiterate?

The early teachings of Jesus are not limited to any unpreserved "oral tradition." Like Diogenes, Jesus probably checked all of the literary units his disciples used and organized them into lists for the disciples to take with them on their missions. It was Jesus who

---

[1]   D. Flusser, *Jesus*, tr. R. Walls (New York: Herder and Herder, 1969), p. 18.

prepared and directed the message. It was the apostles who did most of the preaching.

The chreias have survived as valid written historical reports that tell us what Jesus did and taught. I will demonstrate their historical veracity in the rest of the book. Many scholars have devaluated the historical importance of the gospels, holding that the gospels were composed much later than the time of Jesus. That is true, but the historical value of the chreias attributed to Jesus is not contingent upon the dates when the gospels were finally edited. They had to have been written down during the lifetime of Jesus, no matter when they were finally included into the gospels.

We are now at the beginning of the trail. The next chapter will show us how this material clears up a lot of fog, removes the consensus obstacles that say, "There should be NO TRESPASSING into these fields," and leads us to the statesman, Jesus. Stay tuned.

CHAPTER TWO

ON A CAMPAIGN MISSION

THE ROLE OF THE DEAD SEA SCROLLS.

Before the discovery of the Dead Sea Scrolls, many Christians thought of Jesus as a rather innocent storyteller who embraced everything good and upheld all of the values that we in the Western world value highly. He probably opposed slavery and racial discrimination, championed women's rights and advocated democracy. Although he was called Messiah and king and spoke frequently about the Kingdom of God we did not think of these as being political terms. Then the Dead Sea Scrolls appeared and told us of the volatile, nationalistic, political situation that existed in Jesus' day, and they used terms that occur frequently in the gospels. This has forced us to reexamine Jesus' role in the midst of that history and learn how he could function there at that time and be considered as great and significant as he was. It means that he must have had something to do in this political arena, so we have to stop to think what the words messiah, king, son of God, and Son of man mean. Perhaps he did have something to do with politics after all.

The Dead Sea Scrolls were just beginning to come to the attention of biblical scholars when I began research on the teachings of Jesus in 1955. One of the first insights discovered was that ancient Judaism expected not one messiah, but two. One of these was preparing to become the national high priest and the other was to be the king. This followed the type of David and Zadok in the earliest United Kingdom. As soon as I learned that, I realized that Jesus and John the Baptist constituted a messianic team, prepared to rule the Kingdom of Israel. John was to be the new high priest who would anoint Jesus as the king.

This plan was frustrated when John was arrested, and Jesus was left with the assignment of continuing the program alone. Herod killed John and watched Jesus carefully, holding him under suspicion. Fortunately John had anointed Jesus before John was killed.

There is no report in any of the gospels, saying that Jesus was anointed, but that is implied. In the court of law a person does not have to guarantee that a milk cow gives milk or that a lawn mower can mow grass. The warranty is implied in its name. There are many other things that can be implied, because they always belong together. When two or more things always belong together, when one is mentioned, all the rest are implied. Rabbis call this *geh-zee-ráh shah-váh*. For example, every president of the USA is also the commander-in-chief of the American forces. It is not necessary to mention that fact every time you use the term "president." It is implied. Because all members of the United Methodist Church have been baptized and confirmed there is no need to say that a member of the United Methodist Church has been baptized and confirmed. It is implied. The gospels report that in the presence of John the Baptist Jesus received the spirit, spoke with authority, and was called God's Son. No one had to see the spirit descending like a dove (Matt 3:16; Mark 1:10-11; Luke 3:22; John 1:32). When the oil was poured on Jesus' head everyone knew that Jesus received the spirit and with it messianic authority. This was not just the inward authority that people recognized from his manner and personality, as Braun and Borg contended.[1] This was the legal *ex officio* authority that came from his position as the Messiah and Son of God.

Clement of Alexander called John the spiritual gospel. It was not necessary for Clement to explain to his reading public what he meant by spiritual, because the readers all understood what he meant. In the twenty-first century western world, however, we have to learn that from the gospel itself and its vocabulary in relationship to other scriptural passages that use the term "spirit" to learn what he meant. A few examples will guide us in the right direction.

When Saul received the spirit, Samuel anointed him and he became king. When Samuel anointed David, he received the spirit, and became king. Like Saul and David, when anyone is anointed he receives the spirit. When Jesus received the spirit, spoke with authority, and became God's Son, it is implied that he had been anointed.

Saul lost the spirit when David replaced him as king. Various judges – Gideon, Samson, and Jephthah – received the spirit when they began to rule. When Moses appointed subordinate judges to assist him, he shared with them some of his spirit. When Jesus was with John the Baptist at the River Jordan the spirit came upon him, and he began to speak with authority. This means that he was anointed, but none of the gospels say that. If they had, the Romans would have killed Jesus at once, just as they had beheaded John the Baptist, but it was not necessary to tell Jews that John had anointed Jesus. When they said that he received the spirit and spoke with authority they meant that he had been anointed and was the Messiah.

Following these examples it seems obvious that by "spiritual" Clement of Alexander meant that the Gospel of John was couched in legal terms. In NT times that which today we call

---

1   M. J. Borg, "The Spirit-Filled Experience of Jesus," J. D. G. Dunn and S. McKnight (eds.), *The Historical Jesus in Recent Research* (Winona Lake: Eisenbrauns, 2005), pp. 302-314.

"legal authority" the church called "spiritual power." Modern Christians have always believed that the Spirit was something that was powerful, but we have not known what that power was. We knew it was something we could not touch, see, or hear that was important. Sometimes we thought we could feel it, but we could not define it or be sure it was present. Now that we know that the word "spirit," in some contexts, means something legal, we must stop and think every time we see the word in Scripture and ask if in this context it has a legal meaning. The function of the spirit can be something that provides legal authority, and that helps us understand the real nature of the Spirit. It also provides some perspective for calling some spirit holy.

This chapter gives a coherent picture of Jesus that began with his anointing and continued until his entrance into Jerusalem. He was reported to be carrying on a campaign from the imprisonment of John the Baptist. Jesus was a man who had grown up in wealth, was well educated, trained in business, government, law, and religion before he received further training in commitment under the teaching of John the Baptist. The training from John required him to give up all of his wealth, deny his family that gave him birth and early training, and accept vows of poverty, celibacy, and obedience for the sake of the Kingdom of God. John the Baptist anointed him Son of God and authorized him to be the new Messiah of Israel. Paul said Jesus was descended from David, according to the flesh, and designated Son of God, according to the Spirit of holiness (Rom 1:3-4). This means he was physically born, just as other human beings are, and he was legally authorized and given his official title of Son of God through accepted legal methods.

John was reported to be the leader of a sect called the "Nazoreans." Some members of this sect still live in the Fertile Crescent area and trace their origin back to John the Baptist. Jesus was called "Jesus the Nazorean (*Nah-zoh-raí-aws*)," often mistranslated as the Nazarene (Matt 2:23; 26:71). The monk, Paul, the apostle, was also called a leader of the sect of Nazoreans (Acts 22:8; 24:5). It was probably this sect of whom Jesus became a member when he joined efforts with John the Baptist and became a monk.

This very intelligent, well trained, and committed statesman set out to recruit other competent, wealthy leaders in Palestine who would also make the same kind of commitment. He persuaded them that there was no value as great as the reestablishment of the Promised Land free from foreign rule. He trained these men for the project. They had to proceed directly and carefully, obtaining the necessary financial support and commitment of the citizens. They also had to communicate in a code that Jews would understand, but Romans would not.

It was probably in these training sessions that the disciples learned to take notes and record into chreias both the teachings they learned from reading his writings and from his oral instructions. Later they used these chreias in their promotions. Jesus also taught his disciples parables to use for promotion and composed parables for their own inner use to keep the commitment high among themselves. He probably provided the disciples with written lists of parables to which they added their chreias and carried them with them on their missions. Most scholars think that the parables are valid teachings of Jesus, but they have not shown why. Chreias and parables were not new literary forms that Jesus invented. Chreias were used more than 400 years before Christ. Church fathers and Greek scholars for the next millennium used them extensively. Parables were used in the time of David – a thousand years earlier than Jesus. Jesus used these educational methods very wisely.

The study of chreias in the gospels is fascinating, but most scholars have overlooked it. I will show the coherence of the chreias in relating an outline of Jesus' activities and a group of parables related to the same subject and coherent with the chreias. It was probably because the disciples had lists of parables that Jesus wrote and chreias the disciples recorded to use in their promotions that we still have record of them today. One of the reasons these literary messages are so coherent is that all of Jesus' apostles apparently had the same lists. They were not just individually heard and orally reported.

Although there may be some later expansions, none of these chreias or parables implies a teaching that took place at any time later than Herod Antipas, John the Baptist, Pontius Pilate, Jesus, or in any geographical location other than Palestine. No revolution could succeed in Palestine without the support of Jews in the diaspora, and there is some possibility that Jesus was in communication with Jews outside of Palestine (the diaspora). This is a further indication of his skills as a statesman.

First he had to select and recruit a competent, committed cabinet of leaders. He immediately went to the largest industry in Galilee, the fishing industry, in his local community. There he met leaders who were no stranger to him. The story of his beginning recruitment is told in chreia form. The identification of the character as Jesus is given only in Mark. The context also requires that meaning in Matthew.

CALLING DISCIPLES

> While he was walking along the Sea of Galilee he saw two brothers, casting a net into the sea, for they were fishermen, and [Jesus] said to them, "Follow me, and I will make you fishers of men" (Matt 4:18-19; Mark 1:16-17).

This was not the entire discussion. After all, Jesus was asking these fishermen to make a lifetime commitment that required them to leave their families, give up all of their money, abandon their business, and commit themselves to a new project that was dangerous, difficult, and demanding. The chreia was a "shortcut in memory," designed to summarize the entire story of his task of recruiting. It preserved the teaching of Jesus, just the way Diogenes taught his students to preserve in their memory an entire document by writing down one chreia. These fishermen were to become key leaders assigned to recruit still others. Instead of catching fish they would be recruiting others to be followers of Jesus.

As it was recorded in Matthew, this chreia no longer stood alone, it was included into a larger narrative that told of further recruitment around the Sea of Galilee. In this tour, Jesus successfully recruited Peter, Andrew, James, and John and continued preaching and telling people about the new kingdom that was being planned (Matt 4:20-25). Others became interested in Jesus' program, but Jesus reminded them that this was not an easy program to follow. The recognition of the size of his task and the problems that they were promised is evident in the following chreia.

LEADERSHIP PROBLEMS

> When he had seen the crowds, he had compassion on them, because they *were scattered and torn like sheep that had no shepherd* (1Kings 22:17). Then he said to his disciples, "The harvest is great, but the laborers are few" (Matt 9:36-37).

This is a chreia in which the speaker made the assertion, prompted by the situation that confronted him, rather than in answer to a question. The speaker is identified only by the context in which the chreia was framed. The quotation in 1Kings was from the prophet Micah who prophesied that if Israel and the Syrians went to war against Ramoth-gilead this is what would happen to their armed forces. The king ignored the warning, and the king was killed in battle leaving the army without a general. Jesus recognized the disorganized crowd before him in desperate need of a king. He changed the metaphor from that of a shepherd and sheep to that of laborers and a harvest. The grain was ripe; the harvest was abundant; but there were not enough laborers to bring it in. That is why Jesus selected a cabinet to recruit more laborers for him. This seems to reflect an early experience in the recruitment program.

Luke told the same basic story in more detail, preserving the punch line quotation, but in the process he broke the chreia form.

> After this the Lord appointed seventy others and sent them out in twos before his face to every city and place where he, himself, was about to go. Then he said to them,

"On the one hand, the harvest is great, but on the other hand, the laborers are few. Therefore pray that the Lord of the harvest will send out laborers into his harvest. Go! Look, I am sending you out as sheep in the midst of wolves" (Luke 10:1-20).

Matthew did not give any report of Jesus sending out seventy others to assist in expanding his program, but there probably were other participants. According to Matthew, Jesus limited his activity to Palestine, but Luke was also interested in the diaspora, that is, the countries where Jews resided outside of Palestine. The word "diaspora" means, "scattered," and it refers to the places outside of Palestine where Jews have been scattered.

The seventy are normally understood as those agents that Jesus sent to the diaspora. Since there were traditionally seventy nations in the world, the seventy may have referred to them. These agents had been sent out in groups of two to **every city and place where he himself was about to go** (Luke 10:1). They were there to prepare the way for Jesus' visitation. When they returned with great joy, bringing a good report, Jesus said, "I saw satan falling like lightning from heaven" (Luke 10: 18). When the Greeks came looking for Jesus, and Phillip and Andrew brought them to Jesus, Jesus said, **Now is the hour when the Son of man will be glorified** (John 12:23). Jesus evidently knew that the success of his program depended heavily on the support of the Jews in the diaspora.

There is a strong possibility that Jesus was in close contact with the diaspora. Josephus said there were many thousands of Jews in the Roman Empire. Jesus had not gone there yet at the time this was written, but his plans involved his activity there. Palestine was a small country that was an important land bridge between other countries. It was often ruled by other countries that wanted to control the movement of armies and trade between Egypt and countries to the north and east of Palestine. Jews were never happy about being ruled by others, but whenever they wanted to be liberated from one country they had to get help from another. As early as eighth century Isaiah there was the problem between Egypt and Assyria. As early as the Assyrian captivity of the Israelites and the Babylonian captivity of the Jews there were Jews and Israelites living in the diaspora away from the Promised Land.

When Jews were in Babylon they negotiated with Persia to get Babylon overthrown and the Promised Land returned to Jewish control. When Jews were ruled by the Syrian Greeks, Judas the Maccabee obtained support from Rome to get freedom from the Syrians. There were also many Jews in Syria at the time of the Maccabees who could help weaken Syria from within. Rome successfully delivered Jerusalem from the Syrians only to take control of Palestine itself.

In Jesus' time Palestine was suffering from Rome's strong-arm tactics. There were also thousands of Jews in Rome, many of whom held prominent positions in government and also in business. Any leader in Palestine who was trying to free Palestine from Rome would need the support of the Jews both in Rome and in Parthia. There is no direct external evidence that Jesus sent a group of agents to Rome to obtain support from there, but both Luke and John indicate that there was, and it is reasonable to think that these were valid reports and that there was such a mission. The harvest was ready, and Jesus needed more laborers in the field from all sources.

One of the clues that point to the possibility that Jesus had sent legal agents out into the diaspora to recruit followers and gain support for his program is the existence of Christian churches all the way from Syria to Rome by the time of Paul. Paul did not have to organize all the churches with which he was in communication. There were synagogues in the diaspora that quickly became Christian, including the church at Rome that was there while Paul was still involved in his mission in Asia Minor (Modern Turkey). There were thousands of Jews in the Roman Empire in Jesus' day. Only 300 years later there were enough well organized Christians in Europe to be able to negotiate with Constantine and establish the Holy Roman Empire. The earliest church historian, Eusebius, interpreted the victory of Constantine as the fulfillment of Jesus' ministry – the new exodus and the resurrection of the dead (HE 9:9, 4-5; 10:4, 12).

Jesus knew that he needed many laborers to work in his program, but that did not mean that he accepted everyone who applied. He required very capable, dedicated people. That is shown in the next chreia.

VOLUNTEERS

One scribe, approaching, said to him, "Teacher, I will follow you wherever you go," but Jesus responded, "The foxes have holes, and the birds of the heaven, tents, but the Son of man has nowhere to lay his head" (Matt 8:19-20; Luke 9:57-58).

This unit is a responsive chreia. It was attributed to a particular person, Jesus, but the questioner was not identified. This is normal. The grammarian, Doxapatres, said that there could be only one character in a chreia. The anonymous person that prompts the speaker to speak was not called a character.

"One scribe," is an apparent Semitism. There is no indefinite article in Hebrew. You cannot say, "A scribe" in Hebrew. You either say, "One scribe" or "scribe." The Hebrew then said, "One scribe," and the Greek rendered it literally. Some translators render it, "One, a scribe." Luke does not show the problem, because the word, "scribe," is not in the text. Otherwise Luke's statement varies somewhat from Matthew's, but the quotation from Jesus is the same. A scribe in antiquity held about the same office as that held by attorneys today.

Although Jesus had been anointed Son of God he also had to be in hiding from the Romans as he conducted his campaign. Those who were impressed with his leadership and wanted to follow him and be part of his kingdom would have to survive the way the followers of Judas the Maccabee did in the many honeycombed caves in Palestine. Sometimes even these were not available. Foxes had caves. Jesus did not say, "Birds have nests."

That which birds had was a place to stay at night. Followers of Jesus needed army tents (*kah-tah-skay-nóh-sace*), but he did not have any. By substituting expected words with code terms Jesus was able to communicate with those who had ears to hear and understand the hidden code.

The expression "Son of man" is an expression that can mean just "human being." The Romans would have understood it that way, but for Jews it had a special coded meaning. The Jews who knew Dan 7 would understand that the Son of man was the plaintiff in the same drama of a heavenly trial in which "the horn" played the role of the defendant. "The horn" was Antiochus Epiphanes, and the Son of man was Judas the Maccabee who defeated the troops of Antiochus at Beth-horon the same year Antiochus died in Persia.

The drama of Dan 7 explains theologically what happened that year to make all of these events take place. God held court in heaven and gave Antiochus the death sentence. To Judas he gave the kingdom, the power, and the glory of ruling Palestine. By calling himself the Son of man, Jesus implied that he was a new Judas the Maccabee who would restore the kingdom, as Judas had done. The term, "Son of man," was a code name for the new Messiah, the Christ.[1] To speak to Jews without the Romans understanding the message, it was necessary to use material whose meaning Jews knew but Romans did not. That was Scripture and Jewish tradition. The reports of Jesus in these chreias are consistent.

---

[1]   M. Grant, *Jesus: An Historian's Review of the Gospels* (New York: Charles Scribner's Sons, c1977), 101-104, overlooked all of the coded meaning in Jesus' speech. He held that Jesus did not think of himself as the Messiah and he used the expression "Son of man" 52 times to claim his humanness. P.M. Casey, "Son of Man," Dunn and McKnight (eds), *Historical Review*, p. 324, reached the same conclusion by dismissing the quotation from Daniel (Mark 14:62) as inauthentic and all other references as productions of the later church.

CONDITIONAL VOLUNTEERS

> Another of the disciples said to him, "Lord, permit me first to go away and bury my father," but Jesus said, "Follow me, and let the dead bury their own dead" (Matt 8:21-22).

> Then he said to another, "Follow me!" He responded, "Permit me first to go away and bury my father." [Jesus] said to him, "Let the dead bury their own dead, but you, after you have gone away, announce the Kingdom of God" (Luke 9:59-60).

The name "Jesus" did not occur in this chreia, but that is not important. When lists of chreias were made the name of the character was not mentioned in every chreia, because it was understood and replaced with a pronoun. Luke has turned the Matthean chreia into a brief dialogue that preserves the message. He has also made the quotation sharper by following the "go away" with a responsive "after you have gone away." Furthermore he added the command to announce the Kingdom of God. That was probably not a part of the very brief chreia of Matthew, but it is an appropriate message for the circumstances. The next Lukan chreia mentions Jesus' name, so these two probably belonged to a list.

Both reports remind the reader of the confrontation Elijah had with Elisha. When Elijah was old and needed a person to train as his successor, he selected Elisha. He put his own mantle on Elisha's shoulders. This had the ritualistic effect of offering Elisha his own legal clothing to become his successor as the prophet of Israel. But Elisha had a responsibility to his parents.

One of the Ten Commandments was that a member of God's contract must honor his parents. That meant he was obligated to provide them with food, clothing, and clean garments so that they would not die of neglect (Mekilta, *Bahodesh* 8:1-10), but that they would live long in the Promised Land. Elisha asked permission of

Elijah first to kiss his parents good-by. This was a euphemism. He really wanted permission to care for them until they died. Then he would accept Elijah's offer. Elijah said he did not have that much time to wait. Elisha had either to follow him then, or Elijah would have to find someone else. When faced with the hard choices, he chose to follow Elijah.

Under similar circumstances, Jesus reacted in the same way. He did not have time enough to wait around until someone's parents passed away. Those who followed him had to follow him immediately. The stakes were high; the demand was great; the time was short; the pressure was extensive. The "dead" were not corpses; they were those who were not followers of Jesus. They could take up the responsibility of taking care of the parents of the monks and burying them after they had died. Those who followed Jesus would have to leave their parents, their positions in society and employment, their businesses, their lands, families, and all other things that belonged to the world away from the monastery (Matt 19:28). In NT times monasticism was the highest form of religious commitment. It came into being when the temple either did not exist or it was believed by the faithful to be defiled and therefore not valid. The monastery developed to replace the temple as a pure and holy place where God could be present. It was the only way to be legally and religiously perfect. Jesus accepted that role. He also observed the same kind of Torah expediency ethics observed by the second-century B.C. Hasmoneans when they fought on the Sabbath. They said it was better to break one commandment in order to obtain control of the land where all the commandments might be kept than to observe only one commandment, meticulously (1Macc 2:40-42). Those who joined the monastery would make it possible for the Promised Land to be reestablished where all the chosen people could care for all of their parents the way that the commandment required. Monasticism was not held to be a permanent establishment. It was a temporary crisis measure. Whenever either the tent of God, which David installed (Rev 21) or the temple was reestablished in its purity, then monasticism would be no longer necessary.

It is normal for Matthew to give two examples, apparently to fulfill the requirement that it takes two or three witnesses to make a case valid in court (Deut 19:15; Matt 18:16). Here are two chreias in parallel relationship in the Gospel of Matthew (Matt 8:19-20, 21-22). They probably did not happen at the same place and at the same time, but Matthew put them together from different sources. One was a scribe and the other was called a disciple. A disciple is only a student.

Like Diogenes, Jesus evidently held classes and taught recruits, all of whom began as students. Only after they had been adequately trained and tested were they invited to become apostles, which meant "following him," becoming monks, and being perfect. The word that is translated into English as "perfect" did not mean scientific perfection, as it does for westerners today. It meant keeping all of the rules required for membership in the monastery. The rigor of these demands seem impossible to Protestant Christians today, but monks in NT times were very serious.

Among the students, there were only a few who became apostles by giving all that they had to the monastery. The monastery was called the "poor," because none of the individual monks any longer owned any possession. They had all taken vows of poverty, celibacy, and obedience. Jesus was not willing to modify his conditions and accept the student's offer to take these vows sometime later. Still another recruit was ready to follow Jesus, but he also had restrictions:

> Also another said, "I will follow you, Lord, but first let me put my house in order." Then Jesus said, "No one who puts his hand to the plow and looks back is well-set for the Kingdom of God" (Luke 9:61-62).

The picture given here is of a man plowing with a walking plow. He held two handles of the plow with his two hands and looked straight ahead, with his eyes both on the plow itself and the distant point which should be the end of the furrow. He had to do this to keep the plow in the furrow and make the furrow straight. If he should look back he would move his hands involuntarily and jerk the plow out of the furrow or make the furrow weave. Jesus was asking people to make ultimate decisions that involved giving up everything they owned and treasured – family, home, job, and social status – and become celibate monks for the sake of the Kingdom of God.

Luke modified Matthew's earlier chreia to make it more obvious that this was a reenactment of the Elijah-Elisha encounter (Luke 9:59-60). Luke followed that chreia with this chreia about plowing, calling attention to the activity of Elisha when Elijah found him.

All of the above chreias are related to Jesus' activity in recruiting followers. They are all coherent and picture one character involved in the same kind of activity and responding in the same way. The next three chreias are responses Jesus made to women along the way. They are not directly related to recruiting, but they are not out of character, either.

PERCENTAGE GIVING

> When he looked up and saw the rich people putting their gifts into the treasury, and he saw one poor widow, putting her two mites, he said, "I tell you for a fact that this poor woman gave more than all the rest" (Luke 21:1-3; Mark 12:41-44).

This unit is a chreia whose spokesman is identified only in context. It is slightly expanded in Mark. The chreia does not explain why Jesus thought this woman gave more than all the rest. It was not mathematically true, but in a context where Jesus was asking people to give all that they had to the movement, this woman qualified, even though she did not have many possessions. In the next chreia, Jesus' response to a woman was not as supportive.

MONASTIC CONDITIONS

> It happened while he was saying these things a certain woman from the crowd raised her voice and said to him, "Blessed is the womb which bore you and the breasts which nursed you," but he replied, "Rather blessed are those who hear the word of God and keep it" (Luke 11:27-28).

The Literature. The context of this unit is a little longer than most, giving attention to the situation which prompted the woman to speak as well as Jesus' answer. This is called a double chreia. The name "Jesus" is not mentioned, but it is implied by the context. Jesus responded by being consistent with the monastic vow to reject his family. He was responding by saying that the monastery that adopted him was more blessed than the mother who bore him. He would not acknowledge a blessing to Mary. Instead he responded with a partial quote from Exod 24:7, the response of the Israelites to the offer of the commandments when Moses came down from Mount Sinai. When asked if they would accept them, they said, "We will keep [the commandments] and we will hear (obey) [them]" (Mekilta, *Bahodesh* 5:80). This is called a *hysteron proteron* (last-first) literary form. That which happened last (keeping the commandments) came first, before hearing them. The Sermon on the Mount, pictured Jesus as the new Moses and the new mountain, and it concluded with a reference to "Everyone who hears these my words and performs them" (Matt 7:26).

It was ordinarily considered proper to bless the Messiah, and that was implied in the woman's blessing. By blessing the mother the blessing on the son was implied. One Jewish blessing is as follows:

> Blessed be the hour in which the Messiah was created; blessed be the womb from which he came; blessed be the generation that sees him; blessed be the eye that is worthy to see him (Pesikta Rabbati 149a)

The response attributed to Jesus is not a proverb, which might have been placed on the lips of many teachers in various periods and locations. There was a local incident, which prompted this distinctive saying, although it is no longer possible to know just when this event occurred in Jesus' travels. It might not have happened when Jesus was involved in recruiting followers. Once the discussion was reduced to a chreia, it could be inserted into any part of a narrative. The next chreia has been expanded. It shows still more distinctly than other chreias the way Jesus rejected his family, and his adoption by a monastic order that involved also his disciples.

> While he was still speaking to the crowds, look! His mother and brothers were standing outside, wanting to speak to him. [Some one said to him, "Look! Your mother and brothers stand outside, wanting to speak to you]. He, replying, said to the one who was speaking to him, "Who is my mother, and who are my brothers?" Then, extending his hand to his disciples, he said, "Look! My mother and my brothers, for whoever does the will of my Father in heaven is my brother, sister, and mother" (Matt 12:46-50).

This is a rather long and involved chreia. It may have been expanded in some way. The words, "Someone said to him, 'Look! Your mother and brothers stand outside, wanting to speak with you'" are omitted in some texts. The situation is described at length, and there seem to be two punch lines. In one, the disciples alone constitute Jesus' legal family. In the second one, it may be just anyone who does the will of God, or it may be repetitious, implying that his disciples are the ones who do the will of God. This may be the result of two chreias having been compressed. The Gospel of John also testifies to Jesus' monastic vows. The background of this saying is the story of Elijah and the widow of Zarapath.

The widow had only one son, and he seemed to be on the deathbed. The widow confronted Elijah in distress. She thought

God was punishing her for the way she obtained that child, implying that Elijah was the father of the child as was the case of Elisha and the Shunnamite woman (2Kings 4). God had killed her son because of her iniquity. She came to Elijah in her distress, saying, **What do we have in common?** (*mah leé wah-lah-kháh*) (1Kings 17:18). Literally this means, "What belongs to me and to you?" "What is it that is both mine and yours?" This was a rhetorical question, expecting a negative answer. That which they once had in common was their son, and he was then dead. They no longer had any binding relationship.

On another occasion, the mother that gave Jesus his physical birth came to Jesus, as the son of God, to report a hospitality problem. His mother was approached as one who would have influence with her son. She told him that there was a shortage of wine, and asked if Jesus could do something about the problem. First he quoted from the passage about the Shunnamite's distress, **What belongs to me and to you?** Implying that Jesus and his mother, like Elijah and the widow of Zarapath, no longer had any relationship. That was all ended when he took his monastic vows. Mothers of kings had influence over the decisions their sons' made. For example, Solomon's brother wanted a favor from Solomon, but he did not ask Solomon for it directly. Instead Adonijah asked Solomon's mother to intercede and ask Solomon for the favor (1Kings 2:13-25). Likewise, Jesus' mother was trying to utilize her authority as the mother of the Messiah, but Jesus denied that such a relationship existed. He had legally denied his family for the Kingdom of God.

Many of the teachings of the Sermon on the Mount would make sense only for monks, who have no family and have taken vows of poverty, celibacy, and obedience. For them the contrast was between the narrow road that leads up the cliff to the monastery in contrast to the broad Roman roads that lead to Rome. Existence for monks within the community was "life," and existence outside the community was called "death." Salvation would have been acceptance into the monastery. Destruction would have been the consequences of choosing not to become a monk. It is not certain whether the chreia had the same meaning or not. Furthermore, it is not certain which way the dependency lies. In chreias applied to Diogenes, the punch line sometimes involved a quotation from Homer. Diogenes' students obtained some of the quotations of Diogenes from his writings. The author of the chreia might have formed a chreia from the quotation in the Sermon on the Mount, just as Diogenes' students formed chreias from his writings, or the author of the Sermon on the Mount might have developed his poetry from this chreia in Luke. There are other chreias that confirm the suggestion that Jesus was himself a monk and taught monastic discipline.

> Great crowds gathered to him, and he turned and said to them, "If anyone comes to me and does not hate his father and mother, wife and children, brothers and sisters, and yet even his own soul, he cannot be my disciple (Luke 14:25-26).

The Gospel of Thomas has a similar teaching attributed to Jesus:

> Jesus said, "Whoever does not hate his father and mother cannot be my disciple, and whoever does not hate his brother and sisters and does not take up his cross in my way will not be worthy of me" (Log 55).

The speaker was identified as Jesus only by the general context. The situation is given and the assertion was made. The entire message is succinct. This is therefore a responsive chreia. The point made here is clear – to be a follower of Jesus, a person was required to break all family ties and become part of a celibate order. This probably reduced the context of "great crowds" to a very few zealous followers.

In western society the terms "love" and "hate" are emotional terms that reflect deep feelings either of affection or hostility. As we use these concepts in our daily lives, we become shocked to learn that Jesus taught followers to hate their families. We would normally expect him to encourage them to love their family members. Jesus, however, lived in a world in which "love" and "hate" were legal terms that were closely related to contracts involving responsibility. For example, when Paul told husbands that they should love their wives, he was simply reminding them that they had contracted to do so in their marriage ceremony. That meant that husbands would provide for all of their wives' needs, the way the wives' fathers had done previously. As soon as the new husbands took over this responsibility, the fathers stopped loving their daughters, but that does not mean they no longer had any affection for them.

Wives were not invited to love their husbands, because, in those days wives did not have any authority or ability to provide for their husbands. Therefore they only agreed to be subject to their husbands who loved them (Col 3:18) the way they had been subject to their fathers before the marriage. Legally the bride became the husband's daughter. When Hosea complained that Israel had too many lovers, he was not talking about sexual partners. He meant that Israel had made too many trade and military agreements with other countries, like Egypt or Assyria.

Jacob and Laban did not become lovers until they became enemies. When Jacob left Laban's house he took with him most of Laban's possessions. Laban followed him as rapidly as he could and caught up with him at Mizpah. There Jacob and Laban had harsh words, but finally agreed to disagree and stay in different geographical areas. They confirmed their agreement in two ways:

1) They ate a liturgical meal together, and
2) They set up a pile of stones and agreed that Jacob would stay west of these stones, and Laban would stay east. They would never again enter into each other's territory (Gen 31:43-54).

The contract by which they agreed to be enemies made them lovers, even though they despised one another. Grant did not know the biblical meaning of love and hate, so he mistakenly pictured Jesus in an emotionally angry and hostile relationship with his family.[1]

The Essenes were Jews about which Josephus, Philo, and Hippolytus have written extensively. Josephus was a Jewish historian who lived and wrote during the same century that Jesus did. Philo was an Egyptian Jewish Scripture scholar and philosopher who was a contemporary of Jesus. Hippolytus was a later scholar who was probably dependent on Josephus and Philo. Josephus was one of the greatest historians of antiquity. His work is especially important for providing an accurate historical background for Christian origins. He provided the most extensive and accurate history we have about the Essenes.

One group of Essenes was celibate. Members lived together as monks, segregated from others, forming their own legal family, providing a place for the Lord to be present in the absence of a trustworthy temple. There have been other monastic groups in NT times, such as those described in the Dead Sea Scrolls (1QS). It is because these monastic groups have been described so fully that we can understand the teachings and actions of Jesus and his apostles from a monastic point of view.

All of these monastic groups required their trained applicants to love all of the other members of the monastery. This meant they should provide for them and take care of them as they had previously done with their families, but they should stop all association with the families into which they were physically born. They should not provide for their needs in any way. That meant that they should hate their families into which they were born, even though they had deep affectionate feelings toward them. When they joined the monastery that is what they contracted to

---

[1] Grant, *Jesus*, pp. 126-129, who claimed special skills as a historian, made the same mistake that non-historians make. He thought words in the Near East 2000 years ago had the same meaning as they do in the U.S.A. today.

do. When monks looked after one another's needs, that action was called "works of love."

Jews and Christians in NT times had normal feelings of affection and hostility, but they did not always call it love and hate. Love and hate could be commanded and required by law. Monks were not required to have strong feelings of affection or hostility toward their parents who gave them birth. These feelings are subjectively motivated, but they could not be commanded. It was not their feelings that were commanded, but their behavior. However they felt about the people with whom they were formerly associated, upon admission to the monastery, monks were required to hate them and love only the other monks in the monastery. Even Jews and Christians who were not monks provided for one another's needs, and these were called acts of love. This does not mean that the ancients never used the terms love and hate to express affection or hostility, but that it often had a much stronger meaning with legal implications.

The commitment required of these monks was so demanding that it is difficult for twenty-first century westerners to believe that it actually happened. We have only to read early reports, however, to learn that there were both Jewish and Christian monks in the time of Jesus. They were serious. The demands and teaching of Jesus were similar to requirements and teaching of other celibate communal orders such as the Essenes and the community governed by the Community Rule (1QS) of the Dead Sea Scrolls. It is also similar to the ethics of the Sermon on the Mount, First John, and the sermon of Hebrews 1-12. Monasticism was much more prominent in Judaism of Jesus' time than is normally recognized. It developed at that time as a temporary measure to replace the temple that many Jews and early Christians thought was defiled and therefore invalid. Because monasticism is not as prevalent in western Christianity today as it was then, we tend to overlook its existence in the NT and in early church fathers.

This chreia is coherent with other recruitment chreias that confronted volunteers with high demands for permission to follow Jesus. The same basic teaching is recorded, but not in a chreia.

He who loves father and mother more than me is not
worthy of me.
He who loves son or daughter more than me is not
worthy of me.
He who does not take up his cross and follow me is not
worthy of me.
He who finds his soul will lose it,
And he who loses his soul for my sake will find it. (Matt
10:37-39).

This is another case in which Luke has summarized the poetic passage in Matthew and put it into chreia form by adding a general introduction to give it a context, or Matthew composed a poem based on a chreia. The latter seems more likely. Both units required the listener to give up his own soul. The soul was the seal of membership. It was the seal of belonging. The soul of the world was the one the listener should surrender in order to receive the soul of the community where religious and legal life was possible.

There are many indications that Jesus was himself celibate and advocated celibacy. He told his apostles to call no man "father" on earth. Their only father was in heaven, and they were all brothers (Matt 23:9-10). He never referred to Mary as his mother, but called her "woman" (John 2:4; 19:26). He held that his disciples were his mother and brothers (Matt 12:46-49). That could be possible only legally. Celibate men could not become physical mothers to one another.

He told the Sadducees that in the resurrection there would be neither marriage nor giving in marriage, but all would be like angels in heaven who are celibate (Mark 12:18-25). Jesus' apostles were those who had left all – houses, parents, brothers, sisters, children, and fields – to follow Jesus (Matt 19:27-29), professing at least temporary celibacy. This means that the call to become fishers of men was not a light invitation. It was an emergency measure required in the existing crisis, and the followers had not accepted the call spontaneously with only a moment's notice.

A Priest for the Age. Jesus was born into the family of David, but the author of Hebrews claimed that he was a high priest. How could that be? The monks who volunteered to replace the function of the temple were not all sons of Zadok, but they were ordained as priests. The author said,

> So Christ did not exalt himself to be made a high priest, but was appointed by him who said to him, "You are my Son. Today I have given you birth." As it says in another place, "You are a priest for the age, following the order of Melchizedek" (Heb 5:5-6).

This text implies that Jesus became a priest when he joined the monastery. Part of the liturgy by which he was admitted may have included the texts quoted here. Like Melchizedek and other monks he was without father, mother, or genealogy. He continued as a priest for the age (Heb 7:3). He had denied all family connections when he joined the monastery. In Herod's temple, which was nearby, the high priest entered the holy of holies only once a year and that was done behind the curtain so that no one could see what happened, but in the monastery, where all monks were undefiled priests, the curtain was no longer necessary. There was a new and living way, which Christ opened for the monastery through the curtain (Heb 10:20). Nearby was Herod's temple, which the author said was "made with hands," meaning that it was pagan. The monastery, in contrast, was a temple not made with hands.

The synoptic gospels seem to suggest that Jesus lived in Capernaum, north of the Sea of Galilee. He may have lived in a monastery there, and that monastery may have been of the same order as the one at Zion. These are conjectural interpretations of various texts from different documents that cannot claim perfection. Readers have the right to evaluate them. However these details are considered, that which is likely is that Jesus actually was a very rich man originally, but that he gave up all of his wealth and took vows of poverty, celibacy, and obedience.

When Paul was trying to persuade the Corinthian church to give money generously to the saints at Jerusalem, he reminded them that the churches at Macedonia had set a good example by giving abundantly of their money. Also Jesus Christ, "Though he was rich, for your sakes became poor, that by his poverty, you might become rich" (2Cor 8:9). Paul told of the Macedonians who had given money, Jesus who had given money, and he was asking the Corinthians to give money. This was a financial campaign to raise funds. Paul may have been reporting a historical fact about Jesus that is coherent with other testimonies about his monastic behavior. It was extraordinary for rich people, like Jesus and his apostles, to give up all of their former offices and status in the nation to become monks, without money or status, except in their righteousness before God.

It was especially extraordinary for a man who was anointed as the Messiah, God's legal agent, who was authorized to speak in God's behalf, in his name, and at his responsibility to accept the humble role of a monk. Legally, the agent is the principal, so Jesus was legally God. Instead of entering Jerusalem on a royal mule, as Solomon had done, he came riding on a donkey, following the prophecy of Zechariah (9:9). In a Pauline confession, Jesus was distinguished as one who was legally equal to God, but who still humbled himself, taking upon himself the form of a servant in obedience to God. As a faithful legal agent he acted only in obedience to God, even unto death (Philip 2:5-10). He was certainly an unusual type of messiah. This fact became further evident when he celebrated his last Passover with his apostles.

Before entering Jerusalem, Jesus sent two of his disciples to the city, obviously Zion, in preparation for the Passover there. He told them to meet there a man carrying water. In the ancient Near East, women carried all of the water, with one exception. Monks who lived together alone did all of the housework, including cooking and carrying water. The water near the city was either from the Spring of Siloam or from the Pool of Siloam at the southwest end of Hezekiah's tunnel. When the disciples saw this unknown man carrying water, they were directed to follow him to his residence and there speak to the masculine manager, who would serve Passover to Jesus and his disciples (Mark 14:13-15).

Jesus did not expect the apostles to arrive at a home where the man would introduce them to his wife and children, because he knew the man would lead them to a monastery. Like the managers of other monasteries, this manager was always prepared to provide hospitality for other monks of the same order. In that monastery Jesus apparently celebrated his last Passover with his apostles. The man who carried water in a pottery jar on his head, would not have carried it far, so the monastery probably was somewhere in the City of David, Zion. That small area is now only about 10-acres in size. In New Testament times it was probably larger. It was located west and south of the Spring of Siloam, directly south of Herod's mighty fortress, which now holds the Dome of the Rock and Al Aqsa mosque.[1]

THE RIGHTEOUS REMNANT

> Someone said to him, [Would you tell me] if those who are saved are few? Then he said to them, "Struggle to enter through the straight gate, because many, I tell you will want to enter, but will not be able" (Luke 13:23-24).

Jesus was identified as the respondent only by the general context. While he was interpreting his proposed program to others, there were many questions like this that were asked. This question was raised in a group discussion of some kind. It is not clear whether Jesus was speaking to a large crowd or to only a few when the question was raised. It seems more likely, however, that the

---

[1]   Buchanan, "The Tower of Siloam," *Expository Times*, 115.2 (2003):37-45; "Running Water in the Temple of Zion," *Expository Times*, 115.9 (2004):289-292; "The Area of the Temple at Zion," *ET* 116.6 (2005); Ernest L. Martin, *The Temples that Jerusalem Forgot* (Portland, OR.: ASK Publications, c2000).

question was raised in one of Jesus' classes. Jesus had a network of people who communicated to the masses while he kept himself out of sight from the government leaders. The answer given was not only to the questioner, but also to all who were listening.

The question the twenty-first century westerner asks is "What did he mean by being saved? Saved from what?" The word "save" was used in the FT 44 times to refer to national deliverances, usually in war, 92 times for deliverance of individuals from such difficulties as prison, illness, and injury, 14 times for those with proper qualifications, such as the patient or righteous ones in court. In the Greek mystery cults, those saved were members of the cult.

Those mentioned in the chreia as saved may have been the ones qualified for membership in the new nation – perhaps those who either survived the conflict with Rome and had qualified for citizenship in the new kingdom or had been killed in battle and would be raised, after the gentiles had been driven out, to live the rest of their lives in the Promised Land, free from foreign rule.

Jesus did not say directly whether many or few would be saved, but the statement that many would not implies that only a few would be successful. The Lukan chreia is somehow related to the same teaching in the Sermon on the Mount.

> Enter through the straight gate,
>   because broad and spacious is the way
>   that leads to destruction,
>   and many are those who enter it,
> Because straight is the gate, and narrow is the way
>   that leads to life,
>   and few are the ones who find it (Matt 7:13-14).

THE FUTURE OF THE TEMPLE

A short distance south of Herod's large fortress, where the Muslim Dome of the Rock is now located, was the temple that Herod built. It was constructed on Mount Ophel, directly behind the Spring of Siloam. In recent years archaeologists have found the old wall of Zion, one wall of which was also the wall of the temple. Inside that wall was also found the ruins of the Tower of Siloam. The temple was larger and more beautiful than any temple that had been built on that site before, but many Orthodox Jews refused to enter it. It was called a "sanctuary made with hands" (Heb 9:24), which meant it was "pagan," "idolatrous," "common." The prophet of Rev 21:1-22:5 did not expect the temple to be restored. He anticipated the holy city to contain a tent and an altar. In the next chreia, the disciples asked Jesus about that temple.

> Now when Jesus left, he went away from the temple, and his disciples came to show him the buildings of the temple. He said to them in response, "Do you not see all these things? Truly, I tell you, there will not be left here one stone upon another that will not be broken down" (Matt 24:1-3; Luke 21:5-7; Mark 13:1-4).

This teaching occurs as a chreia in all three gospels. They vary somewhat and have come from different traditions, representing the work of different authors. Modern commentators almost universally fail to comment on these verses. In each of the synoptic gospels there is a later interpretation that follows, telling of the signs of the end of the Roman age that would take place within three and a half years, as it had with the Hasmoneans who fought that long before the temple was cleansed and rededicated. Modern commentators comment only on the later interpretation. The question is, "What did Jesus mean when he spoke these words?" What did he expect? When? How? Why?

Like the expressions of the sermon in Heb 1-12, the prophecy of Rev 21:1-22:4, and some of the literature found among the Dead Sea Scrolls, Jesus may have been offended by the defilement of the temple that was called "a temple made with hands," where the high priest was called "the wicked priest." Jesus may have believed that, since the Romans built it, it was not really God's house, even though the part necessary for ritual was actually constructed by authorized priests (War 15:390). The Romans had the last word of deciding who could be the high priest, and they controlled the garments the high priest had to wear. The office of high priest could be purchased for money. Like Ezek 4 and 5, Jesus may have believed Jerusalem and its temple were so corrupt that they would have to be destroyed before true worship could take place. If it was to be destroyed and in three days reestablished (Matt 27:63), Jesus probably meant that the tent of God and the altar that David established would again be reinstituted at Gihon, there behind the Spring of Siloam.

Solomon had hired the Phoenicians to design and build the temple. It was probably designed to look very much like the temples of Baal. Part of the temple itself was evidently made with wood, because when it was destroyed it was burned. Josephus said at least the roof was made with cedars from Lebanon (Apion 1:110). There may have been more. When the temple burned, it was Jewish soldiers who actually set it on fire, which suggests that they did not think it was very sacred. The altar, however, was made of stones that had not been chiseled. It was huge. Hecataeus, in the 4th century B.C., said the altar was 30 feet long, 30 feet wide, and 15 feet tall (Apion 1:198), just as the Bible prescribed (2Chron 4:1). During the first century A.D., Josephus said it was 75 feet wide, 75 feet long, and 22 ½ feet tall. When Herod had his temple built (20 B.C.-A.D. 66) it was larger than the earlier one, and he may have enlarged the altar as well. Both authorities describe a huge altar. It was not portable, and it would not have burned. In three days, a tent, like the one David installed, could be constructed near the altar, and Jews would have been freed from that pagan temple. Even if the Romans had also destroyed the altar in the City of David, another altar could have been constructed quickly from loose stones. That would have been like the one David had built – only large enough to roast one beast at a time. That small altar would have been adequate for the monastery that was located at Zion and functioned as a temporary temple while Herod's temple stood.

The extensive prophecy in the Book of Revelation (Rev 21:1-22:5) anticipated a new Jerusalem without a temple, but with a tent, just as there had been in the days of King David. The new Jerusalem would come down from heaven to earth (Rev 21:10). It would have an altar with a bonfire burning continually to lighten up the city so that there would be no need for the sun or the moon to give the city light (Rev 21:23). The seer said, **I saw no temple in it** (Rev 21:22). There would be no temple but the tent of God (*skay-náy too-theh-oó*) would be there on the land among human beings in the City of David, just as there had been before the time of Solomon, and God would **tent dwell there** (*skay-nóh-say*) (John 21:3). His presence would not be in a temple, but in the **tent of God**. Furthermore, the sea would no longer exist (John 21:1). The sea involved was not the Mediterranean Sea, the Sea of Galilee, or the Dead Sea. That sea was the bronze sea that was part of the furniture of the temple (1Kings 7:23-39; 2Chron 18:8; Jer 52:17). It would not be there, because the **temple** would be gone. There would be no place in **the tent of God** for a huge bronze basin. Jesus may have agreed with those Jews who thought the temple in Jerusalem was pagan and would have to be destroyed and replaced with a tent.

Whatever the understood meaning of the chreia, the statement of Jesus is coherent with the other chreias quoted here. Anyone recruiting under pressure that lacked the necessary military tents needed, could, without contradiction expect to see the temple destroyed. It is not necessary that this chreia had been composed after the destruction of Jerusalem in A.D. 70. Some faithful Jews, years before, believed that it had to be destroyed. There are enough teachings contained in chreias to make certain that Jesus was himself a monk who had rejected the family into which he had been born and belonged to a new corporation into which he had been born again legally. He also trained his disciples to accept the same discipline. He was involved in a program that was not only local. It involved the hopes and aspirations of the nation.

In one of the earlier chreias it was reported that Jesus was not living in a palace. He had to wander like birds and animals, and he often lacked the facilities that were available to them. In the next chreia it is clear why Jesus' task was hard.

In that very hour, certain Pharisees came, saying to him, "Hurry and leave this place, because Herod wants to kill you." Then he said to them, "When you leave, tell that fox, 'Look! I cast out demons and perform healings today and tomorrow, and on the third [day] will be finished'" (Luke 13:31-32).

The Pharisees were some of Jesus' sharpest critics. They had learned to live with the Romans and profit. They also got along well with Herod. Herod Antipas was a contemporary of Jesus, so the likelihood of this chreia having been a local report, as chreias claim to be, is very great. Pharisees were also contemporary with Jesus. They were intent on keeping peace. Jesus was a problem to them. He broke some of the laws they thought were essential. They knew that Jesus was dedicated to reestablish the kingdom of David, and he had chosen a cabinet that did not include any of the Pharisees. It was not only Herod and the Romans that wanted Jesus out of the way, but so did the Pharisees. When they told him to "leave" he told them what to do "when you leave." This is like the repartee between Amos and Amiziah. Amiziah told Amos to go, walk, get out of Israel. Amos responded that Yehowah had told him to walk to Israel and prophesy to them (Amos 7:15).

It is not certain whether the Pharisees really were trying to be helpful and protect Jesus from Herod or whether they just wanted to frighten Jesus so that he would not be a problem to them. At any rate, Jesus was not intimidated. He seemed far enough along and had enough materials and followers so that Herod could not stop him, as he had stopped John the Baptist. Another chreia in relationship to the Pharisees is this:

Now certain of the Pharisees from the crowd said to him, "Teacher, warn your disciples." But he, replying, said, "I tell you, if these keep still, the stones will cry out" (Luke 19:39-40).

In the context, Luke has this chreia placed at the entrance of Jesus into Jerusalem on Palm Sunday. While people were treating Jesus as the new Messiah, they laid large, flat, palm leaves on the road before him and shouted,

> Blessed is the king who comes in the name of the Lord
> (Ps 118:26)!
> Let there be peace in heaven and glory to the Most High
> (Luke 19:38).

The activity reported in this chreia seems to have occurred very close to the preceding chreia, which also captured the Pharisees' attention. In both cases it was the Pharisees who tried to suppress the movement. In this chreia the time is located near the end of Jesus' campaign. He had gathered such a strong movement that he no longer tried to keep it in hiding. He was ready to confront the Romans at the feast in Jerusalem. That would have been a major undertaking. The Romans permanently kept 6,000 troops in the Tower of Antonia – that huge fortress, just a *stah-dái-ahn* (600 feet) north of the temple in the 35-acre plot that now contains the Dome of the Rock and the Al Aqsa mosque. It was tall and could easily look over both the temple and the City of David to the south. Whenever they wanted, Romans could go down the stairs and cross over to the temple on the two bridges that joined the temple to the fortress.

When Jesus entered the City of David he was no longer announced as the Son of man, in code terms. He entered Jerusalem, following the teaching of Zechariah,

> Look! Your king comes to you,
> Triumphant and victorious is he,
> humble and riding upon a donkey (Zech 9:9).

At that time the apostles were prepared for a military attack. No more attempts were made to keep the disciples still or to warn them in any way. Jesus was not afraid of Herod.

The above teachings were preserved in the literary form that was best known in antiquity as the form through which the teachings, actions, and sayings of great leaders and teachers were preserved. These teachings reflect coherently the sayings of one great teacher, leader, and statesman who lived and acted at a time in Palestine when the nation was under subjection to Rome. That leader was Jesus, a man who was anointed by John the Baptist to become the new Son of God. He had received the spirit, as Gideon, Jephthah, Samson, Saul, and David had when they became tribal or national leaders, and he spoke with authority, recognized as the Messiah of Israel.

These chreias were all coherent. They reflect activity that would have made sense in Palestine. They indicated periods at the beginning, during, and at the end of his recruitment campaign. The time involved was between the imprisonment of John the Baptist and entrance of Jesus into the holy city. This was when Pilate and Herod Antipas were ruling Palestine. The chreias might have come together the same way those attributed to Diogenes did. Some of them may have been taken from the writings of Jesus. Disciples accompanying Jesus on the trail or in the classroom may have written others. None of them requires a time different from that in which Jesus lived or a place other than Palestine. It would be abnormal historical research to treat them as fiction.

After Jesus had recruited "fishers of men," he prepared them for their work. Many of the teachings that are now in chreia form may have been put into chreia form by the disciples during their training period, just as the students of Diogenes did for his teachings. Then they would have been shared so that all disciples had a list of chreias to use in their communication with the local people. Jesus probably also gave them a collection of stock parables for various occasions, which they should use in their promotions. Then he sent them out, not heavily burdened with baggage, and only to the lost sheep of the house of Israel, according to Matthew (Matt 10:5-10). According to Luke he sent others to the diaspora.

Those assigned to Palestine were told not to loiter; they were to announce the Kingdom of God. If they were received favorably they were to stay there for only a short time; if they were not received favorably, they should quickly leave and go to the next town (Matt 10:23). They were under pressure to move quickly, and they had to be cautious, at the same time, not to expose Jesus to Herod and the Romans. This means that the apostles did most of the preaching and promoting, under Jesus' supervisory guidance.

Because most of his actions and teachings took place when Rome was suspicious of any pretending messiah who might lead an insurrection, he had to speak openly in code, and train his apostles to do the same, so that Rome would not suspect him of being a threat. That is the reason he spoke in parables.

THE FUNCTION OF PARABLES

David and Bath-sheba. Parables are illustrations, usually told in story form, intended to apply to something other than the story itself. Parables are almost always not historical facts, but they answer some important questions. Parables were something like the Greek myths or fables. They were small dramas that were not historical reports, but they were successful ways of persuading that communicated some messages better than any other means.

The practice of telling parables is very old. Parables were told in David's time, and there are more than 300 parables recorded in the Babylonian Talmud alone. After David had seduced Uriah's wife, Bath-sheba, and she became pregnant, David tried to cover up the scandal by having Uriah killed in battle. After that Nathan met with David, as the chief justice of the land, to consult with him over a legal detail. Nathan wanted to know how David would rule on the following case.

There was a poor man, who had only one ewe sheep, and he loved her like a daughter. Another man had many herds and flocks. When he had guests and needed a sheep to slaughter for the banquet, instead of taking one of his own sheep he stole the poor man's only sheep. How should the court rule on that case? David replied, he should repay for stealing one sheep, four sheep (Exod 22:1; four for one was also Roman law). But because he did not show mercy on the poor man, he should be given the death penalty as a punitive measure. This is similar to the kinds of rules that apply in most courts in the United States of America today.

1) For deception, fraud, thievery, etc. there are multiple damages.
2) For malice or breach of fiduciary trust, additional punitive damages.

That which David thought was an objective, anonymous, legal case turned out to be a parable. Nathan was not talking about a sheep being stolen, but a wife, who had been like a daughter to Uriah. In antiquity a man's wife was legally his daughter. The offender was not an ordinary rich man, but a king. At the end of the parable, Nathan said, "You are the man" (2Sam 12:7).

The parable got the point across to David, as no other method of expression would have. It was persuasive. If Nathan had simply told David that he had committed a terrible criminal act, David would probably have said it was none of Nathan' business and dismissed him in anger. Parables are little dramas that are used to persuade people about some point. Shakespeare said, "The play's the thing in which we catch the conscience of the king." Shakespeare was good at delivering messages through theater. For the Greeks the myth was the drama of theater. Greeks thought the myth was the method of communication that was more successful than ordinary prose or poetry in getting a message heard. Nathan's small theatrical message was certainly successful. There was probably no other means to draw David's conscience into the situation as well as that parable. David, however, was not the last judge to mitigate the sentence when his own guilt was involved. The parables of Jesus were also skillfully composed.

Rabbinic Parables. Parables are not necessarily historical at all. Most of them are fiction, and some of them do not make sense if taken literally. They are used to answer questions and persuade. Neither the hearer nor the teller understands them as factual. In answer to questions, the rabbis usually responded with, "To what can this be compared?" and then told a parable. For example,

Rabbi Shimon ben Yohai's disciples once asked him, "Why did the manna not come down to Israel once a year?" He replied, "I will give you a parable: This may be compared to a king of flesh and blood who had one son, whose maintenance he provided once a year. [This meant that the son] would visit the father only once a year [to receive his allowance]. Thereupon, [the king] [provided for [the son's] maintenance day-by-day, so that [the son] would call upon [the king] every day. The same is true with Israel. One who had four or five children would worry, saying, 'Maybe no manna will come down, tomorrow, and all will die of hunger.' Thus they were found to turn their attention [day-by-day] to their Father in heaven" (m Yoma 76a).

This parable was not intended to give a factual account of the way kings manage their family economy. It was composed only to answer the question asked. In the parables of Jesus, there is not always the associated question, so the meaning of the parable has to be deduced from other sources. The disciples of the rabbi had their question answered with one parable. The parables of Jesus were composed to be shared with all of the apostles and told over and over again in many situations by different apostles. They all had similar points and were coherent with one another. Therefore most of them are not inseparably attached to specific questions. They were designed to persuade people to Jesus' point of view.

There are 33 parables of Jesus in the gospels, and they are amazingly coherent with the chreias already studied in relationship to Jesus' activity on campaign to recruit followers while under pressure.

The Parables of Jesus. When Jesus began recruiting, he went to leaders of industry and business, just the way politicians do today. He needed capable, well-trained administrators, with lots of money to support his campaign. They were people who had houses and lands (Matt 19:20). Jesus was not just a storyteller who was simply teaching wisdom. He had a purpose and a goal. He sent the apostles out to contact others for two reasons:

1) to get wealthy people to support his program financially, and
2) to persuade these wealthy leaders to become his followers.

Because of these goals, many of the parables are addressed to wealthy people about the use of money, such as the next one about a happy rich man. Jesus lived in a strongly classed society, quite unlike the United States of America. No one in his community could move up from poverty to riches in one generation. Neither could a lower class person associate with the rich and powerful. Jesus' ability to associate with the wealthy and powerful implies that he was himself once one of these rich and powerful businessmen who had good business connections. At one time he associated with them in business and belonged to the same country clubs. He had then given all that he had to this movement, taking vows of poverty, celibacy, and obedience in becoming a monk. Paul implied that this was so. Because Jesus once associated with these rich men, after he became a monk his relationship with them was still good. During his campaign to raise money for the poor in Jerusalem, Paul promoted his cause to the Corinthians by

1) first telling them of the sacrificial giving of the Macedonians toward this project,
2) then reminding them of the "grace of our Lord Jesus, that on account of you, became poor when he had been rich" (2Cor 8:9).

He was asking the Corinthians to give money; he told of the Macedonians who had given money; he also told them of Jesus who had given money. This is one of the reasons he had the authority to send as apostles other formerly rich people in his name to ask other very rich people also to give money. Some of his parables reflect this context.

Business Techniques.

> The field of a certain rich man was productive, and he pondered, saying to himself, "What shall I do, because I have no place in which to gather my produce?" Then he said, "I will do this. I will tear down my granaries and build bigger [granaries], and I will gather there all my wheat and goods. Then I will say to my soul, 'Soul, you have many good things laid up for many years. Rest, eat, drink, and be merry.'" But God said to him, "Fool! This night I will take your soul from you. Then whose will be the things you have prepared?" Thus [it will be for] the one who lays up treasures for himself and is not rich toward God" (Luke 12:16-21).

This was the kind of message the disciples brought to those who wanted to follow Jesus, but turned away, because they had many possessions or those who did not realize how strenuous it was to live like birds and animals without adequate provision. This parable reminded the rich man that it was more important to have a good credit rating with God than to have money invested in banks and produce. One who had taken pains to redeem himself from economic poverty but was not religiously solvent was not at all prepared to face the future. He was a fool. The purpose of the parable was to persuade this fool to reinvest his money in the treasury of merits so that he would have treasures in heaven. This parable was coherent with the next parable about wealth.

> A certain man was wealthy. He wore purple garments and fine linen, feasting sumptuously every day. A certain poor man, named Lazarus, was left at his gate, covered with sores and wanting to be filled from the things that fell from the rich man's table, but the dogs came and licked his sores. Now it happened that the poor man died and was taken by angels to Abraham's bosom. The wealthy man also died and was buried. In Hades, he

lifted up his eyes, being in torment, and saw Abraham at a distance and Lazarus in his bosom. Then he cried out and said, "Father Abraham, have mercy upon me, and send Lazarus to dip the tip of his finger in water and cool my tongue, because I am tortured by this flame."

Abraham said, "Son, remember that you received your good things in your lifetime, and Lazarus, likewise, misfortunes; now he is comforted here; but you are tormented. Besides all of this, there is a great chasm between you and us, so that those who want to cross over from here to you cannot, nor can they cross from you to us."

Then he said, "I ask you then, Father, that you send him to the house of my father, for I have five brothers, so that he may testify to them, so that they may not come to this place of torture." Abraham said, "They have Moses and the prophets. Let them hear them." He answered, "No, Father Abraham, but if someone from the dead will come to them, they will repent." He said to him, "If they will not listen to Moses and the prophets, they will not repent even if someone were to rise from the dead" (Luke 16:19-31).

This parable had to be directed toward the class of the rich man. Lazarus could not have learned anything from it to change his behavior. The same is true of Jesus' teaching that members of his audience should not invite the rich to their meals, because they could pay them back. They should invite instead the poor, the lame, the blind, and the crippled, because they could not pay them back. Those virtues would then be paid back in the resurrection (Luke 14:12-14). If the audience had been made up of poor people they would have been in no position to hold these feasts for others in need. It had to be directed to the rich.

Jews are obligated to help one another in time of need. Here is pictured a very wealthy man who ignored that responsibility. Instead of finding help from other Jews, Lazarus had to turn to the gentiles for support. This should have made another Jew who could have helped him ashamed of himself. The "dogs" here are not four legged dogs that roam the streets. One of the derogatory names Jews call gentiles is "dogs." This insulting practice is also found in the NT. Warning against giving that which is holy to the dogs (Matt 7:6) means "Don't try to convert the gentiles by sharing your religious benefits." The accusation that the "dogs return to their vomit, and the sow to its wallowing pond" (2Pet 7:22), means gentile converts are never reliable. These "dogs" and "pigs" will go back and become gentiles again. The gospels were written when all Christians were also either Jews or Samaritans, so it is normal for Jewish expressions to be also Christian. Today a Christian is not insulted when called a gentile, but nevertheless is insulted if called an SOB, meaning that his or her mother is a gentile (female dog). Feelings are transferred long after original meanings are lost.

The original parable might not have included the paragraph about the brothers and the situation if someone were raised from the dead. That may have been added by later Christians to complain against Jews who did not accept Jesus even after the resurrection. That is not a necessity, however, because Jews believed in the resurrection two centuries earlier, in the time of the Maccabees.

> The Kingdom of Heaven is like a treasure hidden in the field, which a man, when he found [it] hid [it], and from his joy goes and sells whatever he has and buys that field (Matt 13:44).

A kingdom is a territory ruled by a king. A field is a definite piece of ground in a definite location. The same is true of a kingdom, a country, a city, or a state. The field involved in this parable is not just any field. It was a very special field to be compared to a very special kingdom.

Heaven is a euphemism for God. In the parable of the prodigal son, the returning son said, "Father, I have committed a crime against Heaven, and in your sight" (Luke 15:18-19). He did not mean that he had injured and offended the sky. He meant he had treated God badly. The City of God is Jerusalem, the capital of Palestine. The Kingdom of God is an expression that occurs 37 times in Matthew and 32 times in Luke. It is not just the sovereign ruling activity of God,[1] as many scholars assume. A kingdom is not an act or an attitude. It is a country, a state, a place where a king rules. In the gospels, the Kingdom of God is Palestine, the country of which Jerusalem is the capital.

The man who would have been spading in another man's field would have been some kind of hired help. He would have been digging a well, postholes, a trench, or a garden. He would not have been a big businessman, a merchant, or a banker, who regularly invested money. How could such an unskilled laborer find money enough to buy a whole field? Even if he sold all that he had, it would not have been enough, but Jesus was asking very rich men to give all that they had to gain possession of a very special "field" – the Promised Land.

Like other parables, the story told is only an illustration. It was not a historical report, and it was not intended as an end in itself. This was not counsel for day laborers, advising them in economic matters. The point of the parable was not the field but the Kingdom of Heaven, the Promised Land that was then having to function underground. Every Jew should recognize that the Promised Land is filled with treasure. If Jews could only recover that land from the Romans they would be very wealthy. Palestine was not famous for its rich minerals, but it was a strategic land bridge between large nations that had to use it for commerce and defense. Jews could charge high prices for this privilege, and they did. They were constantly bargaining for better terms. This was the kind of parable that communicated in code. Only the Jews would have received the real message. Romans would have thought of it as only a story.

---

[1]   As defined by M. Grant, *Jesus* (New York: Charles Scribner's Sons, c1977), p.15.

For many years scholars have attempted to interpret Jesus in a way that removed all the gospel evidence that Jesus was in any way related to a political movement. One of the earliest was the German theologian, Albrect Ritschl, who called the Kingdom of God the ethical ruling activity of God.[1] There is nothing wrong with upholding a theology that identifies God's will with good ethics, but there is no textual basis for claiming that this theological view is the Kingdom of God. The Kingdom of God is not just a theological opinion. It is a country, a state, a land.

Ritschl's view is widely accepted in theological circles today, but it is unfair to the gospel evidence. Jesus was not just a wise teacher of ethics. He was a good teacher, to be sure, but he was not just a Jewish Socrates. It seriously minimizes Jesus' leadership skills to reduce him to a simple storyteller. He was an outstanding statesman, who was also a good teacher. He was called the Messiah, Lord, king, and Son of God. These are all political designations. A kingdom is a territory ruled by a king. It is not just an ethical ideal, a labor movement, a democracy, or a movement to uphold sexual and racial equality. The Kingdom of Heaven or the Kingdom of God was a territory over which Solomon was once the king. Jesus told parables that were related to that land.

Christians have often thought there was an ethical problem of finding treasure on someone else's property and then making skillful plans of acquiring it without paying its full value. That has not been a problem to conquest theologians, like Christians, Jews, and Muslims who have traditionally thought it was God's will to conquer other countries and take over their land and treasures. We have enjoyed sitting under our own fig trees that someone else planted and reaping crops that someone else has sown and cultivated. Israelites took over the Promised Land from the Canaanites by warfare, in the first place. Christians acquired the Holy Roman Empire in the same way. That is what happened

---

[1]   G. W. Dawes, ed., *The Historical Jesus Quest* (Louisville: Westminster John Knox Press, 2000), pp. 154-184.

when the Christian specialists in conquest (*conquistadores, kohn-kees-tah-dóh-rays*) destroyed the Aztec and Inca civilizations in Mexico and Peru and took the gold and the land. That is the way Christians acted when they found treasure in North America. There is an ethical problem involved, but it is not one that has traditionally bothered Christians and Jews – but maybe it should. The next parable has the same basic teaching.

> Again, the Kingdom of Heaven is like a merchant looking for choice pearls, and after he had found one very precious pearl, he went away and sold all that he had and bought it (Matt 13:45-46).

The parables of the kingdom (Matt 13) begin with the words, "The Kingdom of Heaven is like – a man who sows good seed in a field (Matt 13:24), a grain of mustard seed (Matt 13:31), leaven (Matt 13:33), a treasure hidden in a field (Matt 13:44), a merchant in search of fine pearls (Matt 13:45), or a net that was thrown into the sea(Matt 13:47). In these cases the Kingdom of Heaven is not defined by the first words of the parable. They mean, "The Kingdom of heaven is like a situation in which the following is true."

This parable about the fine pearl is more reasonable than the parable about the treasure found in a field, because this is the way businessmen really act. They are in business to make money. They want to buy at low costs and sell for high prices. The merchant was skilled in recognizing the real value of pearls. He wanted to buy this particular pearl because it was worth more than he would have to pay for it. That is good business. Jesus addressed his parables to businessmen who understood this practice.

The reason Jesus told both of these parables was to remind the listeners that the Promised Land was worth more than anyone could pay for it, but it was then available. Good businessmen would understand this logic. It would be foolish not to extend every possible method to obtain it. This would demand that rich people give up all of their money and possessions, all their family, social, and business responsibilities, and devote themselves completely to this one purpose. That would require that they become monks and follow Jesus. That is what these two parables asked them to do. The next parable discloses the ethics of business.

> A certain man was rich, who had a business manager. Now this [business manager] was reported to him as one who was acting carelessly with his funds. After he had summoned him [the business manager], he said to him, "What is this I hear about you? Give me an accounting of your work! For you may no longer act as business manager."
>
> The business manager said to himself, "What shall I do? For my employer is taking away the office of business manager from me. I am not strong enough to do manual labor, and I am ashamed to beg. I know what I will do so that when I am removed from the office of business management they will receive me into their homes."
>
> After he had invited each one of his employer's debtors, he said to the first, "How much do you owe my employer?" He answered, "a hundred measures of oil." He [the manager] said to him, "Take your bill; sit down and quickly write, 'Fifty.'" Then he said to the next, "How much do you owe?" He replied, "A hundred measures of wheat." [The manager] said to him, "Take your bill and write, 'Eighty.'" The employer praised the crooked business manager, because he had acted wisely (Luke 16:1-18).

This parable has caused Christians a great deal of distress, because it pictures Jesus in some way admiring a crooked businessman for his shrewd action in providing for himself at the expense of someone else. Like many others, we will try to make sense out of this parable in the Jewish business world of Jesus' time. The manager evidently worked for someone else engaged in loaning money at a very high rate of interest. This was customary both for gentiles and Jews loaning money to gentiles. Jews were prohibited from taking interest from one another, but sometimes they did. In the Lukan context, this parable prompted the comment that the children of this age (That is, gentiles and Jews that associate with gentiles) were wiser than the children of light (faithful Jews).

In Judaism of NT times the rules against stealing and exploitation that applied to Jews in their dealings with fellow Jews did not apply to gentiles. In fact it was considered meritorious to benefit from any deal with gentiles. When tax collectors came to John the Baptist, repenting, John told them not to collect more taxes than their Roman overlords required. Jewish soldiers in the Roman army were told not to rob other Jews by violence or false accusation and to be satisfied with the pay they received from the Romans (Luke 3:12-14). These officers normally committed the crimes John here prohibited. John was trying to get them back within the Jewish fold, without demanding that they leave their offices with the Romans.

John did not prohibit any of these Jews from committing similar crimes against gentiles. This is particularly true in dealing with Romans, who were considered enemies in war. Christian and Jewish ethics have some limitations. They are limited to being ethical with their own people. This is part of the apartheid consequences of being a chosen people.

There were Jews who compromised their loyalty to their nation to become rich by exploiting fellow Jews. They were the tax collectors and other officeholders who worked for the Romans. These people were alienated from other Jews who would not try to help them in time of need. They were called "harlots," "criminals," "children of darkness," "gentiles," and other uncomplimentary terms. The middle manager's anxiety was the realization that he belonged to that group of Jews, and that most Jews hated him. He could not receive help as other Jews did

How could he get back into their good graces? He had already lost his position of employment. He had nothing further to lose from taking advantage of his employer in his last hours of business. Therefore, he could concentrate on ways he could use his office to the advantage of other Jews who had been forced to borrow from either a gentile or a Jew who did business with gentiles. This might bring him back within the fold where he could receive normal Jewish care. That which he probably did was to cancel the interest in every case. This allowed the employer to receive his original principal, but not benefit from the loan. Another possibility was that he canceled the amount he had charged to procure the loan from his employer in the first place.

The employer was also probably a Jew who had become wealthy by charging interest to Jews. If he had been a gentile, he would not have praised the middle manager for giving away his income. Jesus understood the situation of these disloyal, rich Jews. He also realized that they really were not complete scoundrels. They still claimed to be Jews, and they could be brought back into the fold. He not only asked them to return; he asked them to give up their money to the monastery that was called the "poor." It was called the poor, because individual monks did not possess anything. They depended on the administration to provide all of their needs. The poor, however, who administered Jesus' program had to have a large treasury, and his campaign involved building up this treasury. Money was a practical necessity in any national program.

The message of the parable was for people in both the situation of the employer and of the manager. There were Jews in both positions. Both should use their positions to strengthen the nation, its citizens, and the movement Jesus led. The parable was intended to bring the wealthy Jews who had wandered away from normal Jewish responsibility back into the fold by making use of their positions of power to strengthen the nation. It was to these wealthy business criminals that Jesus directed his parables. The next parable of Jesus was designed to arouse nationalistic feelings and resentment toward Rome.

> A man was a landlord, who planted a vineyard, surrounded it with a wall, dug a wine press in it, and built a tower. Then he rented it out to tenants and went

away. When the time of the harvest approached, he sent his servants to the tenants to collect his rent. Then the tenants seized the servants: some they whipped, some they killed, and others they stoned. Again he sent different servants, more than the first, and they did the same to them. Afterwards, he sent them his son, saying, "They will respect my son." When the tenants saw the son, they said among themselves, "This is the heir. Come, let us kill him, and we will have his inheritance." Then they seized him, threw him out of the vineyard, and killed him. Now, when the master of that vineyard comes, what will he do to those tenants?" They said to him, "He will utterly destroy them, and he will rent out the vineyard to other tenants, who will give him his rent on time" (Matt 21:33-34; Mark 12:1-11; Luke 20:9-18).

Like other parables, this was given in code. Jesus was not talking about tenants but about something else that the audience understood. If we knew what the question was that he was answering, we would understand for certain who the characters were. Most scholars assume that this is not the teaching of Jesus but that of the later church and that the son who was killed was Jesus and the Jews were the laborers in the vineyard. Like other parables, it is more likely to have been a parable Jesus taught his apostles to tell when they were recruiting followers. It would have applied somehow to national loyalty, commitment, raising money, or building quiet resistance against Rome.

The place to begin is to realize that Jesus was not really speaking about just any vineyard. He was talking about Palestine, God's very special vineyard. Jews persistently believed that they were the legitimate owners of Palestine, even though they were subjects, sometimes of Egypt, sometimes of Assyria, Persia, Babylon, Syria, Parthia, or Rome. These countries did not usually tax Palestine. They paid Jews for allowing them to march across their land in war and commerce. Jews did not think of themselves as ordinary tenants of the land, which these various countries owned, but as the children of the God who owned the vineyard that other countries temporarily rented. Sometimes the dominating country abused the Jews and treated them as if they were inferior tenants, but Jews never acknowledged that.

In Jesus' day it was Rome that first entered to support the Maccabees and assist them in recovering the land, but they later took control of the country, which was God's land. God's son was the ruling king. The last legitimate king to rule was the Hasmonean, Antigonus. He ruled for three years before Herod came with Roman troops and military equipment, conquered the land and killed and crucified God's son, King Antigonus. The parable asked the question, "What do you think God is going to do about this? Do you think this will go on forever? What will he do to those Roman imposters?"

Jews were eager to get the land restored and be liberated from the Romans. That is why people followed Jesus. He was the new Son of God who would lead the nation in throwing out those cruel Roman tenants. Jesus was asking people to give all they had to follow him, and some did. They were willing to give up homes, families, lands, money, and status to support Jesus in obtaining this recovery, but they wanted quick results. There were undoubtedly times when some wondered when it would happen. Had they made a mistake in their judgment? Should they keep up this intense commitment forever? Some may have longed for their former security and comfort and their freedom to run their own programs. They needed to be reminded of the unfairness of their situation and learn the consequences of indolence and disobedience. This is also true of the next parable, which was probably prepared for a wider audience.

> The kingdom of heaven is like ten virgins, who took their lamps and went out to meet the bridegroom. Five of them were foolish and five were prudent. The foolish ones took the lamps, but they did not take oil with them. The wise ones took oil in their vessels with their lamps. As the time for the bridegroom to come was delayed, they all nodded and fell asleep. Then, in the middle of the

night, a cry went out, "Look! The bridegroom. Go out to meet him!" All those virgins arose and prepared their lamps. The foolish ones said to the prudent ones, "Give us some of your oil, because our lamps have burned out." The prudent ones said by reply, "No. There may not be enough for both you and us. Instead, go to the market and buy your own." While they were going to buy oil, the bridegroom came, and those who were ready went in with him to the wedding chamber, and the door was closed. Later on, the rest of the virgins came, saying," Sir, Sir, open for us!" But he, in reply, said, "I tell you under oath, I do not know you" (Matt 25:1-12).

Jews celebrate Passover at night. They celebrate with an evening meal of mazza, bitter herbs, lamb, and wine. Every Jew is obligated to celebrate Passover. Every Jewish host is obligated to admit other Jewish guests into his or her home for Passover and provide the minimum requirements of at least an olive's bulk of unleavened bread, bitter herbs, and lamb. At this meal there is Scripture reading, liturgy, and singing. Jews expect that the Messiah will come some year and join them at Passover, so they open the door and put out a plate of food for him. If the news got around that the Messiah was about to appear, local authorities would get out their security forces to control the revolution, so Jews keep the door closed and do not say they are expecting the Messiah. They say they are putting out the plate for Elijah. Every Jew understands the code and knows that Elijah must come first to announce the Messiah. If the Messiah would come, Jews would invite him to come in, and then they would close the door.

When Jesus spoke of John the Baptist, he said John was more than a prophet. Of those born of women, there was no one greater than John. All the prophets and the law prophesied until John. He was the Elijah who was to come (Matt 11:7-13). Rabbis said that all prophets prophesied only for the days of the Messiah. In code, Jesus told the crowd that they were living in the days of the Messiah. John was the new Elijah who would precede the Messiah.

Everyone could see that Jesus was the one Elijah announced and that all prophets prophesied only of him.

It was customary in antiquity when a great person came to a city that the people of the city would go out to meet him or her. When the Messiah was expected to come, of course, there would be a group organized to go out to meet him. That is the reason the virgins were waiting up with their lamps lighted. They did not know for sure if or when the Messiah was coming, but just in case, they had a reception committee waiting to greet him even at night.

The Messiah is called the bridegroom, because he is the legal agent of the Lord. With the arrival of the Messiah, Jews expected a new contract to be instituted with the Lord. The contract with the Lord was treated as if it were a marriage contract. The earlier contract had been annulled when the Lord drove the Jews out of his temple and sent them into Babylon, just the way a husband would send his wife out of his house to divorce her (Deut 24:1). Ever since that divorce Jews had existed without a contract to show that they were God's people.

When a Jew or Israelite wanted to divorce his wife, he was required to get a legal document of divorce, put it into her hand and send her out of his house (Deut 24:1). That is what the Lord did when he had the temple burned and sent the people into Nineveh and Babylon. Because the contract with the Lord was considered to be a marriage contract, whenever the Israelite corporation, which was thought of as the bride, broke any terms of the contract, it was called being unfaithful. This corporate "bride" had broken faith with her husband, the Lord.

Hosea described this vividly, claiming that Israel had become a prostitute. Lamentation described the situation after Jerusalem had been destroyed. Jerusalem was pictured as initially a pure virgin bride and princess who later became unfaithful, accepted other lovers, and made the Lord angry with his unfaithful bride, so she was abandoned as a divorcee and left without comforters. This unfaithfulness was not personal or sexual. It was national and related to national business and treaties with foreign nations. At the time of the parable, Israel was still divorced from the Lord, but when the Messiah would come, and the new marriage contract was to be established, the people who greeted him would be expected to qualify as a virgin bride again, not compromised with foreign alliances.

Over the years many Passovers had come and gone, but the Messiah had not come. At the time the apostles were telling this parable to the masses, they all knew this, but the apostles were telling them that the Messiah was already there in secret. At some Passover he would declare himself, but people had to be patient. No one knew except the Messiah at which Passover this would happen or at what time of the night.

There were so many code terms in this parable that Romans would not understand that the apostles dared to tell this parable openly without threatening the Romans. This parable encouraged Jews to be ready and not to let up on their preparation. There is a similar message in the next parable.

> Who, then, is the faithful and prudent servant whom his employer set over his household, so that he would give to [the other servants] their food at the proper time? Blessed is that servant, who, when his employer comes, he will find him, doing just that. I tell you under oath that he will appoint him as administrator over all his possessions. But if that wicked servant says to himself, "My employer is held up," and begins to strike his fellow servants, and eats, drinks with drunkards,
>
>> The employer of that servant will come
>> On a day when he does not expect,
>> In an hour when he does not know.
>> Then he will cut him in two,
>> And place his share with the hypocrites (Matt 24:45-51).

This was a management parable, designed for the members of Jesus' cabinet. They had been former CEOs of big business. Now they were subordinate officials of an organization that was not moving fast enough. It would have been easy for any of them to want to run the entire program. They were accustomed to do as they pleased. Now they were taking orders, but they still wanted to participate in the new kingdom. Jesus had not only to recruit new followers and raise more funds continually, but he had to keep harmony within his administration.

This kind of parable confirms earlier evidence that Jesus was working with a group of business people. Big business requires delegation of authority to others. If the manager finds trustworthy middle managers he gives them more salary and responsibility. If the manager makes a mistaken appointment, the sooner he or she learns of the problem and removes it the better. Jesus understood these things the way he never would have if he had grown up in a craft shop. He selected the "fishers of men" because of their wealth and management skills. They all would become middle managers in his program.

The word "servant" in Greek is a term not limited to manual laborers or household workers. Any subordinate official is a servant. The top general of the military services or the ambassador to another nation is a servant for the king. All middle management people are servants to the general manager, who is a servant to the CEO. This parable was designed to tell the disciples that they had to be on duty continually, always in preparation for immediate changes if necessary. The next parable also seems to have been prepared for the disciples themselves.

> Watch, then, because you do not know the day or the hour. For it is like a man who went on a journey. He called his servants and entrusted to them his possessions, to the one he gave five talents, to another two, and to the third, one – each according to his ability. Then he went away on his journey. The one who had received five talents went at once, invested them and gained an additional five. Likewise, the [one who had received] two, gained an additional two. But the one who had received

one went out and dug [a hole in] the ground and hid his master's silver.

After a long time, the master of those servants comes and holds a reckoning with them. The one who had taken five talents came and brought an additional five talents, saying, "Sir, you have given me five talents. Look! I have gained another five talents." His master said to him, "Well done, good and faithful servant. You have been faithful over a few things. I will set you over many. Enter into the joy of your master." The one [who had taken] two talents, said, "Sir, you have given me two talents. Look! I have gained an additional two." His master said to him, "Well done, good and faithful servant. You have been faithful over a few things. I will set you over many. Enter into the joy of your master." Then the one who had taken the one talent came and said, "Sir, I knew you, that you are a hard man, harvesting where you have not sown and gathering where you have not scattered, and, since I was afraid, I went away and hid your talent in the ground. See! You have your own [talent]."

Then his master, in reply, said to him, "Wicked and cowardly servant! You knew that I harvested where I have not sown and gathered where I have not scattered. Then you were obliged to give my silver to the moneychangers, and when I came I would have acquired my [silver] with interest. Take, then, the talent from him and give it to the one who has ten talents, for

To the one who has [earned interest]
 shall be given everything,
  and he will abound,
but to the one who has [earned] no [interest]
 even that [capital] which he has
  will be taken from him (Matt 25:13-20; Luke
   19:12-27).

A talent is an amount of silver that weighs about 75-85 pounds. The discussion here was in terms of high finance, the way anyone would have to consider if he or she were organizing a new government. After he had successfully persuaded many people to give up all of their wealth, there would have been a large treasury. That would have involved careful administration. Fortunately, Jesus had not chosen manual laborers as members of his cabinet. He organized good businessmen who were capable of managing and investing funds. One of the Jewish puns is, "Jesus saves, but Moses invests." According to this parable, Jesus was also involved in investing. In the investment business it is easier to double large sums than small sums, so the one who had been given only one talent for which to be responsible would have been at a disadvantage even if he had tried to invest. He was criticized for making no effort to increase the group's treasury. This was a parable and not a historical report, but it reflects the kind of environment in which Jesus functioned. The next parable was also important for the former big businessmen who had become subordinate officials.

> Which of you, having a servant, plowing or herding sheep, who, after he has come in from the field, will say to him, "Quickly, come and rest?" Rather, will he not say to him, "Prepare something for me to eat? Then, after you have girded yourself, serve me until I have eaten and drunk. After this, you also may eat and drink." He will not thank the servant because he has done that which he has been commanded, will he? Thus, also you, when you have done everything that has been commanded you, say, "We are useless servants. We have done that which we were required to do" (Luke 17:7-10).

This was directed to men who had formerly either owned slaves or had servants to do all of the manual work. They had issued commands, and expected either their slaves or their employees to do as they were required. But these leaders had since joined the monastery where all members were brothers. Monks had to do ordinary housework, cook, clean, wash dishes, carry water and wood, and do other chores that hired servants would do. That was surely difficult for upper class businessmen. They had taken vows of poverty, celibacy, and obedience. They were then the servants and not the CEOs. They had to take orders rather than give them. This was a very different way of life. They probably missed their former status, recognition, comforts, and authority. This was a great adjustment, and they needed reminders from time to time of the conditions of their admission into the order (Matt 20:20-27; Luke 22:24-26; Mark 16:42-43). They were to accept the positions they were given, do the work they were assigned. They were servants, not masters, disciples, not teachers (Matt 10:24-25). When the kingdom came, they would all be cabinet members and hold important offices, but until then, they had no time or occasion to expect royal treatment. The following parable was also prepared for people who had once managed finances.

> Who, among you, wanting to build a tower, will not first, after he has seated himself, count the cost [to see] if he has enough for the completion? Otherwise he might lay the foundation and not be able to finish. Then all those who observe will begin to mock him, saying, "This man began to build and was not able to finish."

Or,

> What king, going out to engage in battle with another king will not first, after he has seated himself, hold counsel [to see] if he is able with ten thousand soldiers to resist the one coming against him with a hundred thousand? If he cannot, while he is still a great distance, he will send a gift of honor and ask terms of peace (Luke 14:28-32).

Both of these parables began with questions, assuming that the listeners knew the logical answer. In the first, Jesus was talking about good business practices for people planning some large construction. These were concepts not undertaken by ordinary stone cutters, bricklayers, or carpenters. The same basic teaching was turned to a king commanding soldiers. Both of these had to sit down and calculate before they began the project. Jesus, however, was dealing with a possible revolution, and he had advisors who were impatient. When would this action begin? How long could they wait? Jesus had to assess his military and financial strength before he could wisely begin any project as large as evicting the entire Roman army from Palestine.

These parables are coherent with chreias demanding the high price for discipleship. Volunteers had to realize that the road ahead was rough. Those who wanted to be perfect had to take all they had and join the monastery, leaving the "dead" to bury the "dead" (Luke 14:25-26). Those who wanted to be perfect were given the note of caution. The project was huge. No one really wanted to fail. It was necessary to wait until all the signs were just right. In any battle there are always the winners and the losers. People involved need to think carefully about which side they choose to support. After the battle there are rewards and punishments distributed. The following parable shows that.

> When the son of man comes in his glory,
>> and all his agents with him,
> Then he will sit on his glorious throne,
>> and all nations will be gathered before him.
> Then he will separate them one from another,
>> just as a shepherd separates the sheep from the goats;
> And he will place the sheep on his right
>> but the goats on his left.
> Then the king will say to those at his right,
>> "Come, blessed of my Father, inherit the kingdom
>>> prepared for you from the foundation of the world.
>>>> for I was hungry, and you gave me [something] to eat,
>> And I was thirsty, and you quenched my thirst;
>> I was a stranger, and you gave me hospitality,
>>> naked, and you clothed me;
>> I was sick and you cared for me,
>>> in prison, and you visited me."

Then the righteous will answer him, saying,
    "When did we see you sick or in prison,
        and we came to you?"
Then, by reply, the king will say to them,
    "Whatever you did to one of these least of my brothers
        you did to me."
Then he will say to those on his left,
    "Leave me, you cursed, into eternal fire prepared
        for the devil and his agents.
For I was hungry, and you gave me no[thing] to eat.
I was thirsty, and you did not quench my thirst;
I was a stranger, and you gave me no hospitality;
    naked, and you did not clothe me,
        sick, and in prison and you did not care for me."
Then they will answer, saying,
    "Lord, when did we see you hungry or thirsty or
        a stranger or naked or sick or in prison, and
            we did not minister to you?"
Then, by reply, he will say to them,
    "I tell you under oath,
    'Whatever you did to one of the least,
        you did to me.'"
Then, these will go away to eternal punishment,
    But the righteous into life of the age (Matt 25:31-46).

Like the drama describing a trial in heaven by the Ancient of Days at Hanukkah, following the victory of Judas and the Jewish guerrillas at the Valley of Beth-horon, described in Dan 7, this poem is a projected judgment to be made after the victorious battle planned in Jesus' day. In Dan 7, the plaintiff was one like a son of man. In Matthew the son of man was also the plaintiff. In Dan 7, the plaintiff was Judas the Maccabee; in Jesus' time, it was Jesus.

This poem could have been read many times to audiences by different ones of Jesus' apostles. The purpose was to encourage those who had been passive observers to become involved. There would be only two groups:

1) Those who had helped Jesus and his followers, and
2) those who did not.

In a movement, such as this, there would have been many degrees of authority. Jesus' apostles were the middle managers, but they probably had subordinate supporters and volunteers, all of whom were supporters of the program. Even the least of these were Jesus' brothers and his legal agents. This parable illustrates the importance of the legal practice of agency. Legally a person's agent is the person himself or herself. The agent acts in behalf of, in the name of, and at the responsibility of the principal. Here the principal was the King Jesus.

In monastic programs, such as the Essenes and those legal agents that Jesus sent out (Matt 10), the missionaries went out without provisions, and they depended entirely on the provisions and hospitality given by non-monastic members of their sect. If they were not provided hospitality, those events would be remembered later, according to this parable. This parable was designed to encourage potential hosts and hostesses to welcome the apostles that entered their area.

In Palestine there are many herds of goats and also of sheep. Sheep are easier to herd than goats. Sheep are ignorant and dependent. They require a shepherd to decide for them where to go and what to do. Goats think and are rather independent, but most shepherds keep one male goat in a flock of sheep. The goat might see some danger the shepherd overlooked. If so, he would run, and all the sheep would follow him and be saved. Jesus' middle managers were expected to be as obedient as sheep, but they also were needed to be able to invest wisely and make decisions like goats. This judgment parable is the longest parable of Jesus, but there is another parable telling about the consequences of the judgment.

> Whenever the householder arises and closes the door, you also will begin to stand outside and knock on the door, saying, "Sir, open for us." Then he will say in reply, "I

do not know from where you have come." Then you will begin to say, "We ate and drank in your presence and you taught in our streets." Then, speaking, he will say to you, "I do not know from where you have come. Leave me, all [you] workers of iniquity." There will be there weeping and gnashing of teeth, when you see Abraham, Isaac and Jacob, and all the prophets in the Kingdom of God, but you are cast out. And they will come from the East, and from the West, from the North, and from the South, and they will recline in the Kingdom of God, and Look! There are [people] of last [rank] who will be first and [people] of first rank who will be last (Luke 13:25-30).

This parable begins with a master of some kind of house closing the door, but it does not tell what the door was, why it was being closed or what the occasion was. When this was first told, it was in response to something everyone knew, but we do not. We have to conjecture the situation on the basis of the story itself. It might be associated with the Passover service of another parable, where the five virgins were excluded when the door was shut. Since it seems to be a very serious and final exclusion, it is probably the messianic banquet that would be associated with the coronation of the king and also Passover. Those who were threatened by Jesus' success were the scribes and Pharisees who would have lost their offices if Jesus succeeded and chose a new cabinet made up of his apostles. The scribes and Pharisees are the ones who are pictured as crying to be admitted. They were the ones who would be displaced.

Those who come from the East, West, North, and South are faithful Jews in the diaspora who had supported Jesus' program from the beginning. In Matthew's account of this event, it followed the narrative about the centurion who wanted his son to be healed. That centurion was obviously a Jew, because he knew the rules of overshadowing that would make it illegal for Jesus to enter his house. The law of overshadowing is a law that says a person who comes under the same roof as a corpse is defiled by corpse defilement. A person who is defiled has something like a black magic spell cast over him or her that is like a disease. Depending on the kind of defilement the person is isolated from orthodox Jews until the spell is broken.

A person defiled with corpse uncleanness must remove himself from contact with all other people, perform the correct rituals, and remain defiled for seven days. After that he or she can be sprinkled with the ashes of the red heifer and be cleansed (Num 19:14-19). The average gentile would never have heard of this law.

The centurion also had built for the local people a synagogue (Luke 7:5). There were many Jews in the Roman army in NT times. John the Baptist told Jewish soldiers in the Roman army not to rob other Jews by violence or false accusation and to be satisfied with the pay they received from the Romans (Luke 3:12-14). This centurion was also a Jew. When Herod died one of his generals, a Jew, led his entire regiment of 2,000 soldiers from Herod's army to join in the revolution against the Roman occupation.

This parable reflects the prophecy of Second Isaiah, which pictures the Jews returning from Babylon. When the Lord comforted his people by restoring the land, then the diaspora Jews would return to Palestine from all of the places where they had been taken, "From the North and the West and from the land of Syene [in the East]" (Isa 49:12). They were not planning on going to heaven, but to Jerusalem. This parable anticipates the prophecy being fulfilled. There in Palestine the diaspora Jews would recline at a banquet with Abraham, Isaac, and Jacob, but there would be local Jews, "sons of the kingdom," like the Pharisees, who would be cast out (Matt 8:11). Being cast out does not mean they would be expelled from Palestine or thrown into the pits of hell. They would be thrown out of their governmental offices and replaced by Jesus' disciples.

All of this would take place in the Kingdom of God, which was the Promised Land, and not anywhere in Rome, Egypt, or Asia Minor. The Kingdom of God was the "Kingdom of Yehowah" over which Solomon ruled when he sat on the throne in Jerusalem (1Chron 28:5). King David was speaking of the United Kingdom, the land from the River of Egypt on the south to the Great River that forms the border of Lebanon on the north, when he said, "Yours is the kingdom, Yehowah" (1Chron 29:11). In one of the Dead Sea fragments there is a prayer for God's people wherever they were scattered and for God's kingdom, that was obviously Judah where the king at the time of the writing was Alexander Janneus (78-103 B.C.; 4Q448 B.C. 8). Jerusalem was the City of God the capital of the Kingdom of God. There is no biblical evidence to refute this, but many fictions have been written to ignore it.

The messianic banquet would have been something like the banquet held by Adonijah at Ain Rogel, just before the death of David. He was there with most of the members of David's cabinet celebrating his anticipated coronation. He was interrupted, however, by the shout, just 300 meters north at Ain Gihon, saying, "Long live King Solomon!" (1Kings 1:5-39). What a revolting development!

SUMMARY

The ancient grammar books that I read, introducing me to the literary form, "chreia," provided just the clue I needed to find valid information of the teachings of Jesus. When these are compared for coherence among themselves and with associated parables and tested in relationship to the land and history of the place where Jesus lived and conducted his ministry, and the people with whom he was associated, it is obvious that we have a solid basis for learning more about the historical Jesus. There are still more chreias and more parables to tell us about Jesus' action and teaching – in fact there is more testable data for learning about the historical Jesus than there is for most other similarly ancient characters in history. This will become still more obvious in the continuing chapters that will provide more illustrations. The next chapter will show dramatically the extensive conflict Jesus had with the Pharisees in his defense of the tax collectors and other businessmen who had broken Jewish law.

CHAPTER THREE

CONFRONTING THE STATUS QUO

CONTEMPORARIES OF JESUS

The Status quo for Pharisees. Jesus set out to change the status quo. He wanted to remove the Romans from their position of ruling power and establish the Kingdom of God in Palestine. This could not come about without changing the status quo from within. The Pharisees were comfortable with the status quo. They were in positions of power and were getting along rather well with the Romans. They were the keepers of the law, and law has a very stabilizing way of keeping things as they are. The law approved the actions of the Pharisees. The Pharisees fulfilled the letter of each law. They gave their tenths that the law required; they observed the Sabbath; and they ate only foods that were approved both by the law and Jewish tradition.

The Pharisees were very critical of Jesus' associates, whom they called tax collectors and criminals. These were upper class people who were members of the best social and business clubs and associated regularly in business with the Romans. Many other

Jews were also critical of this group of people, but Jesus persuaded these upper class CEOs to give 100% of their goods to the monastic community and become monks themselves. This made an impression on many Jews, but it was a threat to the Pharisees. They had belonged to the highest class of religious people, but they could not compete with the demands of Jesus. Chreias and parables preserved in the gospels show the conflict that developed between the Pharisees and Jesus.

Conflict with Pharisees.

> Now it happened, when he was reclining in the house. Now look! Many tax collectors and criminals had come and were reclining with Jesus and his disciples. When the Pharisees saw, they began to say to his disciples, "Why does your teacher eat with tax collectors and criminals?" When he heard, he said, "The healthy have no need for a physician, but those who are ill" (Matt 9:10-13; Mark 2:15-17; Luke 5:29-31).

Like the chreia asking the fishermen to become fishers of men, this chreia is a summary of an event that was more extensive. The Pharisees were not present at the banquet involved. If they had been, they could not have been critical of Jesus for also having been there. They had learned about the event through the "gossip grapevine" and later cross-examined the disciples about it. This chreia reports the event that took place at that time. There may have been more events like this that the Pharisees knew were happening. It was against the law to eat with the unorthodox, even if the food was approved. John the Baptist would never have done such a thing. He was extremely careful about food laws, and Jesus had been trained in the same rigor. The Pharisees noticed the difference.

Before the fall of Jerusalem in 586 B.C. levitical rules had been designed for observance for the priests, primarily for their tasks in the temple. It was liturgically required that they be completely undefiled, because the temple was the dwelling place of the Lord. His presence was contingent upon their observance. Once the temple had been burned, and the upper class Jews and the craftsmen and skilled Jews had been taken into Babylon, Jews there had to find substitutes for the temple and the priesthood. They did not want to be excluded from God's presence, so the laypeople took upon themselves the responsibility of preparing places for God's presence. They had a precedent for this.

When North Israel seceded from Judah, the priests and Levites from Israel fled to Judah, leaving Israel without priests, but temple services continued in Israel at places like Bethel and Mount Gerizim. Israel apparently installed priests that were not from families like those of Zadok, Aaron, or Levi. In Babylon, Jews did the same. They established monasteries with monks from non-priestly families who functioned as priests in monasteries that were temporary temples, and the monks kept themselves as undefiled as the priests who served in the temple at Zion. They took vows of poverty, celibacy, and obedience. Other lay people who were married also kept their houses as undefiled as possible and still have families.

They kept their kitchens as undefiled as the altar and their homes as ritually pure as the temple. They kept their own bodies and clothes undefiled and refused to admit into their homes guests that were not as observant as they. Those guests they accepted were considered "worthy" and those not accepted were "unworthy." These restrictive people were very careful where they went, what they ate, with whom they associated, and what and whom they touched. When they returned to the Promised Land, after their exile into Babylon, they continued their exclusivity. Some of their religious descendants were the Pharisees.

Those engaged in international business, of course, could not be as careful as that. They had to do business with people of other nations and religions. They associated with them socially and ate with them. That made them outcasts and unworthy from the liturgical point of view. Jesus and his disciples had been reared in this class and were therefore considered unworthy. Jesus, however, had later joined a monastic sect led by John the Baptist and was trained in all the Levitical exclusiveness. Since that was true, Pharisees expected Jesus to be as exclusive as John and they were.

Jesus had one goal in mind – the establishment of the Kingdom of God in Palestine. To obtain that kingdom he had to have the kind of resources available only among the upper class leaders. They had the money and the talent. Therefore, Jesus did not set out to train people in exclusivity. After they had joined the monastery, these rich men became financially "poor." They depended on the monastery to provide their needs. Some scholars claim that monasteries required monks to give up all of their money so that their minds were not distracted from spiritual thoughts. That was not the main reason for the demand. The monastery had to provide social security for the members as long as they lived. Members were divorced from the families that gave them birth. The monastery needed this money for very practical reasons. Jesus also needed money for his movement. Scholars have misunderstood this and identified these apostles with Americans like Abraham Lincoln who learned to write with charcoal on the back of a shovel. Jesus' apostles, however, did not grow up in nineteenth century America. They were Near Easterners where class lines were distinct. They would not have had the money Jesus needed if they had not been associated with wealth all of their lives.

Jesus concentrated on that which was necessary for restoring the kingdom. He did not alienate them by carefully detailed liturgical forms. He taught these men to give up only their families, social and business responsibilities, and their material possessions for the sake of the Kingdom of God. That was a tremendous amount, but it was the kind of support he needed and they were able to provide. He also showed them how to use their talents to promote that kingdom and recruit other leaders to participate in it. Jesus was not training kindergarten children in catechism. He did not have to teach them how to read and write. He taught his disciples how to take notes and write chreias, and he taught them parables to use in their tasks. Like Jesus, the apostles were all well educated people who were able to write down all of this material. That is probably the reason it has been preserved until today.

Because some of these businessmen had cooperated with the Romans and even collected taxes for them, they were not very loyal nationalists when Jesus first met them, but he realized their potential. He also knew that they were truly faithful Jews who had adjusted to the environment, because they thought they had no choice. He correctly thought that when they were given a choice they would abandon their Roman connection and dedicate themselves to be stronger nationalists than the Pharisees had ever been. Jesus recognized their problems, and he came to them as a physician to restore them to health and benefit from their healed contribution.

Jesus taught his disciples only that which they needed to know to recruit more followers and prepare the citizens for the Kingdom of God. In order to bring in the Kingdom of God, Jesus would have to act as the Messiah and establish a new contract between God and his people. He would do that by acting as God's legal agent, establishing a new legal corporation, and performing the necessary legal liturgy to form a new contract between God, as the groom, and his people, as the corporate bride. Legally, Jesus would become the new bridegroom in God's behalf. He was still with his disciples who were the sons of the bridegroom, and as his apostles, they were still working to establish the Kingdom of God. The goals Jesus had in mind were political – not just psychological. As Peuch said,

> In many passages in the Gospels, from the narratives and the answer to Caiaphas, we find such formulas as the Son of God, the Son of the most High, the Messiah, the Son of Man, the king of Jews. These titles show without a doubt that Jesus was regarded as the king Messiah.[1]

---

[1] E. Peuch, "Messianism, Resurrection, and Eschatology," *The Community of the Renewed Covenant*, eds. E. Ulrich and J. Vanderkam (Notre Dame: U. of Notre Dame Press, c1994), p. 243.

Still in conflict with the Pharisees, the following chreia was written with Jesus as the character.

> The Pharisees and scribes were coming to Jesus from Jerusalem. They asked, "Why do your students transgress the tradition of the elders? For they do not wash their hands when they eat bread. He answered them, "Why do you transgress the commandment of God because of your tradition (Matt 15:1-3)?

This is a chreia, but it does not tell which commandment the Pharisees broke for the sake of their tradition. At the time when the chreia was written, the Pharisees, Jesus, and the first readers all knew what commandment was intended, but the later gospel editor realized that his readers would no longer know that, so he explained what he thought the commandment was. He was probably mistaken, and so his addition suffered from the kind of errors the later church was able to make. Schweitzer thought these mistakes could not be recognized and distinguished from the valid teachings of Jesus, making research on the historical Jesus impossible, but here is the interpretation of the chreia made by the later church.

> For God said, **Honor your father and your mother** (Exod 20:12, and **Let the one who curses his father and his mother receive the death penalty** (Exod 21:17). You say, "whoever says, '[by the] gift [on the altar], [may the following unexpressed curses come upon me] if you receive any benefit from me,' he will not honor his father or his mother, so you overrule the commandment of God for the sake of your tradition" (Matt 15:4-6).

Curses were a normal part of oaths. Oaths usually had these parts:

1) A sacred being or object (the gift on the altar) by whom or what the oath was taken.

2) A list of curses the oath-taker was willing to accept (here understood but omitted).

3) *If* he did not do as he said or if that which he said was not true (here, if he provided for his parents in their old age). Many times the oaths were minted, omitting the curses, because they feared that even expressing them out loud might make them happen. Instead they allowed them to be understood, as was done here.

The original oath might have been something like this:

> *Kohr-báhn* (by the gift on the altar),
> [May the following unmentioned curses come upon me],
> If I provide any benefit to my parents.

When oaths like this were made the Pharisees upheld the oath, and the parents were neglected, breaking the commandment to honor their fathers and mothers. This commandment required that children provide their parents in old age with food, shelter, and clean garments (Mek *Bahod* 8:1-4).[1] There were many monks in NT times in sects like those of 1QS, the Essenes, the Pharisees, the group represented by the Sermon on the Mount, or Hebrews 1-12, or First John. These monks took vows of poverty, celibacy, and obedience, which required them to break the commandment to honor their parents. The member of the later church who wrote this addition to the chreia held that Jesus opposed this monastic practice, but that is not so. Jesus asked his followers to take all they had and give to "the poor" members of the monastery who no longer owned anything, personally (Matt 19:21). His disciples had left houses, lands, and family to follow Jesus (Matt 19:27-29),

---

[1] Buchanan, *The Gospel of Matthew* (Lewiston: Mellen Biblical Press, 1996), pp. 654-55; "Jesus and Other Monks of New Testament Times," *Religion in Life* (Summer, 1979).

and they were required to call no man on earth "father" (Matt 23:9).[1] Using the same chreia the Gospel of Mark interpreted it as follows:

> **The Pharisees and** certain of **the scribes** gathered together, **coming from Jerusalem**, and when they saw some of **his disciples** that they **were eating bread with common hands – that is, unwashed** – (for **the Pharisees** and all Jews if they do not **wash their hands** they do not **eat**, holding fast to **the traditions of the elders**. Also from the marketplace if they **do not wash**, they do not **eat**, and many other things they hold to, that they have received, washing cups, dishes, and pans). Then **the Pharisees and the scribes asked him, "Why do your students not observe the traditions of the elders?" Then he said to them**, "Well has Isaiah prophesied about you hypocrites, as it is written, 'This people with their lips honor me, but their minds are removed far from me. They worship me in vain, teaching teachings [that are] **the commandments** of human beings,' **abandoning the commandment of God**, you **hold to the traditions of** human beings." **Then he said to them, "You have rejected the commandment of God** so that you could **keep your traditions**" (Mark 7:1-9).

This is a typical literary unit, consisting of the chreia which Mark has expanded in a commentary written later on a chreia in which Jesus was the character, and its commentary is easily distinguished from the teaching of Jesus as a later addition, with the intertexts recognized, once it is related to the corresponding

---

[1] Buchanan, "Jesus and the Upper Class," *Novum Testamentum* 8 (1964):195-209. and *Jesus the King and His Kingdom* (Macon: Mercer U. Press, c1984), pp. 171-190.

chreia. There are also other expansions of some of the gospel chreias.[1] There are 25 chreias in the gospels. These, together with whatever commentaries have been associated with them, provide an important method of distinguishing the teachings of Jesus from the additions of the later church. Most scholars speak of the later church in depreciative terms. That is not a reasonable assumption with which to begin. It was normal for chreias to be texts for sermons. Chreias were used as texts even in Diogenes' day, and chreias are still used today by ministers, preachers and rabbis as texts for fuller development and interpretation. Scholars have a right to pass judgment on each expanded chreia to discover whether the later church interpreted the chreia correctly. Many times the church also quoted the chreia first so that the reader had a basis for judgment.

Here in Matthew there are two different teachings. One of these is the chreia that includes the sayings of Jesus. The other is attached to it, but it is obviously not the saying of Jesus. Instead it is the interpretation of the chreia by the later church. Mark has expanded the chreia itself to include its interpretation. The exact location of the event in the chreia is not given, but it was close enough to Jerusalem for the Pharisees and scribes from Jerusalem to have come to Jesus. This was not an event that took place in the later church somewhere outside of Palestine.

The criticism that the Pharisees and scribes (attorneys) directed to Jesus is clear. The disciples of Jesus did not wash their hands, ritually, before they ate, a tradition that the elders decreed should be done. This was a criticism similar to the objection that his apostles did not fast or observe dietary rules. Jesus did not try to claim that his disciples were not guilty of the offenses of which they were criticized. His goal was too important to be distracted by these less important details. In this instance he did not answer the question asked at all. He just returned the *ad hominem* attack – and even that is not clear at this point. An *ad hominem* argument is

---

[1]   These are shown in *Jesus the King*.

an attack against the opponent, personally, rather than the topic debated. It usually consists of a personal insult of some kind.

The author of the interpretation did not approve of the popular monastic practices of the early church. Vows of poverty, celibacy, and obedience involved the promise that upon joining a monastery, the volunteer would give all of his possessions to the monastery, and from then on give all of his earnings to the monastery. The author of the exegesis of this chreia obviously opposed monasticism. Since the chreia did not say what commandment the Pharisees broke, the interpreter was free to choose whichever one he thought was reasonable, and, since ancient courts required two witnesses to prove a case, he supported his argument with two scriptural texts.

Matthew's explanation of the meaning of the chreia is false. Jesus did not oppose monasticism. He was himself a monk. One of the chief messages of his campaign was to get wealthy men to give up all they possessed and join his monastery. Either Matthew did not know this, or he knew but objected and chose a teaching of Jesus to give authority to a teaching that opposed Jesus' teaching. Many interpreters, both before and after the time of Jesus, have used texts to support a point different from the text. Because the early church sometimes misrepresented Jesus, scholars have concluded that they might have invented and misrepresented all of the sayings attributed to Jesus. That is no longer a valid conclusion.

In any event, we are left with the chreia itself to learn what Jesus intended, and the chreia does not say or even imply what that is, so from this chreia we can learn only

1) that Jesus was criticized by the scribes and the Pharisees because his disciples did not observe purity rules about hand washings,
2) Jesus did not refute their claim, and
3) Jesus only accused the Pharisees of being still less observant than his disciples.

They broke not only the tradition of the elders, but they broke the commandments of the Scripture itself. The chreia did not say which commandments. The person who wrote down the chreia understood all of the details. He wrote the chreia only to remind the reader of that which he or she already knew. In the twenty-first century we can conjecture which commandment Jesus accused the Pharisees of having broken, but we can never know, because the text does not say. Jesus was under Pharisaic attack for neglecting ritualistic details, and he responded by telling parables. An associated parable was about the weeds and the wheat.

John the Baptist and Jesus. The disciples' behavior shocked not only the Pharisees, but also the disciples of John the Baptist.

> Then the disciples of John approached him, saying, "Why do we and the Pharisees fast, but you and your disciples do not fast?" Then Jesus said to them, "The sons of the bridegroom are not able to fast as long as the bridegroom is with them" (Matt 9:14-15; Mark 2:18-20; Luke 5:33-34).

This is another responsive chreia. The speaker is identified; the situation that prompted him to speak is given; and the character's answer is quoted. Mark's unit is slightly expanded, but the answer of Jesus is identical. Luke's version has almost ceased to be a chreia as it is adjusted to fit into a larger context. Chreias stand alone and are independent of their contexts into which later editors include them.

The disciples who came to Jesus were the students of John the Baptist. John was no fictitious character made up by some later church for some imagined purpose. He was a historical character, a contemporary of both Jesus and Herod Antipas. Not only the gospels, but also Josephus wrote about John the Baptist. Herod had him killed. Jesus had been one of his disciples. This chreia was put in written form before it was necessary to say who this man, called John, was. All the readers would have known. The author did not even have to mention the fact that he had been killed, because all the first readers would have known that. Had this document been created by the later church the author would also have to have told why anyone should have been fasting at that time. All of this speaks for the reliability of this document and its message as a quotation from the historical Jesus.

Jesus said of John the Baptist that he was the greatest of all people ever born of women (Matt 1:11). Jesus said further that all the prophets prophesied until John. Since rabbis said that all prophets prophesied only for the days of the Messiah, Jesus obviously intended to say in code that he and his listeners were living in the days of the Messiah. That, of course, was a coded way of saying that Jesus, himself, was the Messiah (Matt 11:13). Another way Jesus had of saying the same thing was to say that John was the messenger that Malachi prophesied would come to prepare the way for the Messiah (Mal 3:1). Jesus also said that John was the Elijah who would precede the Messiah (Matt 11:14).

The disciples of John were mourning, as were also the Pharisees, because John was no longer with them. The text did not say John had died, and it did not say why these people were fasting, but mourning was accompanied by fasting, and the disciples of John were fasting. They knew that Jesus had been also a disciple of John. That is why they wondered why the disciples of Jesus were not also fasting. This is the kind of respect one might normally expect of a faithful student. Jesus answered that his disciples differed from the disciples of John the Baptist, because their teacher was still with them. They were not obligated to fast for their teacher as the Johannine disciples were. Jesus, however, said more than that in code. Instead of calling himself a teacher of his disciples, he called himself the bridegroom. How did he mean that when he was a monk who had never been married? The answer is in legal concepts.

Jesus was anointed as the Son of God to establish the Kingdom of Heaven. He was not commissioned to keep the Sabbath, train his disciples in all sorts of dietary laws and purity rules or to take time out from his work to mourn and fast. He had to limit himself to his one project and his one goal for which John the Baptist had anointed him. That was more in keeping with his responsibility as a disciple of John than mourning and fasting because of his death. Jesus was working under the pressure of time. He could not take time out to fast; he could not allow volunteers to wait until their parents died and then become followers. He did not observe the Sabbath day the way the Pharisees thought was proper. He justified this behavior on the basis that he was the Father's legal agent. God worked every day. Since he was under God's assignment to act in his name and in his behalf, he should be doing that which his Father was doing. It was legitimate for God's legal agent to be working on the Sabbath (John 5:17). There was also another factor at work here. If Jesus mourned publicly it would tell the Romans how closely he was identified with John the Baptist. That would be unnecessarily dangerous.

PARABLES ON THE PATHWAY OF JESUS

Parables of Patience. Parables are not historical reports. They are told for definite purposes, and the purposes for which they are told determined their real meaning. They became parts of collections that the disciples took with them on their missions. This means, at this late date, far removed from the event, we have to conjecture the context and meaning from other situations that occurred at the same time and the customs of that time. We are likely to make mistakes, so we need to check the parables for time, historical events, geographical locations, and coherence among themselves and with the chreias. One of the parables, attributed to Jesus is this:

> The Kingdom of Heaven is like a man sowing good seed in his field. While people slept, his enemy came and sowed weeds in the midst of the wheat and went away. When, however, the stalk grew and produced fruit, and then also the weeds became evident. The servants of the manager said to him, "Sir did you not sow good seed in your field? From where, then, does it have weeds?" He said to them, "An enemy has done this." The servants said to him, "Do you want us, then, to go out and uproot

them?" He replied, "No! Lest while you are gathering the weeds you uproot also the wheat. Let them both grow until the harvest. Then, in the time of the harvest, I will tell the harvesters, "Gather first the weeds, and tie them into bundles to burn, but the wheat gather into my granary" (Matt 13:24-30).

Like many other parables, this story is not completely rational in itself, because the parable is not designed to give lessons in agriculture. Farmers do not normally suffer from outsiders sowing weeds in their fields. Weeds just come up voluntarily, and they do not cause alarm and suspicion that enemies planted them. This deviation was made to alert the listener to the fact that this was intended to tell about something other than weeds and wheat. What was the field? What was the wheat? and what were the weeds in the obvious metaphorical use of the terms?

Since other parables and chreias show Jesus in conflict with the Pharisees, defending the tax collectors, this seems like the place to begin. In the parable of the treasure hidden in the field, the field was the Promised Land, and it probably also had the same identification here. The "weeds," which Jesus was defending, were probably the Jewish tax collectors who worked for the Romans to sap the land of its resources so that the "wheat" could be starved. The Pharisees wanted to get rid of all of them – a rigorous weeding program. The Pharisees thought these "weeds" were criminals, and they blamed Jesus for associating with these characters. The tax collectors were not criminals because they had not broken any Roman law, but they were criminals in the eyes of the Jews, because they had broken Jewish laws. Jesus was able to convert some of them, get them to repent and become powerful, national leaders.

In NT times tax collectors seemed to be popping up like weeds everywhere in the Promised Land. Initially, the tax collectors were normal, neighboring Jews. They did not grow up voluntarily, like weeds, first of all. The enemy, Rome, came in and recruited them. Weeds grow up from weed seeds. They cannot be changed. They are weeds from the beginning to the end. That was not so of the tax collectors. They began as Jews, and they might be changed again to become faithful Jews. All they needed was a good physician to heal them of their diseases. The normal way of getting rid of weeds in a wheat field was to wait until harvest and then burn them. This is regularly done in the Near East. Not only do farmers bundle up grown weeds and burn them, but after harvest they burn the entire field to rid the field of weeds. Jesus was allowing for the fact that he would not be able to convert all of the tax collectors, but he argued for patience. Tearing them out early would damage the country and deprive the land of their potential, so he advised, "Let them both grow until harvest."

The harvest of a revolution would take place after the war was over and the field general gathered his troops together and paid rewards to the heroes, punished the saboteurs, and sold the enemy captives into slavery or led them in victory parades. That was the great judgment day. Another similar parable is that of the various kinds of fish in a sea.

> Again the Kingdom of Heaven is like a fish net, thrown into the sea. It gathers from every kind [of sea creatures]. When it has been filled, they draw it up onto the shore. Then they sit down and gather the good ones into a container, and they throw out the worthless ones (Matt 13:47-48).

The analogy here is not between the Kingdom of God and a fish net. This means that the Kingdom of Heaven is like a situation in which a fish net was thrown into the sea. In this parable, Jesus was also talking about the kinds of people in the Promised Land. He probably did not tell all of these parables in sequence at the same occasion. These parables were given to all of the apostles to tell when they were out on promotional tours of duty. Different disciples told different stories at different times.

Of the "sea creatures" involved, some were tax collectors; some were Pharisees; some were Sadducees; some were Essenes. The Pharisees wanted to get rid of the tax collectors at once, excluding them from the Kingdom. They wanted to preempt the judgment. This would require a military revolution.

Jews who fished in the Sea of Galilee were not authorized to eat all sea creatures. Only those creatures that had scales and fins were approved by dietary laws (*kah-sháyr*). That does not mean that other sea creatures did not live in Palestinian waters. They did, and in the same way, tax collectors continued to live on Palestinian soil, even though Pharisees did not like them. The turtles, frogs, eels, catfish, and other creatures were forbidden to Jews for food, because they did not have scales and fins. Fishermen, however, were not able to select which creatures they would admit into their nets. They had to take everything that came into the net.

Those who couldn't stand to touch unapproved sea creatures could never become fishermen, and a person who would not touch weeds could not be a farmer. It was only after the net had been pulled in that the fishermen were able to sort out the good fish that had scales and fins and separate them from all the others (Lev 11:11-13). It was like the weeds and the wheat. Farmers and fishermen had to wait until the correct time to do the sorting. That time always came, but it could not be rushed without adverse consequences. Jesus used these parables in conflict with the Pharisees to persuade them that they also should be patient with the tax collectors and criminals with whom Jesus associated. Wait and see what the result was at the judgment. Those tax collectors by then might become respectable, devoted, committed patriots. Jesus expected them to become even important national leaders, replacing the Pharisees in their offices.

By the time these parables were told, Jesus had probably already been very successful in recruiting tax collectors that Rome had employed and that the Pharisees wanted weeded out. Jesus knew that they were very talented people. One of them, Zacchaeus, was not only a tax collector, but a chief tax collector and very rich. He volunteered to take half of his possessions to repay and amend for all his previous injustices, so that he had no unpaid fines to confront the state. The rest he would give to the poor, which probably meant he would contribute it to Jesus' monastic movement (Luke 19:1-10). Jesus had been very successful and learned the wisdom of recruiting these tax collectors, "criminals," "harlots," "weeds," and unapproved "sea creatures." They were the most competent leaders in all Palestine. Jesus was still defending the tax collectors when he told the next parable.

> How does it seem to you? If a man has a hundred sheep, and one of them goes astray, will he not leave the ninety-nine on the mountains, and after he has gone, look for the one that has wandered? If he finds it, I tell you under oath that he will rejoice more over it than over the ninety-nine that did not go astray. Therefore, it is not the will of your Father in heaven that one of these little ones perish (Matt 18:12-13).

Luke expanded this parable enough so that no one could misunderstand who the lost sheep were: "I tell you that there will be joy in heaven over one criminal who repents more than ninety-nine who have no need of repentance" (Luke 15:7). The little ones were the newly recruited disciples. They were attending Jesus' classes, but they were just learning. They had not yet become monks, but they were preparing themselves. Pharisees were hostile to them, but Jesus recognized their potential.

The sheep who needed no repentance were the same as the ones who had no need of a physician. These were the Pharisees who were constantly troubling Jesus for his association with the tax collectors and criminals, who were the lost sheep and those in need of repentance and of a physician (Matt 9; Luke 15:1).

Only an unusual shepherd would be willing to leave a flock of sheep to get lost, while he is looking for a lost one. Sheep are not very intelligent. They depend on someone to watch them constantly if they are not penned inside a fence or a building. This is not a lesson in animal husbandry, but a parable, and Jesus was not really talking about sheep and mountains, but Pharisees and criminals on the Promised Land.

The house of Israel, however, is called a flock of sheep, so the listeners would readily know that Jesus was not speaking about real sheep. It is not a good idea to leave sheep unattended, but there was no danger in leaving the numerous law observant Pharisees unattended in the land of Palestine. These were not criminals but experts in keeping the law. They were the people who thanked God that they were not like others. Jesus conceded their righteousness many times, maybe satirically, but nonetheless he started the argument with the same presuppositions as the Pharisees. Since that was the case, then how should this Jewish criminal be treated in the Promised Land?

The few upper class businessmen who had associated with the Romans and made money, often at the expense of local Jews, exerted enough power to demand attention. The Gospel of Thomas (107) version of this parable called the lost sheep the largest of the flock. If only these could be motivated to repent and direct all of this power and wealth in the direction of the Kingdom of God, it would make a real difference. The leadership and wealth of each one of these would contribute more to the liberation of Palestine than a hundred ordinary Jewish citizens who faithfully paid their taxes.

Therefore Jesus encouraged the Pharisees to cease from their efforts to stop his program by distancing these upper class leaders from Israel's national security program, asking them, instead, to rejoice with Jesus and note the joy in heaven that occurs over the repentance and restoration of one criminal to the faithful. Jesus told still more parables with the same point.

> What woman, having ten drachmas, if she loses one drachma, will not light a lamp and search the house and look carefully until she finds [it]? When she has found the lost coin, she will invite her friends and neighbors, saying, "Rejoice with me, because I have found the drachma which I had lost." Thus, I tell you there will be joy in heaven before the angels of God over one criminal, repenting" (Luke 15:8-10).

Like the parable of the lost sheep, this parable concludes with the finder rejoicing and inviting in all the neighbors to celebrate. This does not make good sense. The shepherd that has to kill two sheep or a fatted calf for the festival does not come out ahead, financially, by rescuing one sheep. The same is true of the woman who finds one small coin. This is not enough for a very elaborate celebration. In both cases that which was really lost was the tax collector whom Jesus had modestly, perhaps in understatement, called "one of the least," "a criminal."

Here he was represented by a small coin. Although the tax collector was belittled and depreciated by the Pharisees, in reality, the tax collector was a very rich man, who could more justly be called an "especially large sheep," as the Gospel of Thomas did. It was proper and good business for Jesus to celebrate their inclusion with banquets. Those occasions were bases for joy and for the kind of banquets and rejoicing Jesus seems to have been enjoying when the Pharisees criticized him for eating with criminals and harlots. In this context the harlot was not a sexual prostitute. It was a Jew who associated with gentiles. The dog, on the other hand, was the gentile who associated with Jews. Both dogs and harlots were association insults orthodox Jews used with the intention of offending.

The Pharisees implied that Jesus' apostles, who were celibate males, were criminals because they associated with gentiles in business or society. They used the sexual insult to make the offense of association seem more distasteful.

If the tax collector really fit the classification the Pharisees gave him, then these celebrations make no sense. Jesus' understatements may have been made deliberately to make the analysis of the Pharisees look ridiculous, just as the parable of the Pharisee and the tax collector in the temple did.

Luke identified the lost coin with the tax collector, just as he did the lost sheep. This is evident from the fact that he also used this parable to illustrate the chreia about the sick who needed the physician. The Pharisees did not complain to Jesus only about his neglect of Pharisaic law. They resented the implications of his actions. How could he overlook the experience and training in government the Pharisees exhibited? How could he drag into government a cabinet of newcomers who had training only in business and tax collecting? In answer to this question, Jesus told the story of the employer and his laborers.

The New Jacob and Esau.

> For the Kingdom of Heaven is like a man who owned property, who went out every morning to hire workers for his vineyard. He agreed with the workers on a denarius a day, and he sent them out to his vineyard. When he went out about the third hour, he saw others standing in the market place, idle. He said to them, "Go work in my vineyard, also, and whatever is just I will give you." So they went out. He went out again at the sixth and the ninth hour and did the same. About the eleventh hour, when he went out, he found others standing, and he said to them, "Why do you stand here all day idle?" They said to him, "Because no one has hired us." He said to them, "Also you go to my vineyard." When it was evening, the lord of the vineyard said to the manager, "Call the workers and pay their wages, beginning with the last [and continuing] until the first."
>
> Those who went out at the eleventh hour received a denarius each, and those who went out first considered that they would receive more, but they also received one denarius each. As they received it, they grumbled against the landowner, saying, "These last worked one hour, and they received the same as we who worked and bore the burden of the heat of the day." But he answered and said to them, "Friend, I have not been unjust to you. Did you not agree with me for a denarius? Take what is yours and leave, but I want to give this last one also the same as you. Am I not permitted to do what I want with what is mine" (Matt 20:1-16)?

In monarchies there are no labor unions to hold strikes. The CEO alone decides what is just. The parable did not discuss those who came after 6:00 A.M. and those who came before 5:00 P.M. Only those who came early and those who came late were considered, because they fit the needs of the parable. Those who came early were the Pharisees who complained about their treatment. The tax collectors and criminals of Jesus' cabinet were the ones who came in late. They did not complain about their wage. Neither did they express surprise. They just took it and left. Jesus implied that the Pharisees should also take their just dues and leave. As the new Son of God he was authorized to make his own choices without consulting them. And he evidently did.

The Pharisees agreed that it was near the end of the age. The Kingdom of God would soon come. They had no suspicion that God would reverse Jesus' decision. If he allowed the tax collectors into the kingdom, they would be admitted, and the Pharisees could not prevent it. They hoped, however, that they could persuade Jesus to change his mind beforehand. The next parable is also one about laborers in the vineyard.

> How does it seem to you? A man had two sons. He came to the first and said, "Son, go out today and work in the vineyard." He, by way of reply, said. "I will, Sir," but he did not go out. After he had come to the second, he said the same. But, by way of reply, he said, "I do not want to." Later, after he had repented, he went away [and worked in the vineyard]. Which of the two did the will of the father?" They said, "The second." Jesus said to them, "I swear to you that the tax collectors and harlots will precede you into the Kingdom of God" (Matt 21:31).

In this parable both sons were expected to go work in the vineyard. The oldest son said he would but did not. The younger son refused but later repented and worked. The last line of this parable identifies the sons with the tax collectors and the Pharisees. The older son was the Pharisees. He was recognized as the one with the birthright, who accepted the responsibility but neglected it. The younger son was the tax collector, who first denied his family responsibility, took employment with the Romans, but later repented and actually came back to the family and worked in the nation the way the Pharisee was supposed to do, but did not. The Pharisees proudly gave their tithes, but the tax collectors gave all that they possessed and devoted themselves to the discipline of the monastery. That should have embarrassed the Pharisees.

The parable should have embarrassed them still more, because the Pharisees proudly claimed their heritage from Jacob, the younger son. It was Jacob who outwitted the older son and acquired all of his birthright privileges and family blessings. Jesus, however, told this story in a way that pictured the Pharisee as the older brother who was left without a blessing or a birthright while the tax collector was the one who outwitted the Pharisee and took his inheritance. What a revolting development! The next parable has the same message.

> A certain man had two sons. The younger son said to his father, "Father, give me the portion of [family] property that falls to me." So [the father] divided for them [the sons] his possessions. After not many days, the younger son gathered all [his possessions] and went away into a distant land. There he scattered his possessions, living wastefully. After he had spent everything, there was a great famine in that country, and he began to be in need. He went and attached himself to one of the citizens of that land. [The citizen] sent him into his fields to herd hogs, and he was eager for his stomach to be filled with the husks, which the hogs ate, but no one gave him [permission to do so].
>
> After he came to himself, he said, "How many servants of my father have more bread than they can eat, and I am here perishing in famine. After I have arisen, I will go to my father, and I will say to him, "Father, I have committed crimes against Heaven and before you. I am

no longer worthy to be called your son. Make me as one of your hired servants." Then he arose and went to his father. While he was still a long distance away, his father saw him and was moved with compassion. He ran and embraced and kissed him. The son said to him, "Father, I have committed crimes against Heaven and before you. I am no longer worthy to be called your son." His father, however, said to his servants, "Quickly bring out the first robe and put it on him, and put a ring on his hand and sandals on his feet. Then bring the fatted calf, slaughter [it], and let us eat and be merry, because this son of mine was dead, and he came to life. He was lost, and has been found"; and they began to celebrate.

Now his older son was in the field, and as he came he drew near to the house, he heard music and dancing, so he called one of the servants and inquired what these things might be. He said to him, "Your brother has come, and your father slaughtered the fatted calf, because he received him well." He was angry and did not want to enter, but his father came out and begged him. He answered and said to his father, "Look! All these years I have been serving you, and I never deviated from your commandment, but you never gave me even a kid that I might celebrate with my friends, but when this son of yours, who consumed your wealth with harlots, came, you sacrificed for him the fatted calf." He replied to him, "Son, I always have you with me, and all my possessions are yours, but it is necessary to rejoice and be glad, because this your brother was dead and came to life; he was lost and has been found" (Luke 15:11-32).

This parable uses many idioms that are not normally known by non-Jewish groups, and familiarity with these idioms is necessary to understand the parable. The term, "hog," is frequently used insultingly, to refer to a gentile. It was not *kah-sháyr*. It did not chew the cud. The situation here was probably one in which the son had to look for employment among gentiles and would gladly have eaten food that was sold in the open market, which would not have been approved by Jewish laws (*kah-shåyr*). "Harlot" is the name given by orthodox Jews to liberal Jews who associate with gentiles. It implies that they mingle with gentiles sexually as well as socially and in business. The Pharisees called Jesus' celibate male apostles "harlots." These were clearly unfair insults, but they were normal, and Jesus took their meaning for granted.

Religiously, "life" can take place only within the contract, and according to some Jews, it can only occur on the Land restrictively to include those who are faithful to their Jewish heritage. The term "dead," correspondingly, is also used metaphorically. It refers to those who are not circumcised or who have become apostate. Certain sects believed that all Jews of other sects were dead. When the younger son left his secure orthodox surroundings to live among gentiles, he was considered "dead" by rigorous, law abiding Jews. He was also "lost." His return meant a restoration to the contract where life was possible. He could feast on food that was acceptable to orthodox Jews. He was home, so he was no longer lost.

A son in antiquity who asked for his heritage was saying he wanted his father to die, because he would rather have his inheritance than his father. This type of insult would be unbearable in Near Eastern societies. Younger sons did leave home in search of better working and living conditions, but they did not normally take their heritage with them. Most of them had to go into business of some kind and associate with gentiles in commerce, because most of the family possessions would go to the oldest son who would also become the family chieftain. The experience of the younger son was called being dead, becoming a harlot, and living with hogs, but it was often necessary for the son who did not have the birthright to the most of the family property nor the blessing that gave him official leadership in the family corporation.

If a father had only two sons in antiquity, and the father died. The family wealth was divided into three parts. The older could choose which of the three parts he wanted most. The other two parts were given, one to each son. That was the heritage. The blessing was that the older son also became the tribal chieftain and had dictatorial authority over the rest of the family. The younger son in this parable had already taken his one portion, so he would get no more. The oldest son would still inherit what was left of the family wealth, so the father said to the older son, "All my possessions are yours," but the younger son still was allowed a place in the family.

The parable did not go into detail about considering the possible justification of the younger son for his actions, because it was understood that he was not justified. This parable was composed to defend the tax collectors. They had left home and were eating with gentile "hogs." Should these ever be allowed to leave their tax offices and be welcomed back into Judaism? The position of the older brother, the Pharisee, was that this was absolutely unfair – especially the celebration of their return. If they were accepted at all they might be acknowledged as servants.

There are enough reports of Jesus feasting and celebrating the recovery of the lost tax collectors and other criminals to suspect that there really were banquets held, celebrating the repentance of these upper class businessmen and their commitment to the Kingdom of God. These banquets may have been associated with Jesus' recruitment programs. The Pharisees reacted to these banquets negatively, and Jesus, in turn, told parables like this to respond.

In the story of Jacob and Esau, Esau was never pictured as a criminal. He was the one who stayed at home within the family corporation at Hebron, while Jacob left to live in a foreign land with his uncle Laban. In fact Jacob was more devious and unprincipled that Esau, but Jacob was more intelligent and therefore more successful than Esau in obtaining the family possessions. In the parable of the prodigal son, it was the prodigal tax collector that emulated old Jacob, and it was the Pharisee who was like Esau and was therefore left outside, refusing to come in. By separating himself from the tax collector, the Pharisee was also separating himself from the kingdom.

The old Jacob and Esau were reconciled the way Jesus hoped his contemporary sons of Jacob could be reconciled after Jacob also repented and returned. After he had wrestled with the angel at Peniel, instead of lining up his troops to fight Esau, he fulfilled the requirements of the Day of Atonement. He first sent many cows, goats, and donkeys loaded with gifts to Esau as punitive payments to cover his damages, hoping that this would atone (*ah-kah-pehr-áh*) (Gen 32) Esau to him. Then he returned to Esau his birthright and blessing, so that Esau could return to Hebron as chief of the Abraham Corporation. Just as the father in the parable said to the older son, "Son, I always have you with me, and all my possessions are yours." The implication of the parable is that the Pharisee would continue to have a place in the kingdom, but Jesus' apostles would also.

Jacob himself moved from Peniel to Shechem, a city just a little west and north of Peniel, and started a new family corporation there. Like the later tax collectors and wealthy businessmen associated with Jesus, old Jacob returned to the land and was accepted. He gave up all of his claim to the family property at Hebron and his right to become the family chieftain after the death of their father, Isaac. He moved to a different place and began his own family corporation. His new land was called Israel, and his new name was Israel. The brothers were reconciled and there was room enough for both on the land.

The parable of the two sons in the vineyard occurs only in Matthew. The story of the two sons in the story of the prodigal son occurs only in Luke. There is no dependency apparent either way. Both seem to be independent parables. That means they came through separate lines of tradition. With all of the other parables coherent with these two, the odds are very great that Jesus taught something like this in reaction to his conflict with the Pharisees. They were both probably included in the list of parables that Jesus prepared for his apostles, but only one was preserved by Luke and the other by Matthew. There is no possibility that one was copied from the other. The same basic message was preserved in two independent parables. They are coherent with other parables, such as the weeds and the wheat, the good and worthless fish, the lost sheep and those still in the fold.

The Business of Atonement. Jesus was obviously in conflict with the Pharisees, and he was skilled in his ability at refuting them. The next parable relates the Pharisees to the tax collectors on the question of judgment.

> There were two men who went up to the temple to pray. The one was a Pharisee and the other was a tax collector. The Pharisee stood and prayed thus to himself, "God, I thank you that I am not like other men – extortionists, unjust, adulterers, or even as this tax collector. I fast twice a week; I give tithes of all that I acquire." Then the tax collector, standing at a distance, did not want even to raise his eyes to Heaven, but beat on his chest, saying, "God be merciful to me a criminal." I tell you, this man will go down to his house justified, rather than the other" (Luke 18:10-14).

There are ten days between New Year's Day and the Day of Atonement in the Jewish calendar. Those are the days when Jews reexamine their behavior for the previous year to consider the things they did that might have made them guilty of some criminal activity. The goal was to have all penalties paid or pardoned before that time. If they had not reconciled themselves with victims of their injury, it was necessary for every Jew to confront every victim of his or her criminal acts and learn what he or she might do to obtain forgiveness. This had to be done before the end of the Day of Atonement. After they had become reconciled with all the individual Jews they had injured, there were still the unpaid fines to the state that were to be satisfied in terms of sacrifice. In this parable the tax collector and the Pharisee were in the temple during the few days before the end of the Day of Atonement. This was their last chance to settle their accounts outside of court to avoid the following judgment.

The Pharisee did not worry, because he recognized himself as an upstanding citizen who had committed no crimes, but he had not become reconciled to his brother, the tax collector, whom he frequently offended and attacked. One of the requirements of the Day of Atonement was that the believer must first settle his account with the brothers he had injured before his sacrifice could be accepted, just as Jacob had done with Esau. The Pharisee did not consider his attitude to the tax collector a crime, but Jesus did, and he declared that the tax collector would have his case settled out of court, but the case of the Pharisee would go to court and face the judgment. The next parable deals with banqueting and conflicts with the Pharisees.

> Again Jesus answered and told them a parable, saying, "The Kingdom of Heaven is like a man who is a king, who prepared a wedding for his son. He sent his servants to call those who had been invited to the wedding feast, but they did not want to come. Again he sent other servants, saying, "Tell those who have been invited, 'Look! My meal is ready; my bulls and fatted animals have been slaughtered; and all things are prepared. Come to the wedding feast!'" But they rudely went away, one to his own field, another to his place of business, [and the rest seized the servants, treated them dishonorably, and killed (them). Then the king became angry, and after he had sent his troops, he destroyed those murderers and burned their city]. Then he said to his servants, "The wedding feast is ready, and the invited ones were not worthy. Go, then, to the secondary roads and whomever you find invite to the wedding feast." When those servants had gone out into the ways, they brought together all whom they found, evil and good, and the bridal chamber was filled with those reclining.

The bracketed words seem to be a later addition to the parable. Both the content and the style are different from that which precedes and that which follows. The later message which had been intruded seems to reflect either the historical situation in Judea after Herod's death and before Archaelaus had clearly been established ethnarch of Judea and Samaria, or the period just before the fall of Jerusalem in A.D. 70.

Without the additions of the later church (Matt 22:6-7, 11-13), this parable tells of only one event, a wedding feast for a prince. The parabolic clue of the wedding and the prince was that the prince was the new Messiah who would renew the wedding contract that God had made with his people, but had afterwards annulled when he sent them out of his house (Deut 24:1) into Babylon and Assyria. Those who had been invited were expected to participate in Jesus' program to bring in the Kingdom of God.

The king first sent his servants to tell people they would be invited when everything was ready, so this invitation would come as no surprise. Then, after everything was prepared, the servants went again to these same people to tell them to come, assuming that they would be ready, but they all made the same kind of excuses that Gideon accepted (Judge 7:2-7; Deut 20:5-9), offered by soldiers to exempt themselves from military service, so that only the committed would be involved in the war. These references may have been included in the parable intentionally to give the listeners, who had ears for special code, the clue that Jesus was talking about a wedding ceremony that would take place, but this also involved a war and the people invited offered excuses allowed in the rules of holy warfare. Gideon's war was amazingly successful with only a few dedicated soldiers, and Jesus intended that this revolt would be, too. Jesus' invitation first went out to the major leaders of the country, the Pharisees, but they refused. Then he went to the upper class businessmen and tax collectors, and they came. They were the dedicated few on which the Kingdom of God depended.

This parable is like others that show a conflict between Jesus and the Pharisees in relationship to the tax collectors and criminals that joined Jesus' program. Like other parables, the Pharisees are shown as the first that were invited. They were the first that were invited to work in the vineyard; they were in the father's house before the prodigal son returned home. They were excluded by their own choice.

There is another parable that follows this one just because it also tells about a feast to which people were invited. It was customary for ancient editors to put together works that were similar in some way. Such items as Beatitudes, Psalms, parables of the Kingdom, and chreias were organized together. The same is true of these two parables, even though they have different emphases for different purposes.

> After the king had entered and looked over those reclining and saw there a man who was not dressed in wedding garment, and he said to him, "Friend, how is it that you have entered here without a wedding garment?" Then he was silent. The king said to the servant, "After you have bound him hand and foot, throw him out into outer darkness" (Matt 22:11-13).

Many scholars have tried to make sense of this parable without noticing that it is separate from the one before it. It is an independent unit. This was a different situation. In this case everyone was expected to come well dressed. They were not asked to come as they were when the servants found them. The wedding garment was a term used for baptism, because it qualified a person for communion. The baptism that preceded the Lord's Supper was something like the wedding garments that people were expected to wear at the messianic banquet when the new contract was performed. After baptism, the new Christian put on a new, clean "wedding" garment as the second step of his or her initiation. St. John of Chrysostom invited those coming to be baptized to come as those being invited to a royal banquet where one would receive a wedding garment. Essenes bathed and changed into special white garments before each meal. This was a separate parable, which was appropriate for some other occasion. Another beautiful parable now has an identity problem. It may once have also been a conflict parable between Jesus and the Pharisees.

> A certain man went down from Jerusalem to Jericho, and he fell among brigands who disrobed him, whipped him, and went away, leaving him half dead. By chance, a certain priest, going down that way, seeing him, went by on the other side. Likewise a Levite, coming to that place, when he saw him, went by on the other side. But a Samaritan, while traveling, came to the place where he was, and when he saw him, had compassion. He came to him, bound up his wounds, pouring on oil and wine. Then he put him on his own donkey and brought him to the inn and took care of him. The next day, he gave the innkeeper two denarii and said, "Take care of him, and whatever you charge, when I return I will repay you" (Luke 10:20-35).

Ever since the secession of Israel from Judah, there was animosity between the Israelites (Samaritans) and Jews. The setting for this parable was in Judah. It was a place where the man who came to the aid of the wounded traveler frequented. What was a Samaritan doing there? How did he happen to have credit with the innkeeper in Judah? These questions challenge the identity of the main character of the parable.

The hero of the story was obviously a rich, traveling, businessman who was known in Jericho and had credit with the innkeeper. He was not a priest or a Levite, because he dared to touch a person who was half-dead. He did not fear corpse uncleanness the way priests or Pharisees would. This story seems more appropriate if the hero were understood as a tax collector or criminal associated with Jesus. The tax collectors and criminals with whom Jesus associated were criticized for being careless about Levitical defilement. The good thing about a tax collector or criminal, however, was that he could help people in need, the way strict law observers, like the Pharisees, could not.

This parable might initially have been a defense of the tax collectors with whom Jesus associated rather than a Samaritan.

With the tax collector, who was thought by the Pharisees to have been worse than useless, this parable would parallel the parables of the two sons and the weeds and wheat parables as literary units designed to make the Pharisees and their priestly colleagues look bad. It would also have justified Jesus' association with those who were not considered worthy. It also supported Jesus' willingness to let himself be defiled in order to be the good physician to the sick and to rescue the tax collectors and criminals that were lost. He rescued those who had left the fold and were half dead. The editor, Luke, favored the Samaritans and may have changed the tax collector or criminal into a Samaritan to suit his own editorial purposes.

All of the chreias and parables in this chapter are coherent. They reflect a situation in which Jesus was in conflict with the Pharisees who tried to sabotage his movement by blaming him for associating with tax collectors and criminals. He did not deny that he did, but he gave answers that are preserved in chreias and parables that were repeated by his apostles that justified Jesus' action. His answers also made the Pharisees, whom Jesus acknowledged to be legally righteous, look silly. Some of these parables show satire and ridicule. All are cleverly designed and portray an author who was a very intelligent debater with good ethical motives. Literary productions of this sort do not reflect an origin in community gossip groups, as scholars like James Dunn claim.

The apostles did most of the preaching. The details can only be conjectured. They probably met with Jesus from time to time to report their success and problems as they confronted the Pharisees and the disciples of John the Baptist. It was probably after one of these reports, that Jesus asked, "Who do men say that the Son of man is" (Matt 16:13)? At those times, Jesus counseled them in ways to respond when they confronted those problems again. The apostles, then, may have written down the advice in chreias and recorded the parables that are still preserved. None of these chreias or parables mention any time before or after the time in which Jesus lived nor any geographical location outside of

Palestine. When mentioned, the territory was Jerusalem, Jericho, Siloam, and the temple, the vineyard, and the field.

The people mentioned in the chreias were Pharisees, citizens of Israel or Judah, priests, Levites, and other citizens of Palestine. There is no need to conjecture that any of these documents had its origin in the later church, somewhere outside of Palestine. These chreias and parables were not developed out of community gossip sessions, talking about the impression Jesus had made upon them. The care and literary skill shown in these documents can hardly have been spontaneously developed from some oral tradition that was later written down by untrained community groups. These documents reflect study, care, and choice wording that have been planned by a skilled literary author. Just because they do not have Jesus' notarized autograph on any of them does not justify anyone in holding that Jesus was an unskilled illiterate person who could neither read nor write and was therefore not the author of the statements attributed to him. The same scholars who assume that Jesus and his apostles could not read or write assume that Plato, Aristotle, Socrates, Diogenes, Philo, Paul, and all of the rabbis and authors of the Dead Sea Scrolls were literate.

All of the teachings in these two chapters are in chreia or parable form. In one of the chreias, the contemporary historical character was John the Baptist, a well-established contemporary of Jesus, reported in the works of Josephus. Others were Pilate and Herod. Geographical references in the parables are all inside Palestine. All materials are amazingly coherent in character, time, and location. The odds are very great that these are valid teachings of Jesus, organizing and carrying out his program in conflict with the Pharisees. The most reliable are the chreias, and the parables are coherent with them.

There are still other teachings similar to these that are neither in chreia or parable form. If they were not valid teachings of Jesus, then the later church in a reliable fashion added them. They were not fictional. The assumption that the church had evil motives and deliberately falsified their own teachings as the teachings of

Jesus has been widely claimed but not carefully demonstrated. Now there is a large body of demonstrated teachings of Jesus to use as a backdrop against which to test other teachings attributed to Jesus for their coherence and learn how accurately the church represented Jesus in other literary forms that can not be as easily tested as the chreias and parables.

RELATED TEACHINGS NOT IN CHREIAS OR PARABLES

Sabbath Problems.

> At that time Jesus went through the wheat field on the Sabbath, and his disciples were hungry and they began to pluck heads of wheat and eat. When the Pharisees saw, they said to him, "Look! Your disciples are doing that which is not lawful to do on the Sabbath!" Then he said to them,
>
> ["Do you not know what David did when he was hungry and those with him? How he entered the house of God and ate the loaves of the presence, which was not lawful for him to eat or those with him, but for the priests, only (1Sam 21:1-6)? Or, have you not read in the law that on the Sabbath the priests abandon the Sabbath in the temple and are innocent? I tell you that something greater than the temple is here. If you had known what (the text) 'I want mercy and not sacrifice' (Hos 6:6) (means,) you would not have persecuted the innocent]. For the Lord of the Sabbath is the Son of man" (Matt 12:1-8).

This appears to have been a chreia at one time. It has a long introduction, but otherwise would be a chreia if the bracketed section were omitted. The bracketed section seems to be a later church expansion, arguing the case still further. Matthew regularly supported arguments with two witnesses. Here the one is the authority of David over Scripture, and the other the precedent of the priests regularly breaking the Sabbath, as the disciples were doing. Monarchs made law. Since the apostles were both breaking the Sabbath and eating, neither of these texts alone would have covered the offense. David and Jesus were both monarchs and both confronted with items of hunger. These legal justifications were probably the additions of the later church. Jesus simply said, as the Messiah, he had the authority to deal with the Sabbath as he chose, just as David did and just as the following text assumes. In the Gospel of John, Jesus is quoted as saying. "My Father works until now, and I work" (John 5:17). In that gospel Jesus is pictured as God's legal agent about 40 times. A legal agent acts and speaks in the name of, in behalf of, and at the responsibility of the principal for whom he functions. Legally the agent is the principal. Therefore Jesus reflects only the activity and will of God, and God works on the Sabbath. Therefore Jesus is justified in working on the Sabbath.

> Which man among you, who has one sheep,
>   and it falls into a ditch on the Sabbath,
>   will he not seize it and pull it out?
> How much more valuable, then
>   is a man than a sheep (Matt 12:11-12; Mark 3:4:
>   Luke 6:9).

This is an *a fortiori* (to the greater) argument. An *a fortiori* argument defends the truth of some point by relating it to a much weaker or smaller point that has already been accepted. If even that small thing were true, then how much the more so would this point that is stronger and bigger be true. Here the small, weak object is the sheep. If this situation is true of the less valuable object, a sheep, how much more for a more valuable object, a person. Jewish legalists in NT times were not agreed on whether or not a sheep should be saved on the Sabbath. Some (CD 11:13-14) say, "No." Rabbis (Yoma 85a; Shab 128b; Beza 3:4) say, "Yes." Luke has a similar argument.

The Lord answered and said, "Hypocrites! Each of you on the Sabbath day, will he not loose his cow or his donkey from his manger, and lead them out to water? This is a daughter of Abraham whom Satan bound – Look! Eighteen years! Was it not necessary that she be released from this bondage on the Sabbath day"(Luke 13:15-16)? I tell you under oath that the tax collectors and the harlots will precede you into the Kingdom of God, for John came to you in the way of righteousness, and you did not believe him, but the tax collectors and the harlots believed him. When you saw, you did not even repent and later believe in him (Matt 21:31-32).

This is a Matthean addition to the parable of the two sons in the vineyard. The Pharisees failed to respond not only to John, but also to Jesus. According to this teaching, Jesus did not start a program that was completely different from John's when he went out to the wealthy businessmen. There had been communication between John the Baptist and these so-called "harlots" before Jesus began his campaign. Esau accepted the repentance of the old Jacob. When he returned the two brothers were reconciled, but the Pharisees did not accept the tax collectors and wealthy businessmen who repented – even later. This agrees with the report that the soldiers and tax collectors came to John, asking for permission to repent and be baptized (Luke 3:10-14).

There are still other teachings and accusations of Jesus against the Pharisees (Matt 23:1-36). There is nothing anti-Semitic about these sayings. They are anti-Pharisaic from an inner Jewish point of view. They are the harshest sayings recorded of Jesus. They are well organized and coherent among themselves, but there are some reasons for thinking that some of them, at least, are later than Jesus' time and are not completely coherent with the teachings of the chreias and the parables. The woe against Pharisees on the technical matter of taking oaths presumes the existence of the temple, and, therefore, was probably composed before A.D. 70 (Matt 23:16-22). On the other hand, it pictures Jesus involved in precisely the kind of legalistic detail, which he blamed the Pharisees for entertaining. The accusations against the Pharisees for all the bloodshed from the blood of innocent Abel to the blood of Zechariah (Matt 23:35) may be a reference to the mock trial of a righteous wealthy man, named Zechariah, whom the zealots killed after he was pronounced innocent by the court. This happened near the end of the war of A.D. 66-70 – too late to have been a saying of Jesus. There is one more parable that tells about Jesus' campaign that is not directly related to the Pharisees.

Three and a Half Years.

> A certain man had a fig tree planted in his vineyard, and he came looking for fruit on it, but he did not find [any]. He said to the vinedresser, "Look! For three years I have come looking for fruit from this fig tree, and I do not find [any]. Dig it up! Why does it keep land nonproductive?" Then, by reply, he says to him, "Sir, let it go also this year until I have cultivated around it and fertilized [it]. Then, if it produces fruit the following year, [well and good], but if not you may dig it out" (Luke 13:6-9).

Jesus was pictured as a man in a hurry. He had only a small amount of time to accomplish his goal. He did not have time to rest on the Sabbath. During the Maccabean Revolt, there was a 3½-year period between the defilement of the temple and its rededication in 164 B.C. Jews thought this was the divinely ordained period of "birth pangs of the Messiah." After 3½ years had passed in the war with Rome (A.D. 66-70), Jews surrendered. The same was true in the Bar Kochba Revolt (A.D. 132-35). This parable did not really deal with the time in which some fig tree had lived without producing fruit, but the time Jesus had spent in campaign without the underground Kingdom of God having become a public reality. It was during this period that all of these chreias were written and all of these parables were told throughout the Promised Land. Jesus was engaged in a political program.

CONCLUSIONS

There are still other chreias and parables in the gospels, but the ones given above are those associated either with Jesus' campaign to recruit followers and raise funds or his conflict with the Pharisees and the disciples of John the Baptist. These are related to historical figures of Jesus' time, such as Herod Antipas and John the Baptist. They are also related to geographical locations, such as Jerusalem, Jericho, Siloam, and the temple area. There is not even the slightest implication of any activity of Jesus that took him outside of Palestine or at a time, later than the reign of Pontius Pilate and Herod Antipas. They are so coherent it would take a great deal of credulity to think that anyone in a later church, somewhere in Egypt, Rome, or Asia Minor could have composed this literature, fictitiously, about Jesus and never have shown any inconsistency with each other and the social and political conditions in Palestine of Jesus' day that these texts reveal. What other ancient rabbinic, historical, poetical, rhetorical, or philosophical literature has ever been expected to be defended like this for its genuineness? Almost all of this other literature is assumed to be valid, but if it were subjected to the kind of doubts that have been applied to the gospels, how much of it could survive? Like political programs still today, Jesus faced two great challenges:

1) recruiting competent leaders and
2) raising funds to support the program.

Jesus worked arduously and effectively to solve both of these problems. Since he was introducing a new program, it was quite normal for him to have conflict with the old order that he was planning to replace. This involved his conflict with the Pharisees. The most difficult task of all was that of conducting this entire program under the watchful eye of Rome without revealing either the events or the goals to the Romans. The next chapter will show how this happened.

CHAPTER FOUR

UNDERCOVER EVANGELISM

POLITICAL PROBLEMS

The Kingdom and Rome. The biggest problem Jesus confronted was the fact that he had to undertake this project without the Romans discovering it. How could he organize a movement designed to evict the Romans from the Promised Land, enlist the support of all the patriotic Jews in the land, confront the leading Pharisees, and organize the support of Jews throughout the Roman Empire without disclosing this fact to the Romans? There were Roman soldiers and intelligence agents everywhere. Jesus depended on well-established Jewish traditions. Years before the time of Jesus, Israelites and Jews had lived under the rule of the Egyptians, Babylonians, Persians, Syrians, and Parthians, as well as the Romans. They had many years of experience in communicating in code. Children were trained in the Scripture and tradition. Before celebrating their bar Mitzvahs boys learned secret terms that suggested earlier history, liturgy, or legal concepts. This code was called "the mysteries of the Kingdom of God" (Matt 13:11; Luke

8:10; The Gospel of Thomas 62) or the *gnôh-sees*. Rabbis called this the oral Torah (*toh-ráh shuh-buh ahl-péh*)or the memorized Torah. Talmon said correctly,

> We must assume, on the one hand, that an indefinable part of biblical legislation was actually passed on from generation to generation without ever being committed to writing.[1]

It was understood that God forbad Jews from writing down this secret material, because it was the mystery designed only for the just, which meant only for trustworthy Jews. Disclosing this secret material to gentiles was called "giving that which is holy to the dogs" or "casting your pearls before hogs" (Matt 7:6). By knowing this code Jews could use ordinary terms to communicate special meanings, and they did. If Romans ever learned these code terms, however, the codes would lose their effectiveness. These were the mysteries that legalists were expected to keep on the tips of their tongues. This trained them well for the use of riddles or parables.

Jesus took advantage of this training and prepared parables through which he could communicate without the Romans understanding the messages. Jesus also avoided crowds. Instead he trained apostles to travel throughout the land, and he possibly sent agents to communicate with Jews in Rome, Egypt, Parthia, and Syria. These could meet with Jews in small groups that would not attract Roman attention. Jesus evidently gave his agents lists of chreias and parables that were stories with slight distortions as clues to allow Jews to listen for the hidden meanings.

Communication with John. One chreia was told of the occasion when John the Baptist was imprisoned for insurrection (Ant 18:116-19).

---

[1]   S. Talmon, "The Community of the New Covenant," *The Community of the New Covenant*, eds. E. Urbach and J Vanderkam, c1994), p. 16.

> After John, in prison, heard the works of the Messiah, he
> sent through his disciples, saying, "Are you the coming
> one, or should we anticipate someone else?" Jesus replied
> to them, "Go, report to John the things you hear and
> see: **The blind receive their sight**; the lame walk; the
> lepers are cleansed; **the deaf hear**; the dead are raised;
> **and the poor receive the good news;** and blessed
> is the one who is not made to stumble because of me"
> (Matt 11:1-6).

This is a report in a chreia. Jesus was the character. The situation
that prompted him to speak was given, and the quotation of his
answer is reported. John had anointed Jesus to be the new King of
Israel. John was to be his high priest. Then John was thrown into
prison, and Jesus had done nothing, so far as John could see, to
get him out. Was Jesus the new Saul, rather than the new David?
Had John, like Samuel, made a mistake? Would John have to
anticipate another true leader of the nation? All this was implied
in the simple question they asked. Jesus replied by simply telling
them the things he had been doing – none of which would have
frightened the Romans.

If Jesus had actually raised corpses physically, it would have
attracted more attention than he really wanted. But he was
speaking in code. The "dead" that he raised were the tax collectors
and criminals he converted and restored to the nation. That
means that in Jewish terms the tax collectors had been "dead,"
and he caused them to return to the contract community and
be revived. These extreme metaphors were used to show what a
great distinction there was between those who were members of
the community and those who did not belong. Throughout the
Bible there are two kinds of life and two kinds of death. Physically
a person was born without choosing it and the same person died
without planning it. These were involuntary conditions. There
was also another life and death that was much more important.
A person could be born again, legally, and enter into the life of
the contract community. A person could choose this kind of life

and qualify to join the community that had a contract with God. If that happened he or she would acquire a soul and become spiritually (legally) alive. Those who lived only physically were spiritually dead. They did not have souls. Jewish and early Christian life began with baptism. If those who had been born again were ever expelled from the community they would lose their souls and die legally. That was the worst kind of death. It meant these people no longer belonged to a community that was greater than themselves. Members of the contract community worked very hard to keep from being defiled, chiefly because it meant the punishment associated with defilement was the requirement of being at least temporarily isolated. People who think only in terms of physical life and death have trouble understanding and believing in the resurrection, as Christians and Jews profess. They miss the religious significance of resurrection.

When Constantine, with the support of Christians, became emperor of Rome, all of a sudden Christianity was transformed from being a subversive group in Rome to becoming the religion of the nation. Eusebius described the event by saying Christians had been not only half dead, but altogether dead, even foul and stinking in their tombs, but God raised them up (HE 10:4, 12). This was the kind of resurrection Jesus expected John to understand through his coded message. Instead of a physical resurrection, it was a resurrection of the legal body of Christ, the church corporation. Ezekiel spoke of the restoration of the Babylonian Jews to the Promised Land as a resurrection of dry bones from a battle field. The dry bones were restored to life. Hidden, among the list of things Jesus provided was a quotation from Isa 29:18-20:

> In that day, **the deaf will hear** the words of the book; from the gloom and darkness, the eyes of **the blind will see; the poor will increase in the joy** of the Lord, and the **humble of men will rejoice** in the holy One of Israel.

Jesus wanted John to recognize this hidden quote, but the real message John needed to hear was the one that was not mentioned, but one John would have understood. The quotation continued, **for the terrible one will come to nothing, and the scoffer will be finished, and all those who watch to do evil will be cut off.**

Who were the **terrible one,** the **scoffer,** and **all who watch to do evil**? The terrible one was probably Herod Antipas who had put John into prison and later had him killed. He also probably qualified as the "scoffer" in the next parallel line. Those who "watch to do evil" might have been the Roman agents sent everywhere to spy on Jesus, watching to catch Jesus in some threatening act.

Jesus concluded with the encouraging words, "Blessed is the one who is not made to stumble because of me." That should have meant to John, "Don't give up hope! Things are moving favorably. I will get there as soon as I get things organized," but before that could happen, Herod had John killed in prison. If Jesus' communication with John had not been said in hidden code, Herod would have had Jesus killed at the same time John was killed. When the news came to Jesus that John had been killed, again he responded in code. He just said, "This is the one about whom it is written, **Look! I am sending my messenger before your face, who will prepare your way for you**" (Mal 3:1; Matt 11:10). Those who remembered the Passover liturgy knew that Elijah was expected to come to prepare the way for the Messiah who would follow. Malachi prophesied that. In code, Jesus said not only that John was Elijah, but that he was the Messiah who had come. The Romans, however, would not have known that. The next chreia deals with the Kingdom of God.

The kingdom within.

> When he had been asked by the Pharisees when the Kingdom of God would come, he answered that and said, "The Kingdom of God will not come by observation, and they will not say, 'Look here! or there!' Look! The Kingdom of God is in your midst" (Luke 17:20-21).

Some interpreters argue that this meant that the Kingdom of God was a mystic feeling that took place in a person's mind or heart. Jesus, however, was not simply a mystic dreamer. He was a skilled statesman, well trained in law, religion, literature, business, and government. He talked about a political kingdom that already existed underground and would later take place on the Promised Land. The Pharisees knew that, but at the time of this discussion the Pharisees did not see any government in action. Who was the king? Where was his throne? Where was the kingdom? Jesus could not tell them outright where this kingdom was and when it would be established, but he could allude to it.

It was right there on the Promised Land, in their midst. It already had a functioning program. There was already a king and his cabinet. They had a treasury and troops already standing by in secret. There were secret agents in foreign countries, planning for outside support. This was an undercover government that would someday appear to everyone, but in the meantime it existed in the midst of the Jews in the Promised Land. Currently, Jesus and his disciples had to speak of this kingdom in hidden concepts, such as the next parable.

Stories in Code.

> The Kingdom of God is like a man who throws seed in the ground and sleeps and rises night and day, but the stalk shoots up and grows in a way he does not know. Mysteriously, the land produces grain, first the blade, then the stalk, then the full grain in the stalk. When it yields the grain, **he puts in the sickle, because the harvest is ready** (Joel 4:13; Mark 4:26-29).

According to the old Pentacontad calendar that was still used by some Jews in NT times, unleavened bread was eaten after the end of the old year, right up until New Year's Day, the very day that later became Christian Easter. On the first day of the New Year there was a special ceremony for cutting the first of the New Year's grain. The ceremony was so important that it was retained even after the lunar calendar was accepted and New Year's Day was changed to autumn. According to the old calendar New Year's Day always fell the day after the Sabbath, but that was not so according to the lunar calendar. According to the lunar calendar, this day might even fall on the Sabbath. If it did, fundamentalist Jews, who did not observe the lunar calendar, still conducted the ceremony.

> People from neighboring towns gathered and when it was dark, one of the agents of the court said, "Is the sun set?" The crowd then answered in unison, "Yes!" Three times the question was asked and answered in unison. Then he said, "Is this a sickle?" They answered, "Yes!" This was also done three times. The same procedure was followed with a basket. Finally, he asked, "Shall I reap?" and the crowd answered in unison, "Yes!" This procedure was also followed three times before the agent of the court put the sickle into the new grain (mMenahoth 10:3). Then they cut the new grain and brought it into the temple court in baskets. There it was parched and ground into flour. It could be consumed after it had been properly tithed and the priests had received their portions (mMen 10:4).

On New Year's Day it was also believed that the Lord sat in judgment on his people and the gentiles. If the nation had been righteous, the Promised Land would be restored. If it had been criminal it would continue under foreign rule. Judgment would take place in the land of Israel when the enemy would be gathered in the Kidron Valley and on Mount Scopus and the Mount of Olives, just as the Assyrian soldiers had been assembled, just before their destruction in the time of Isaiah and Hezekiah. (Isa 37; 2Kings 19). If Israel had been righteous there would be a verdict in its favor, and the enemy would be utterly defeated through God's judgment (Ezek 38:19-29). There had been once such a judgment when thousands of Assyrian soldiers had gathered on Mount Scopus and the Mount of Olives. The Assyrians' spokesman stood at the upper conduit of Fuller's Field urging the population to surrender before they captured the city. Following Hezekiah's instruction, the people did not answer one word. Hezekiah obviously had a trap set for the Assyrians. When Hezekiah consulted his chief military intelligence officer, the prophet Isaiah, Isaiah told him not to worry. Everything was in order as planned. These Assyrians would all be gone by the next day. That which Hezekiah and Isaiah both knew was that all of those soldiers depended for sustenance on the Spring of Siloam for water. All the Jews had to do was poison the water and they would all die. The next day 185,000 Assyrians lay dead in the Kidron Valley. (Isa 37; 2Kings 19).

Before the Assyrians gathered on Mount Scopus and the Mount of Olives Hezekiah had the famous tunnel constructed so that the spring water was turned into the city, but the government authorities of the City of David evidently also planned a trap. They constructed a pond outside of the city that could be filled from inside, regularly flowing. That provided water for the Assyrian soldiers outside of the city. This pipe, however could be stopped from inside the city so that the pond contained only stagnant water that could also be poisoned from inside the city. That was their way of defending the city.

The Scripture does not give all of these details. They are conjectured from the events that are known to have taken place. National military officers do not usually publish their defense techniques, but after the death of the Assyrian soldiers Jewish leaders knew that the Spring of Siloam offered them security. Any enemy that attacked Jerusalem would gather in the Kidron Valley where the soldiers had access to the water. If they lined up again in the Kidron Valley they could be expected to be treated the same way the Assyrians were. It was probably in that confidence that Joel made his famous prophecy, describing the war in terms of a harvest scene.

> Sanctify war, stir up the mighty men.
> Beat your plowshares to swords,
>   and your pruning hooks into spears . . .

Let the nations arouse themselves
   and come to the Valley of Jehoshaphat . . .
For there I will sit to judge
   all the nations round about.
Put in the sickle, because the harvest is ready.
Come; tread the grapes, for the press is full
   and the vats overflow . . .
Mobs, mobs, in the Valley of Verdict –
The Day of the Lord is near
   in the Valley of Verdict . . .
The Lord roars from Zion,
   and utters his voice from Jerusalem.
The Lord is a refuge to his people,
   a stronghold to the people of Israel.
So you shall know that I am the Lord your God
   who dwells in Zion, my holy mountain.
Jerusalem shall be holy, and foreigners
   shall never again pass through it.

This was probably the Scripture Jesus had in mind when he composed the cleverly designed parable of the way grain grows. Jesus' parable seems innocent enough. It is simply a rural account of the way grain grows. The one who is trained in the mysteries of the Kingdom of God, however, would recognize the final line, which is a quotation from Joel, and realize that Jesus was speaking of the destruction of the enemy and not of grain. The author of one of the visions in Revelation also anticipated a destruction in the Kidron Valley, near the temple, when the enemy nations would be harvested with a sickle, like grain (Rev 14:14-20).

Those who had ears to hear this parable knew that Jesus was referring to a very special New Year's Day celebration when he mentioned putting in the sickle. Only those who knew the mysteries of the Kingdom of Heaven, which were all Jews who were trained in knowledge of Scripture and Jewish tradition, understood this parabolic language. The Valley of Verdict was the Kidron Valley, the Valley of Jehoshaphat, just east of the temple in the City of Zion. There the nations, like Assyrians or Romans, could gather, but they could always be poisoned when they used the only water source in the area. The attack of the Assyrians ended with 185,000 corpses scattered around the Kidron Valley and surrounding mountains. Neither Joel, the seer of Revelation, nor Jesus, ever forgot that experience. All of this was involved in this simple agricultural parable. The harvest involved cutting down the gentile enemy soldiers who would come to take Zion. Jesus was telling his listeners that he would **put in the sickle** when the **harvest was ready.** That was not expected to require a very long wait. This was another way of saying, "The Kingdom of Heaven has come near" (Matt 3:2; 4:17; 10:7). Those who wanted to know what the Kingdom of Heaven was like had to know all of this scriptural history. Of course, the Romans would have missed this entire message; just the way many NT scholars miss it today. A similar communication appears in the next parable.

> The Kingdom of Heaven is like a grain of mustard seed, which a man took and sowed in his field. On the one hand, it is the smallest of seeds, but on the other hand, when it is grown, it becomes greater than the vegetables, and becomes a tree, so that **the birds of the heaven come and dwell in its branches** (Dan 4:12, 21; Matt 13:31-32; Mark 4:30-32; Luke 13:18-19).

This parable also seems innocent. It would probably give the Romans no basis for suspicion, but farmers would know that mustard seeds do not grow up and become trees. They grow up and become mustard plants. That oddity in the story, however, would give the Jewish listener the clue that he or she should listen for a scriptural quotation that would provide the intended message. This was the quotation from Dan 4. The listener, who did not remember the full message of Dan 4, could go back and read it to learn that this was a dream of a tree whose dominion extended to the end of the earth, just the way Cyrus' little kingdom expanded to include all of Media and Babylon, and Alexander the

Great's kingdom expanded from the little country of Macedon to include Egypt and parts of India. This was the Kingdom of Heaven (Dan 4:22).

In the parable the tree was a kingdom once ruled by Nebuchadnezzar, but after it passed through the control of several other kings, was finally given to the Jews under the leadership of the Son of man (Dan 7:13), exactly at the time when Judas won the famous Battle of Beth-horon and returned to Jerusalem to cleanse the temple and begin recovery of the Promised Land. The "Babylon" of Jesus' day, in the opinion of Jews was Rome. The way Daniel interpreted the dream was that the king's empire would "depart from him" (Dan 4:31). God rules the kingdom of men and will give it to whomever he chooses (Dan 4:25, 32). This was a kingdom that the Most High would give to whomever he chose (Dan 4:17, 25, 32), and the ones he chose were his chosen people.

The Romans would have missed all of that, just as Jesus intended. Jesus had to be very clever to have composed parables like this for his apostles to propagate. Another clever parable is the following:

> The Kingdom of Heaven is like leaven, which a woman took and hid in three measures of flour until the whole [dough] was leavened (Matt 13:33; Luke 13:20-21).

The importance of the leaven metaphor is that leaven is very infectious. Leaven is not simply something purchased at the store to add to flour to make bread rise, as it is in the West. Leaven is moisture that touches flour, and it is important for Passover bread that the bread be made of flour that had not touched moisture from the time the grain headed out until it was mixed just before being put into the oven. There must elapse no more than eighteen minutes between the times the flour is moistened until the loaf is put into the oven. Most Jewish bakers can do this in eleven minutes.

In between the time of the heading and the time of the mixing, the wheat must be under constant surveillance by the orthodox, who guard it in the field, while it is being gathered, threshed, ground into flour and stored until it is mixed for baking. If it ever becomes the least bit moldy, it must be discarded. Vessels that can hold water must be broken. If a small bit of flour that is suspicious of having been leavened should fall into a pot of unquestionably unleavened flour, it would require that there be at least sixty times as much unquestionably unleavened flour to neutralize it. This neutralizing process is called *káh-shehr-eye-zing*

Because leaven was so infectious, it was used metaphorically to describe political movements. The apostles were warned to watch out for the leaven of the Pharisees, Sadducees, and Herod (Matt 16:6; Mark 8:14-15; Luke 12:1). Jesus reminded the apostles that these groups were infectious and were propagating their doctrines everywhere. Rabbis complained to the Lord,

> Master of the ages, it is revealed and known to you that we want to do your will. Who is hindering? The leaven that is in the dough and subjection to the gentiles. May it be your will that we may escape from their hands (bBer 17a).

When leavened bread is desired, there is no need to hide the leaven that is used. It can just be added, and once it is added, it will work quickly and effectively. At the time this parable was composed the Kingdom of Heaven was all underground. The flour was all ready until the moment the leaven was added. Then it would suddenly appear. It was like the grain that was ready for the sickle. At the right time the Messiah would make his appearance, on a New Year's Day or Passover. Then everything would break loose, and the Romans would find out too late that the entire Promised Land was under the control of the new Son of God. The Romans would not realize that all this was being said when this parable was being told. Getting things ready for the "leaven" in complete secret from the Romans, however, was not easy. This is shown in the next parable.

> How can anyone enter the house of a strong man and seize his goods, if he does not first bind the strong man?

> Then he can plunder his house (Matt 12:29; See also Isa
> 49:24-26; Ps Sol 5:4).

One of the nursery stories told to many American children is a parable about a mouse counsel. The mice were losing their population because of a cat, so they had to make plans to protect themselves against the cat. Some mouse came up with the suggestion that they tie a bell on the cat, so that the mice would hear when the cat was approaching. Every mouse agreed that this was an excellent suggestion. The question was, "Which mouse would tie the bell on the cat?" That ended the discussion. Jesus was raising a similar question, but he was also making plans to get the project accomplished. The strong man was Rome, but that did not mean the task was impossible. After all, Jews had had experience in international negotiations, and sometimes extraordinary things could be accomplished without bloodshed. A good example of this was in Babylon.

Only the upper class Jews and people trained in crafts had been taken into Babylon, and some of them quickly rose to positions of power there. Nehemiah, for example, became cupbearer for the king (Neh 2:1-20). When Nicotris was queen of Babylon, she fortified the city by diverting the Euphrates River into a lake north of Babylon. While the riverbed was dry, she fortified the city and had the riverbank lined with bricks to prevent invasion. Afterwards the river was returned, and Babylon was well protected. All went well until Cyrus of Persia reapplied the same technique, dried up the river, and invaded the city suddenly on a feast day, when most of the leaders were drunk, and overtook the city with very little blood shed.

This was planned with careful intelligence work inside Babylon, with Cyrus' agents inside the city keeping him informed of the events and conditions there. This all happened as a surprise to the Babylonians but not to the Jews. Before the event, Second Isaiah anticipated it and called Cyrus of Persia the new Messiah and deliverer of the Jews (Isa 43:14; 44:6; 22-23; 47:4; 48:17, 20; 49:7; 50:2; 52:9; 54:5, 8; 59:20; 60:16; 62:12; 63:16). Cyrus had agreed in advance to allow the Jews to return to Palestine in exchange for their intelligence work in Babylon (Isa 45:1-3). Jews had successfully put the bell on the cat and obtained the restoration of the Promised Land. Jesus may have planned something like this.

There were thousands of Jews in Rome at the time of Jesus, and many were in strategic positions of finance, shipping, military, government, and business. Jesus was evidently skilled in working together with leaders such as these. He knew that there was no way to initiate a successful eviction of Rome without first having the entire stage set, with all of the characters in place. Therefore, he sent out his apostles to tell Jews parables like this to let them know what he had in mind. He did not have to tell everyone the details of the plan, but this parable had many possibilities without the Romans knowing anything about it. At the same time, he had probably sent other agents to Rome to get the stage set.

Communication in drama. The drama of Nathan with David and the court drama of Dan 7 were earlier techniques of communication that Jesus perfected in his parables. The church continued this method. One of the undercover means of propagating the belief that Jesus was destined to be a great Messiah is reflected in the virgin birth narratives that employed the kind of stories with which ancients were familiar. Most great men were recognized for their leadership after they had gained their positions, but miraculous birth narratives were attributed to them later. Leaders like Sargon of Akkad, Xerxes of Persia, Moses, Alexander the Great, and philosophers like Pythagoras and Plato were held to have been virgin born. The Matthean birth story is much like that of Sargon, more than two centuries earlier. These birth stories were not based on scientific observation nor understood to be historical reports, but they were expressions of faith told in mythological terms.

The Greek myth was considered the highest form of communication. The myth could reach people with important messages as no other method could. This was the drama of the theater. Some very important messages are difficult to communicate. How can you explain what it is like to fall in love to someone who has never fallen in love? How can you explain what it is like to have a spouse or an only child to die, if the other person has never had the experience. Some people resort to music or poetry, but one of the best methods is through the drama – to act it out in a play.

This was like the Greek myth, and Christians were not about to allow this good method of communication to go untapped. It was a method early Christians were prepared to use. They knew it had been used before by Sargon of Akkad and Alexander the Great and others, but they wanted to tell how great Jesus was and what his destiny had been. They could not shout to the housetops that Jesus was destined to be the new king to overthrow the Romans and reestablish David's kingdom, but they could dramatize their feelings through birth stories, and they did. These dramas were appropriate for use in celebrations, as they have been used ever since.

The authors of the birth narratives in Matthew and Luke were able to enter into this practice in relationship to Jesus, and in the process tell rather subtly that Jesus was the Messiah that was expected to follow David as ruler of the Promised Land. Like the parables of Jesus it escaped the notice of the Roman intelligence. Jesus, like David, was to have been born in Bethlehem, and like Moses he narrowly escaped death in infancy, and a flight to Egypt rescued him (Matt 2). Mary's son was expected to be called "Great, Son of the Most High, and the Lord will give to him the throne of his father David, and he will rule over the house of Jacob for the age" (Luke 1:32-33). Jesus' mother, Mary, like Hanna, recited poetry that predicted her son as one who would "put down the mighty from their thrones" (Luke 1:52). The secret hopes expressed in these stories told Jews who Jesus was and what he was expected to do, and the Romans missed their political implication. Politics were essential to Jesus' program. It is a mistake for Christians to argue about whether or not Mary was really a physical virgin and miss the important point of the drama. The authors were dramatizing their belief that Jesus was the greatest of all the statesmen that ever lived. He was greater than Sargon of Akkad, Xerses of Persia, or Alexander the Great. He was destined for greatness from the very beginning.

SUMMARY

Jesus started his recruitment program with the realization that a government had to have money, so he recruited wealthy businessmen first of all. The next chapter will discuss the way in which he did that.

CHAPTER FIVE

THE HEAVENLY TREASURY

THEOCRACY IN ACTION

The Religion and the Nation. Israel was not just a religion; it was a nation. It was organized like other governments. Initially, leaders like Moses and Samuel were both religious and governmental leaders. Israel's theology, and consequently Christian theology, was patterned after Israel's governmental system at the time of its formation. Since Israel's early government involved a king with his counselors, a judicial system with the king as the highest judge, a collection of laws, some ambassadors, a treasury, and a military force, it was assumed that God functioned in the same way. God himself was the great king and also the highest judge. He governed by the same laws and rules Israel considered valid (inspired). He had a troop of heavenly angels that became involved in all of Israel's wars. He had a legal accounting system that kept track of all of Israel's crimes and also the crimes of all of Israel's enemies. God also had a banking system. That was the agency that kept track of all the crimes committed, the fines paid, the fines left unpaid, and current balances on hand or deficits.

Because of this, Jewish and Christian theology are both filled with metaphors taken from governmental concepts. From the judicial system we learn about God's kingdom, his judgment, and his court system, all about punishment and pardon. We also have financial banking terms in our theology. Bankers can loan money; they collect interest; they can foreclose. They can also forgive notes without requiring that they ever be paid. If loans are paid, they are said to be redeemed. That means that they are cancelled. The one who redeems a note is called the redeemer, even if he or she is not the one who took out the loan in the first place. If the banker forgives the note, he or she is the redeemer. When people commit crimes, these are crimes both against other people and against the government. The criminal is required to settle with both. To the state the criminal has to pay fines, go to prison, or be punished physically. To the injured party the criminal has to become reconciled by doing whatever the victim requires for satisfaction. In a theocracy, such as Israel, God is the final judge and the final recipient of assigned fines or sacrifices.

Jesus was familiar with these governmental concepts both in relationship to the management of a nation and also in terms of ethics and the will of God. He knew how money was raised, invested, and spent. He was planning to rule the Kingdom of Heaven on the Promised Land. Therefore he had to teach citizens correct behavior to live in such a kingdom and also how to please God. All of this was taught in hidden imagery.

The Innocence of Children. The following teaching is preserved in a chreia.

> At that time the disciples came to Jesus, saying, "Who is great in the Kingdom of Heaven?" After he called a child, he stood it in their midst and said, "I tell you under oath,

> if you do not turn and become as the children, you will
> not enter the Kingdom of Heaven" (Matt 18:1-3; Luke
> 9:46-48a; expanded in Mark 9:33-37).

Jesus was not encouraging adults to become senile and lapse
into second childhood. This message was much more important
than that. It had to do with crime and punishment, guilt and
innocence, repentance, reconciliation, and forgiveness. It was the
legal significance of children that Jesus encouraged.

In ancient Judaism girls were taught only three laws:

1) how to light the Sabbath candles,
2) how to give the tithe of everything cooked, and
3) how to observe menstrual purity.

Neither boys nor girls were considered part of the Jewish community
until they had been baptized, and for boys, also circumcised. From
eight days until the bar Mitzvah boys were not legally responsible
for their crimes. Their fathers were. Girls continued to be free from
all responsibility except for the fulfillment of the above three duties.
Their fathers were responsible for them until they were married.
After that their husbands were responsible.

Therefore children (those under twelve or so years of age)
were legally innocent, no matter what their behavior. That
was the condition required for admission into the Kingdom of
Heaven. It was not the age of children or the irresponsibility
of children that Jesus wanted his followers to achieve. It was
the guiltlessness. Adults could achieve the status of innocence
by repenting and meeting all of the demands of the Day of
Atonement. The Day of Atonement was designed to give
believers their last chance to settle their cases out of court so as
to avoid the negative possibilities of the Day of Judgment. Some
Rabbis provided generous assurances of the ease with which
Jews could receive the decree of innocence and become new

creatures on the Day of Atonement. They would become as free from crime as if they had never performed a criminal deed, but the rules of the Mishnah are not as much relaxed about it as the later rabbis.

It says, "The Day of Atonement effects atonement only if he has appeased his fellow Jew" (mYoma 8:9). This is consistent with the Sermon on the Mount. That which is important is that the Day of Atonement is the time when Jews could be born again, legally, become new creatures, have all of their crimes pardoned and settled out of court. When that was done the adult Jews became legally free from guilt and as innocent as children before the Bar Mitzvah.

The point of Jesus' message, recorded in this chreia, was that the Kingdom of Heaven had no room for people who were still guilty of outstanding crimes that had never been reconciled, punished, or pardoned. This declaration is consistent with other teachings of Jesus in parables. He encouraged patience and forgiveness to get all offenses settled out of court before the judgment, but insisted that at the judgment the bad fish would be thrown out and the weeds would be burned. The promises made to Abraham were contingent upon the Israelites keeping their side of the contract. Jesus did not intend to demand less than the contract made with God.

Among the visions of Zechariah was one in which all of the accumulated guilt of the Promised Land would be packed into a large bucket with a heavy lid on top to contain it. Then it would be transported to Babylon. Then Babylon would have the burden of guilt to pay (Zech 5:5-11), leaving the Promised Land free from crime. Ezekiel visualized the Lord sending a troop of terrorists into Jerusalem to slaughter all of the wicked Jews who resided there, leaving only the few faithful ones who were specially marked, allowing no criminals in the city (Ezek 9:1-11). Jesus was intent on fulfilling all of the requirements of the contract for the Promised Land. One of the chreias, attributed to Jesus, is preserved in Matthew (twice), Luke, and Mark.

Then certain of **the** scribes **and Pharisees** answered him saying, "We want to see **a sign from** you." **He, answered and said to them,**

Then **the Pharisees and** Sadducees tempting, asked him to show them **a sign from** Heaven. **He answered and said to them,** [When it is evening you say, "(it will be) a good day, because the sky is fiery, and in the morning, (it will be) stormy, because the sky is threatening red]

"An evil and adulterous generation looks for a sign; a sign will not be given it, except the sign of Jonah, the prophet" (Matt 12:38-39).

"An evil and adulterous generation looks for a sign; a sign will not be given it, except the sign of Jonah" (Matt 16:1-2a, 4).

Now the Pharisees came out and began to interrogate him, seeking from him a sign from Heaven, tempting him. After he had groaned in his spirit, **he said,**

While the crowds were gathering,

he began to **say,**

"Why does **this generation look for a sign**? [May all these unmentioned curses come upon me] if **a sign will be given** to this generation" (Mark 8:11-12).

"This is an evil **generation**. It **looks for a sign,** but **a sign will** not **be given** it, except the sign of Jonah (Luke 11:29).

These are all responsive chreias in which the identity of the character is implied by the context. The Matt 16 chreia is one in which the bracketed words are all explanatory additions of the later church to illustrate the point. Mark's version differs more than the rest, since it is given in the form of an oath, but all versions make it clear that Jesus was not going to give the kind of sign the questioners asked.

The nearest clue to the sign the Pharisees asked is the reference to the sign of Jonah. Jonah wanted all of the people of Nineveh to be destroyed, and he preached to them telling them how wicked they were and the certain destruction they would face. They repented, so God forgave them and did not destroy the city, and Jonah was angry that he did not. The Pharisees wanted all of the tax collectors and criminals that were associated with Jesus destroyed, but when Jesus called them they repented, and Jesus argued that they were forgiven. That was the only sign Jesus would give the Pharisees.

Repentance and the Temple Area. The sign the Pharisees probably wanted was for Jesus to do something miraculous, like striking a rock to make water appear, opening the sea, bringing down bread from heaven, or cleansing someone from leprosy, as Moses had done. They wanted him to prove that he was the real Messiah by such signs as these. The next two chreias are very important to NT research.

> Some were going along at the same time they were telling him about the Galileans whose blood Pilate mixed with their sacrifices. He answered and said to them, "Do you think that these Galileans were worse criminals than all [other] Galileans because they suffered these things? No! I tell you, if you do not repent, all of you will perish in the same way.

Or

> Those eighteen upon whom the Tower of Siloam fell and killed [them]. Do you think they were worse criminals than all [other] men who lived in Jerusalem? No! I tell you, if you do not repent, all of you will perish in the same way" (Luke 13:1-5).

This is a unit comprised of two parallel chreias, which some editor put together and abbreviated by omitting one of the situations that prompted the speaker to speak. The assumption is that both responses arose at the same occasion, and that may have been true. This is one of those literary units that allows us to test it for geographical and chronological validity.

Pilate was mentioned here. He was the procurator of Judah from A.D. 26 to 36. This event is also reported to have taken place under the same Roman procurator that crucified Jesus. Therefore this concurs both chronologically and geographically as an event that could have happened in the life of Jesus just as it is reported. It is also consistent with the behavior expected of Roman procurators, especially Pilate, and that of patriotic Galileans at the time (Ant 17:213-18; 18:55-59; 20:105-12; War 2:3; 9:4; 5:1-5). There were many attempts to overthrow Rome during those years, and Galileans were known for their participation in rebellious activities. Rebellions normally occurred during festivals, when mobs of Jews gathered at Jerusalem. Rome was always prepared for such a rebellion by keeping an entire legion of soldiers at the Roman fortress of Antonia, permanently, just a few hundred feet north of the temple and connected to it by two bridges. Romans tried to curb revolts at early stages by killing only a few Galileans in the temple area. It seems as if the Galileans had taken over the temple, which was also a fortress, motivating the Roman soldiers to cross the bridges and kill the Galileans, but the details are not given.

The place where sacrifices were made and the place which Jewish terrorists often tried to conquer the Romans was the temple at Jerusalem. New archaeological discoveries have uncovered remnants of the Tower of Siloam and the old wall adjacent to it. It is only 500 feet south of the Spring of Siloam, and also very near to the temple, perhaps no more than one or two city blocks away. Solomon was anointed at this spring, called the Spring of Gihon at that time. It is the same spring as the Spring of Siloam. David installed the Tent of God at Gihon, and he also constructed an altar there. Solomon's temple replaced the tent in the very same area. The temple was so close to the spring that Ezekiel spoke of the water flowing out from the temple, down the Kidron Valley and the streambed, through Wadi Qumran, to the Dead Sea where it would sweeten the water of the Dead Sea, because this water flowed out from the temple (Ezek 47). Enoch spoke of the water that flowed under the temple, probably through the shaft and tunnel that ran from the spring to the temple area. Describing the temple of Zion before its fall (A.D. 70), Tacitus said,

> The temple was built like a fortress . . . There is an ever-flowing spring tunneled under the hills into collecting pools and cisterns (Hist 11.12).

Aristeas (ca 285 B.C.) explained how the landscape of the temple area was designed with paved stones and gutters to carry away the blood washed down from the sacrifices. He described an inexhaustible (*ahn-éhk-lape-taws*) spring water system. The fresh water was so accessible to the temple that the blood of the sacrifices was flushed away instantly. He said the water flowed under the temple and that the system was indescribably (*ah-dee-ay-gáy-tohn*) well developed, with lead-lined, plastered cisterns, and countless pipes.[1] The seer of Revelation anticipated a restoration of Zion to its former condition. There would be

> Rev 22:1a river of the water of life, bright as a crystal, flowing from the throne of God and of the Lamb, 2in the middle of the street of the city.

In the Old City of Jerusalem small gutters are made in the center of streets, with the streets sloping from the outsides to the center. At the entrance of Gezer there is a large cement gutter in the middle of the street. This position was necessary, because the streets were narrow. There was not enough room for gutters on the side. The entering chariot had to straddle the gutter, just as the gutter in the middle of the street that flowed out from under the threshold of the temple. This was probably the kind of gutter

---

[1]   Eusebius, *Preparation of the Gospel* 9:38.

Aristeas saw years before. The city of David was small and narrow, so the streets there would not have been wide enough for gutters anywhere except in the center of the street.

There was an inexhaustible supply of water gushing into the temple for use in sacrifices (Aristeas 87-89). During the reign of the Hasmonean, Simon, as high priest and leader of the nation, there was still a large number of Syrian soldiers stationed in the citadel of David at the south end of the City of David. The citadel was so close to the temple that the very presence of the soldiers in the citadel defiled the temple that was nearby, on Mount Ophel near the spring (1Macc 13:52). Among the Dead Sea Scrolls was one called the temple scroll (11QT 32:12-15). It concurs with Aristeas that water was necessary for sacrifices. There was in the temple area a bathing place for the priests to bathe before they participated in the services. Water was required to wash away the bath water. There was a canal to bring water for bathing and also to wash away the blood from the sacrifices into a hole that vanished into the land. That hole may have conducted both the bath water and the mixture of blood and water into the Kidron Valley. It was important that it could vanish before the blood defiled anyone. Yadin noticed the way this conduit had to function. He also showed how consistent this report was with Ezek 47 and the Mishnah that said there were two holes where the water and blood ran and both led down into the Kidron brook (mMiddoth 3:2). Yadin also called attention to the altar on Mount Carmel where there was a similar canal that brought water around the altar to wash away the blood (1Kings 18:32-33). Nevertheless, he did not raise the question, asking how this could function from the so-called "temple mount" location.[1]

---

[1]   Y. Yadin, *The Temple Scroll* (Jerusalem; The Israel Exploration Society, 1983) I, p. 223-25.

It is no longer reasonable to think of the temple as having been in the area where the Dome of the Rock is now located, inside Herod's fortification. Both incidents reported in Luke's chreias are reported to have occurred within the borders of Zion. Both the temple and the Tower of Siloam were within the walls of Zion, the City of David. In NT times this city was a little town south of The Dome of the Rock. That which remains of the city is now only about 10 acres in size. In earlier times it was larger. Just north of this little town was the Tower of Antonia with its huge walls, where Jesus was tried by the same Pilate, by whose command the Galileans' blood was mixed with their sacrifices in the temple. These events are nowhere else recorded in history.

The proximity of the temple to the Tower of Siloam, the Spring of Siloam, and David's Citadel that was later taken over by the Syrians during the era of the Maccabees is evident in the air photograph of the City of David on the following page. Photo by Dr. Richard Cleave, Rohr Productions, LTD.

Because these stories have not been reported in the Gospel of Mark, scholars have erroneously thought that they were later additions of the church designed to meet the church's own local needs and attributed falsely to Jesus. Try to imagine where and when that could have been done! At a time when there were no newspapers, no radios, no telegraphs, no cell telephones, no TVs, no airplanes, no railroads, no automobiles. How far away from Jerusalem could those chreias have been composed without further details? Which Galileans? When? How? Which eighteen men from Jerusalem? How did the Tower of Siloam fall? Why did Pilate mix Galileans' blood with their sacrifice? How long after the events could those eighteen be mentioned in writing without further description? Five? Ten? Twenty? Fifty? A hundred years?

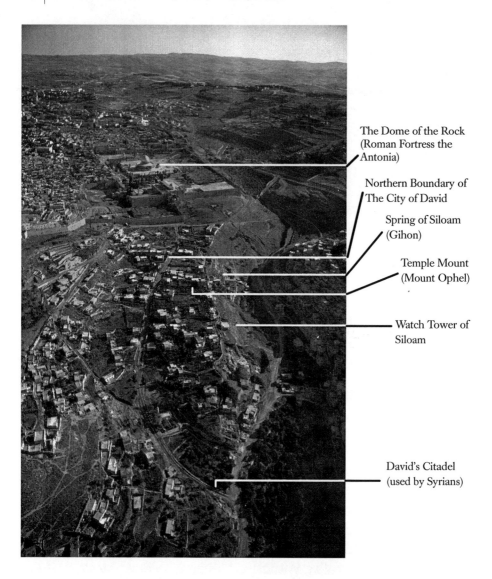

The Dome of the Rock (Roman Fortress the Antonia)

Northern Boundary of The City of David

Spring of Siloam (Gihon)

Temple Mount (Mount Ophel)

Watch Tower of Siloam

David's Citadel (used by Syrians)

Just test your own memory. There was a time, within the last sixty years, when anyone in the USA could refer to the expression "wrong way Corrigan," "Payola on TV," "those 92 who were killed," or "the Amtrack accident," and be readily understood, without explanation. Even though we have good means of communication, today, and these were widely known expressions, they are no longer known by many people. People who say any of these things, today, nearly always have to explain the situation that prompted the expressions and tell what they mean.

Now think of the way things would have been in the Near East two thousand years ago. What church in Rome, Spain, Asia Minor, or Egypt could or would have invented these reports and written them down the way they are, without further details? What might have been their local needs to compose such chreias? If they had been written for the needs of some distant church at some later time, those needs would have to have been written with the story to have any alternative value to any conjectured distant church.

Students of great teachers, soldiers of great generals, or secretaries of great kings traditionally wrote chreias. They were written to preserve important events in the lives of those great people. They were short cuts in memory, composed to remind people of things they already knew, but might have forgotten. Details were not given, because the readers already knew all the details. All they needed to have was a chreia to remind them of the associated stories. These were shortcuts in memory.

All of these points come together to reach the conclusion that these chreias had to have been put into written form very soon after the events happened and very close to the city of Jerusalem. These are the very earliest, verifiable reported events in the recorded life of Jesus – earlier than the letters of Paul or the Gospel of Mark. The odds that this conversation actually took place and that these recorded words are the words of Jesus are very high.

Forgiveness in the Monastery.

> Then approaching, Peter said to him, "Lord, how many times will my brother commit crimes against me and I forgive him? Seven times?" Jesus said to him, "I do not say to you, 'Until seven times,' but 'until seventy-seven times.'" (Matt 18:21-22).

This is clearly a chreia. Jesus is addressed as Lord and identified as the character of the chreia. His answer is given in quotation, and the entire unit is brief. The Lukan account has the same meaning, but it is not in chreia form.

> If your brother commits a crime, warn him;
> > if he repents, forgive him.
> > > If he commits crimes against you seven times a day,
> > and seven times he turns to you, saying, "I repent,"
> > > you must forgive him (Luke 17:3-4).

Peter was one of Jesus' apostles and a member of his monastery. He was not speaking of his relationship to all people in general, but to some other member of the monastery, a legal brother, that seemed to be asking for forgiveness all of the time. Peter may have been a judge subordinate to Jesus, just as Nathan was to David. He had to make decisions on matters of discipline. How would Jesus decide on such a case?

Jesus applied the rules of the Day of Atonement to this situation. Since pious Jews believed that the arrival of the Kingdom of Heaven was contingent upon every legal crime being cancelled – even the smallest offense, every effort had to be made on the part of every criminal to have his or her crimes corrected. The Day of Atonement was set aside to enable Jews to accomplish this result. It was their opportunity to settle their crimes out of court so as to avoid the punishment that might be given on the Day of Judgment.

There were three factors, which the Day of Atonement theology required for the cancellation of crimes.

1) God, through the agency of the state,
2) the criminal through repentance and compensation, and
3) the victim through acceptance of offered terms of reconciliation and forgiveness.

When the criminal is repentant he is required to contact the victim, apologize and offer terms of compensation. This can be negotiated. If the criminal came to the altar with his sacrifice to pay his fine to the state for an injury he had committed and then remembered that he had not cleared everything with the victim, then he was required to leave his sacrifice there at the temple and go, find the victim, and become reconciled with him before offering his sacrifice (Matt 5:23-24). If the victim refused to accept any terms, the guilt of the criminal would remain unresolved, and the case would go to court.

It is at the point where the criminal had not yet received release from the victim that Peter raised the question. Suppose some other Jew continued to injure him – especially a legal brother – and continued to ask for forgiveness. Did this not seem to be a plot to justify continued crime? Would that fellow Jew be seriously repentant? Did he deserve to be forgiven? Was he not just planning to continue criminal activity and counting on liturgical procedures to avoid punishment?

Jesus taught that the criminal was not the primary factor in this system. The real need was to restore the kingdom. All other things were minor. Therefore it was necessary to get criminal cases settled out of court before the Judgment Day. Suppose the criminal was insincere in his request, the nation was still in need of cleansing. Whatever could be done to clear the nation's record should be done, even if it were thought to be unfair. The easiest and surest way to have all crimes of the nation obliterated was to forgive them all. That would be like Zechariah's picture of Israel's crimes all being put into a strong vessel with a heavy lid and sent to Babylon. Of course they would soon be committed again, but the rabbis said that if all Jews were reconciled of their crimes for just one day, the kingdom would come. That day, of course, would be the Day of Atonement. In order to make this happen, from the criminal's point of view, crime must be stopped. From the victim's point, it must be forgiven, even up to seventy-seven times. That was the point from which the question was asked. The next, brief parable compared two debtors; just as other parables compare two brothers, two kinds of sea creatures, or two kinds of vegetation. Instead of crime and forgiveness it deals with obligation and forgiveness in terms of money.

> A certain creditor had two debtors: one owed him five
> hundred denarii and the other, fifty. Since they were not
> able to pay, he forgave them both. Which of them will
> love him more? (Luke 4:41-42).

This is very similar to the parable Matthew told more extensively.
Luke seems to summarize the Matthean parable: The Matthean
parable teaches that the forgiven debtor will finally face the
judgment if his repentance is not sincere, and its significance
understood. The Matthean parable might have been told to a
different audience from that of the Lukan parable

> The Kingdom of Heaven is like a human king who
> wanted to settle accounts with his servants. When he was
> beginning to settle, one was led to him who owed him ten
> thousand talents. Since he was unable to repay, the lord
> commanded that he, his wife, his children, and all that he
> owned be sold and [the proceeds from the sale] be paid
> to him. The servant, then, prostrated himself before him,
> saying, "Be patient with me, and I will pay it all back to
> you." Since the lord of that servant had compassion, he
> released him, and forgave him the loan.
>
> Then, after he had left, that servant found one of his
> fellow servants who owed him a hundred denarii. He
> seized him and choked him, saying, "Pay back what you
> owe!" His fellow servant fell down then and begged him,
> saying, "Be patient with me, and I will repay you." But
> he did not want to. Instead, he went out and threw him
> into prison until he paid the debt. Then, when his fellow
> servants saw the things that had happened, they were
> very much disturbed, so they reported to their lord all
> the things that took place. Then the lord called him in
> and said to him, "Wicked servant! All that debt I forgave
> you, since you pleaded with me. Is it not necessary that
> you be merciful to your fellow servant, just as I had been
> with you?" Then his lord was angry and gave him over

to the torturers until he should pay back all that he owed him. Thus also my Father who is in heaven will do to you, if you do not forgive each one his brother in your minds (Matt 18:23-25).

The term "human king" probably has the same meaning as the rabbinic "a king of flesh and blood." This was a reference to a human king, sometimes a gentile king. Terms here are financial, because debts and forgiveness are financial concepts. In theology they often refer to the treasury of merits and demerits in heaven. The notion that crimes must be punished or pardoned implies that crimes not punished accumulate in their demerit. Some crimes have to be punished by death, maiming, or whipping, but money or goods can satisfy other crimes. Crimes that can be punished and satisfied by money require fines in terms of sacrifices to the state. If these are not regularly paid, the debts accumulate and can be foreclosed. These are called "iniquities." Ben Sira warned his readers, "Pay back your neighbor when the loan falls due" (Sira 29:2). One of the fragments of the Dead Sea Scrolls warns of the damage that comes to people if they leave their debts unpaid. "If you borrow men's money for your poverty, do not let there be [rest for you] day or night nor rest for your soul until you have restored to your creditor [your debt]. Do not lie to him, lest you bear iniquity" (4Q417, frg. 1:1, 21-23).

The parable of the unforgiving servant reflects the same anxiety about the burden of the unpaid debt, but from the perspective of creditor and his necessity to forgive. This probably refers to the brothers in the monastery, although, from a broader concept, all sons of Abraham are brothers. It could have been directed to the unforgiving Pharisees and the same principle would apply. The huge debtor would have been the Pharisee, and the small debtor, the tax collector, as is probably intended in the Lukan parable. It is much more fitting, however, in a monastery where every brother was expected to be perfect, and brothers were expected to counsel one another for crimes they might have seen each other committing to enable the offender to request forgiveness and the community be free from crime.

The financial numbers used are probably hyperbolic for rhetorical effect. A talent is about 75-85 pounds of silver. Ten thousands of these would have been a lot of money. Josephus said that the taxes for Coele Syria, Phoenicia, Judea, and Samaria all totaled 8,000 talents. Jesus' disciples were formerly CEOs in big business or held governmental positions, such as tax collectors. They were used to dealing with large sums of money, but this parable spoke in terms that would have been considered a huge amount, even for them. In this parable the king is God, so hyperbole is proper. Micah said,

> With what shall I come before Yehowah [on the Day of Atonement]? . . . Will Yehowah be pleased with thousands of rams, with ten thousands of rivers of oil (Micah 6:6, 7)?

Both Micah and Jesus recognized that forgiveness was necessary in such a relationship. Micah concluded that it was impossible for him to compensate God for the crime he had committed against him, but he also realized that God did not require adequate payment. He asked only for him to act justly, love mercy, and walk humbly with God. With such a relationship most crimes could be settled out of court, as Jesus required.

In Jesus' parable, God was the huge creditor; and Jews – maybe even specifically monastic Jews – were the large debtors. The crimes they had committed while in big business were much greater than the small crimes monks committed against one another. When, like the very rich chief tax collector, Zaccheus, they chose to follow Jesus, they probably paid multiple damages for all their deception and exploitation and gave the rest to the monastery, which became the treasury for the new kingdom. Jesus then assured them that their crimes had been forgiven, and he argued with the Pharisees for their forgiveness. They had become a community of forgiven criminals.

At the monastery, however, they were obligated to continue to live without legal guilt. They were required to remind one another of their offenses that they might not have noticed themselves. This might have become a nit-picking society of crime and forgiveness and raised community problems if carried to the excess. Jesus said they should be generous in forgiveness. When they joined the monastery, they had been forgiven all their earlier crimes. How much more, then, should they be willing to forgive one another – even up to seventy-seven times; even seven times in one day! Life in the monastery was more intense in all of its law observance than the rest of Judaism, but it followed the same rules with the same goals. It may have been intended as a temporary measure to fulfill all the demands of the Kingdom of God until the Kingdom of God was established, and a legitimate temple was constructed where God could reign in purity.

Jesus was obviously prepared to bend every muscle and develop every corner of the requirements to bring the Kingdom of God into public fulfillment. This required careful planning, studying of the Scripture, employing excellent political strategy, and training his followers in character and dedication. He was not just trying to bring about a military revolution. He was trying to fulfill the will of God, as he understood it. His devotion still demands utmost respect and admiration.

The chreias and parables show Jesus counseling his apostles both in political strategy and in religious doctrine and character. He was preparing for the Kingdom of God where no criminals would be allowed. All guilt would have to be removed; all crimes would have to be punished or pardoned. Reconciliation among the citizens was required.

Just think about it! All of the chreias reported in this book so far have reported only events and sayings that took place within the borders of Palestine – Jerusalem and the Sea of Galilee. There Jesus was associated with Herod Antipas, Pilate, and John the Baptist – people known to have functioned during the lifetime of Jesus in the same land of Palestine. All of these chreias coherently picture an intelligent, religious, and patriotic statesman, moving quietly and organizing carefully, while planning the establishment of a new government that would rule this same land without the imposition of the Romans. He recruited very well trained leaders who committed themselves to this project at a very high cost to themselves in terms of family, money, society, and previous employment. This all had to have been done underground. He used coded speech and avoided conflicts with Herod. The parables and some of the chreias are told in relationship to the Pharisees, scribes, and Sadducees who were known to inhabit Palestine and hold leadership positions in Palestine at the time of Herod Antipas, John the Baptist, and Pilate. The parables are all coherent with these chreias and reflect the same conditions, in the same land, and at the same time.

This is enough to make the reader realize that Jesus does not come to us as one unknown, as Albert Schweitzer claimed. This is enough well composed and accurately reported data to demand careful attention. We have no literature testing the validity of the stories of such leaders as Socrates or Rabban Gamliel as is here tested of the sayings of the historical Jesus. We do not need a non-existent oral tradition or "the silences of Jesus" to conjecture a picture of Jesus. It is not necessary to fabricate fictions or fairy tales about Jesus or to treat all of this psychologically as if it were an inkblot test to reflect our own feelings, prejudices, and political identification. The valid historical reports are adequate to be read for their own historical content

All of these chreias and parables naturally fall into the same four categories that are mutually supporting. They are so coherent among themselves that they tend to overlap, one literary unit falling into two categories at the same time. These are:

1) Those showing Jesus recruiting and maintaining a very committed staff of apostles to be his new cabinet of government officials,
2) those picturing Jesus in conflict with the Pharisees on the question of accepting repentant tax collectors and criminals into his staff,

3) those that indicated Jesus' methods of communicating with Jews in a coded way without being discovered by the Romans, and

4) Jesus' teachings about repentance and forgiveness of crimes.

The next chapter will show that Jesus was not only a very skilled and competent statesman, but he was a man who was devoted to God to whom he trusted all of his life and possessions.

CHAPTER SIX

THE LORD OF THE HARVEST

THE EFFECTIVENESS OF PRAYER.

When Jesus saw the crowds who looked like sheep without a shepherd, he prayed that the Lord of the Harvest would send more laborers into the fields to help with the required program. Jesus immediately went to work himself to make fishers of men of the leaders of the fishing industry. He recruited tax collectors and upper class criminals to assist in his program. These were "white collar" criminals from a Jewish point of view. They had associated with gentiles in their businesses. They did not observe the Jewish dietary laws or other liturgical requirements. Jesus recruited these because he believed that it was God's will. He told his followers, "Do not be afraid . . . it is your Father's good pleasure to give you the kingdom" (Luke 12:32). It was because of his faith in God that he believed that the acquisition of the Kingdom was attainable. This was the Promised Land and the Jews were the chosen people, but, of course, there were problems.

Chreias in Faith

> Then, after the disciples had arrived, they said to him, "You know that the Pharisees, after they heard the report, were offended." He said in reply, "Every plant which my heavenly Father has not planted will be uprooted" (Matt 15:12-13).

This is a chreia. Jesus was recognized as the main character from the context. The situation that prompted Jesus to speak was given, and his answer was quoted. The entire unit is very brief. The situation given indicates that the disciples had returned to meet with Jesus after they had completed one of their missions. They reported to him the way the people were responding to their promotion. When they told him of the pharisaic response, he gave the answer reported here. The disciples, then, wrote this discussion down in chreia form, so that they could use it again, later. Again he used farming terminology. Like the parable of the weeds and the wheat, it would be only the wheat that would be stored in the granary. The weeds would be gathered and burned at harvest time. Jesus implied that the Pharisees were those whom his Father had not planted, so he would not have to worry about them. The following subject may also have been discussed at one of these private meetings:

> The apostles said to the Lord, "Add to our faith." The Lord said, "If you had faith like a mustard seed, you would have said to this sycamine tree, 'Be uprooted, and planted in the sea,' and it would have obeyed you" (Luke 17:5-6; Matt 21:21; Mark 11:22).

In the preceding context, the Lord's followers were called "disciples." Here they are called "apostles." They are obviously the same people. Initially Jesus began with disciples, students. After he had trained them adequately, he appointed them as apostles. Apostles are legal agents who are authorized to speak and act in the name of the principal (Jesus), in his interest, and at his responsibility. Jesus authorized his disciples to extend his ministry. Matt 5-7 describes Jesus teaching; Matt 8-9 picture Jesus performing miracles that involved healing. The next step was to give his apostles authority to continue these activities, casting out demons, healing, raising the dead (enrolling new members), and announcing the Kingdom (Matt 10:1-2, 5-8). That authority was probably given before Jesus sent these former businessmen out to preach, promote, and recruit in his name. When they told these parables and quotations from the chreias, it was the same, legally, as if Jesus had been speaking orally himself. After Jesus had healed the affliction of the man's son by casting out the demon, the disciples were impressed. They asked about his technique.

> Then, approaching, the disciples said to Jesus, alone, "Why were we not able to cast it out?" He said to them, "Because of your little faith. I tell you under oath, if you had faith as a mustard seed, you would say to this mountain, 'Be moved from here, there,' and it would be moved, and nothing would be impossible for you" (Matt 17:19-20).

The Lukan version was a chreia; the Matthean version is not. In the Matthean version Jesus apparently rebuked his apostles because they had less faith than a mustard seed, which is a very small seed. In the Lukan chreia, however, he may have meant that they had more than enough faith to do that, which was required of them. Jesus was confident that God would do a lot for his people with very little faith. The idea that the sycamine tree or the mountain would be moved for them seems hyperbolic, except for the prophecy of Zechariah.

Zechariah said that on the Day of Yehowah the Mount of Olives would be split in half with the eastern half separated from the western half. Then the western half that is visible from Jerusalem would be divided again so that the southern part of the mountain would be moved farther south, and the northern part farther north, leaving a great valley between these two parts of the Mount of Olives (Zech 14:1-5). Zechariah visualized the way he expected this to happen. The picture given here will show the shallow valley that now exists between the two halves of the western part of the Mount of Olives. Zechariah expected this valley to widen. These were only part of the great natural miracles Zechariah expected on the Day of the Lord, similar to the exodus from Egypt and in the battle against Sisera (Judges 5). Zechariah's expectations were grandiose, but his descriptions were geographically and topographically accurate.

Jesus knew the Scripture, and he was evidently stationed somewhere near the Mount of Olives, perhaps in the City of David, so that his listeners would see the Mount of Olives when he said "this mountain." Both he and his listeners would have realized that he was speaking of the Day of Yehowah when Zechariah said these things would happen. Jesus' message seems to have been that the Day of Yehowah would come by faith. Both Zechariah and Jesus expected miracles to take place, introducing the age to come. This is consistent with the belief that God would pull out all of the plants that he had not planted. God was in charge.

> A certain ruler asked him, saying, "Good teacher, what good must I do so that I will inherit life of the age?" Jesus

said to him, "Why do you call me good? None is good
except One, God" (Luke 18:18-20; Matt 19:16-17).

This is clearly a chreia. There is nothing unique about this response.
Jesus simply told the questioner that which he already knew. That
which was impossible with human beings is possible with God
(Matt 19:26; Mark 10:27; Luke 18:27). This was a basic part of
Jewish creed. The same belief is expressed in the following parables.
Life in the age was life in the age to come – the age that would
follow the current evil age. In the age to come the Kingdom of
God would be a reality on the Promised Land.

Parables of Potential.

Look! A sower went out to sow. While he was sowing,
some [seeds] fell along the path, and after the birds came,
they ate it. Others fell on rocky ground where there was
not much soil. They sprouted quickly, because there
was no depth of soil, but when the sun shone, it was
scorched, and because it had no depth of soil, it withered.
But others fell among the thorns and the thorns came up
and choked them. But others fell on good ground, and
produced grain, some a hundred, some sixty, and some
thirty fold (Matt 13:3-8; Mark 4:4-9; Luke 8:5-8).

This is not good counsel in agronomy. Parables seldom are, even
though they use farm terms. Good farmers do not scatter seed on
rocky places, in fencerows, in roads, or other places where grain
cannot grow. But the seeds of the Kingdom, which Jesus' apostles
were sowing, could not be that specific. They had the Roman
soldiers and spies all around watching everything they were doing.
They had to speak in such a way that the well-trained Jews would
get the message fully. Other Jews would understand parts. Those,
like the Romans, would think the message was about something
else altogether. That is why these former tax collectors and upper
class businessmen had to be trained in telling stories in parables.

Jesus told them that this would not be 100% successful, but if they kept scattering the seed, God would bring them a harvest, and it would be adequate.

It was normal in Jesus' day to compose parables related to farming. Even the big cities in Palestine are close to the land, and some of the feasts of Judaism are related to crops. Isaiah compared victory after a battle to a harvest of grain;

> As men rejoice in harvest time
> As they rejoice when they divide the spoil (Isa 9:2).

A psalmist compared the difference in feeling between sowing and reaping.

> Though a man may go forth in tears,
>   when he sows the seed,
> He will come again, rejoicing,
>   carrying with him bundles of grain (Ps 126:6).

John the Baptist compared the Messiah to a harvester, coming with a winnowing shovel in his hand (Matt 3:12; Luke 3:17). Joel described an anticipated battle in the Kidron Valley, at the edge of Zion, in terms of harvesting both grain and grapes (Joel 3:9-17). In Samaria, Jesus found the fields white with harvest.

Jews of NT times believed that time moved in cycles. Day followed night, and then another night appeared. One week came to an end only for another week to begin. Every unit of time came to an end before another unit began. Feasts followed one another in regular sequence. When the growing season came to an end there would be a harvest. Then, the next spring, there would be a sowing season again. Ages rotated in the same way. They grew old and came to an end to be followed by other ages. Therefore Jews were sure that this evil Roman age would come to an end, and there would be a harvest, when Jews would divide the spoils, and a new age would begin when the Kingdom of God would exist openly in Palestine. God was in charge, and he could be trusted to make all of these things happen in their proper time in the cycle, just as surely as day follows night and harvest follows growth. Another parable strengthens the argument.

> Which one of you will have a friend, and he comes to him in the middle of the night and says to him, "Friend, provide me three loaves, since my friend has arrived from a journey, and I do not have anything to set before him." That one, from within, by reply would say, "Do not trouble me. Already the door is closed, and my children and I are in bed. I am not able to get up to give you anything." I tell you, even if he will not get up to give him anything because he is his friend, because of his desperate situation, he will rise and give him whatever he needs (Luke 11:5-8).

The friend in this parable may have been just any next-door neighbor, or he may have been a shopkeeper who normally sold bread during store hours. Therefore the needy neighbor knew he had bread on hand. The problem was that this was after hours, the shop was closed, and the family was in bed. This was not the time to come expecting to conduct business, but there was the question of hospitality obligations. Everyone in the Near East knew about these. When a guest came, the host was under extreme social pressure to meet all of his needs. Consider, for example Rahab's willingness to betray her entire town to protect the Israelites whom she had accepted as guests into her home (Josh 2), Lot's willingness to forfeit his virgin daughters in order to protect his guests (Gen 19:1-8), or the Danite's willingness to provide equally for his Levitical guest (Judges 19:1-26).

I first learned about Near Eastern hospitality in 1957 when I was riding an old white mule, bareback, from Bethlehem to Khirbet Wadi Zaraniq, a ruined monastery on a shelf of a cliff about half way between Bethlehem and the Dead Sea. I was riding behind Dr. Aune Dajani, the head of the Jordanian Department of Antiquities. Dr. Dajani was a handsome Jordanian, dressed in a khaki uniform with a red kaffia and a red saddle on his bay horse with a black mane and tail. I casually said, "Dr. Dajani, you look nice on that horse." He got off the horse immediately and asked, "Do you want it?" I said, "No, I would not look nice on it. You do." He got back on the horse, but I wondered about that. I had never been offered a horse before.

When I returned to the American Schools of Oriental Research at Jerusalem, I asked our chef, Omar, what he would do if we were walking together in the market place (*sook*) and I said I liked his necktie. He responded at once, "I would give it to you." I asked why. He told me that the social pressures were so great in Jordan that if he failed to do so, the news would get around, and he would become a social outcast. Then he gave me examples. When a host accepts a guest into his home (there were no hostesses there in those days), he is responsible for all of the guest's needs and desires. The guest does not have to say he wants or needs something. The guest has only to look at it, and the host must offer it to him. It is the host's duty to sense the guest's needs and provide them, at almost any cost. The good host was trained to sense his guest's needs without asking. For reasons like this hosts did not allow their wives to be present where there were guests. If the guest smiled at the wife, the host would be obligated to give her to him.

This was the implication of the parable. Any person would feel a pressure to help a neighbor in need, but when faced also with hospitality demands, the host was obligated to leave no stone unturned. Also the neighbor was expected to understand the pressure and respond accordingly.

Furthermore, the reputation of the whole village would be injured if a guest could not find hospitality there. It was considered an honor for the entire village for a guest to lodge there over night. Therefore the host would make unusual requests of others and be willing to pay unusual prices for needs rather than treat a guest improperly. The friend who had been awakened also realized that this was an unusual situation for which he, too, had some responsibility. He could not leave this man and the entire village to be embarrassed in this rude way. This was a community crisis so the man awakened in the middle of the night could be expected to help meet the extenuating circumstances.

The implied teaching of this parable is an *a fortiori* argument (how much the more so). If a neighbor or local businessman would respond this faithfully to another person's need, how much more would God respond when his chosen people called on him in their crisis?

There may have been another important point to his parable. Jews in Jesus' time thought time moved in cycles. Things that happened before would happen again. By knowing earlier history, Jews thought they could match current events with some period in the past and then know what events would follow in the future. There was a three and a half year period between the defilement of the temple and its cleansing by Judas the Maccabee. When something happened, such as the defilement of the temple, Jews would expect a war for three and a half years, just as there had been during the Maccabean Revolt. Jews would also expect the liberation from the ruling nation to follow after three and a half years. If the time exceeded three and a half years, then they were prompted to give up and assume they had misread the signs. That may have been the point of this parable of the visitor who came late at night – after the expected time. If so, then the point would have been that God would not mistreat his people. He could be expected to honor the rules of hospitality, even if the expected time was over. Another similar argument deals with an unjust judge.

> There was a certain judge in a certain city that neither feared God nor deferred to human beings. Now there was a widow in that city, and she came to him, saying, "Vindicate me from my adversary!" He did not want to at that time, but afterward he said to himself, "Even if I do not fear God nor honor human beings, because of the trouble this widow causes me, I will vindicate her, so that she will not finally wear me out by her coming" (Luke 18:2-5).

Both Jews and Christians were warned not to take their problems to a gentile court (1Cor 6:1-11). Paul referred to gentile courts as the courts of the unjust (1Cor 6:1). Gentile judges of flesh and blood were contrasted to Jewish and Christian judges who were legal agents of God. Just as rabbis often meant a gentile king when they told parables of a "king of flesh and blood," so Jesus probably meant a gentile judge when he told a parable of a judge who did not fear God. This was not a personal attack on the character of one special judge. It was the evaluation Jews would give of all gentile judges. Since they were not Jews they did not fear God, in Jewish opinion, so they would not show favoritism to Jews.

This makes the *a fortiori* argument all the more extreme. This was not just a crooked Jewish judge who could be bribed by those who had money. He was a gentile judge who would not show special favor to God's chosen people. Although Jews were warned not to go to gentile judges, sometimes that was the only recourse some Jews had. A widow was chosen for the main character of the parable, because another woman would have had a husband, father, or older brother to defend her. This widow was not able to bribe any judge even if one had been susceptible to bribery. There was nothing she could do but be persistent and make a nuisance of herself until the judge vindicated her. That was the point of the parable. When Jews went to the gentile courts, sometimes the gentile judges actually vindicated Jews in need. Jews probably knew of instances when that happened, even though they despised gentiles.

NT scholars have differed greatly in defining the character of the widow. Was she rich and feisty? Was she poor? Did she actually threaten the judge with physical injury?[1] These suggestions are all beside the point. She was chosen because she was defenseless. She had no father, brother, or husband to defend her. She could only cry for help. Like other parables, this is a hypothetical situation.

---

[1]   Wendy Cotter, "The Parable of the Feisty Widow and the Threatened Judge (Luke 8:1-8)," *NTS* 51 (328-43).

The real teaching is not about the ways widows and judges react, but the way God responds to his people when they cry to him day and night, as believers really do. When my wife, Harlene, and I lived in Jerusalem during the Yom Kippur War, we lived only about a block away from an oriental Jewish synagogue. During the war we could hear men shouting their prayers to the tops of their voices 24 hours of the day, convinced, as Jesus was, that this would be effective.

Luke put this parable in a context comparing the widow's incessant pleading to the prayers of the chosen people to a just God who would show favoritism to his chosen people. Luke probably made the correct implication. The appeals people make to juries or judges in modern courts are called "prayers for relief." A prayer to a human judge is aptly compared to prayers to the judge of all the earth. Approximately a third of all of the Psalms are prayers for relief. This is another parable by which Jesus encouraged his disciples and others to trust God not to leave them abandoned in their time of need. One of the rabbis offered a similar argument.

> **If they cry aloud to me I will surely hear their cry** (Exod 22:23). Whenever he cries I will hear, but if they do not cry, I will not hear. The Scripture says, **I will surely hear their cry** in any event. Then why does the Scripture say, **if they cry aloud to me I will surely hear**? Except that I will hurry more to punish when someone *cries* than when he does not **cry.**
>
> Now look! These words constitute an *a fortiori* argument. If when an individual **cries** the Lord **hears his cry,** how much more so when the congregation **cries** (Mekilta, *Nezikin* 18:74-81).

This is consistent with modern courts of law. The offense of a corporation is considered greater than the offense of any one member of the corporation. Likewise the power and influence of the corporation is greater than the power and influence of any one member.

In addition to chreias and parables, there are instructions attributed to Jesus that are coherent with these. Jesus reminded his listeners that two sparrows were sold for a penny, yet neither of them would fall to the ground unnoticed by the heavenly Father. But God's chosen people are to be treasured much more than sparrows (Matt 10:29-30). God has counted even the hairs of Jewish heads (Matt 10:30). God clothes even the lilies of the field and he feeds the birds of the sky. Therefore God's chosen people need have no anxiety about whether or not he will provide for them adequately (Matt 6:25-34).

SUMMARY

Chapters 2-6 do not contain all of the teachings of Jesus, but they are the ones that have the most solid academic basis of being genuine. In fact most ancient historical characters whose sayings are accepted by most people without question cannot have their sayings justified as carefully as these. Most of the teachings of the rabbis, for example, cannot be nearly so well justified. There are other teachings of Jesus that are not recorded in either chreia form or in parables. Many of those are undoubtedly genuine, but that cannot be taken for granted, just because they have been recorded in the gospels. They must be tested for their coherence with this core group of valid sayings. The reason we examine every word reported about Jesus is that Jesus is more important to us than Julius Caesar, Plato, or Rabbi Johanan ben Zakkai. It makes a difference to us whether the report is true or not.

The problems scholars raise constantly is that it is impossible to distinguish the teachings of Jesus from the additions of the later church that preserved the writings. With this basic information, some writings of the church can clearly be distinguished from the teachings of Jesus. For example, some chreias of Jesus are shown in the gospels together with their fuller interpretation. The interpretation is the work of the church that recorded the material. The chreia is the text employed.

It is no longer reasonable to be as skeptical as has been the custom. Not only are these teachings valid, but the testimony of the church should not be dismissed out of hand as being fraudulent. The church is no more likely to be fraudulent in its reporting than the secular Greek and Latin editors and historians who have preserved the works of ancient figures like Julius Caesar, Socrates, or Alexander the Great. The more of these chreias and parables a person reads the more impressed he or she becomes with the skill, dedication, talent, and religious devotion of this leader, Jesus. The chreias and parables have been tested and shown to be the most valid teachings of Jesus, but they are not all of his teachings. They provide the basis for testing other teachings attributed to Jesus and also other teachings of the church. There are other teachings that are coherent with the chreias and parables, many of which can be considered reasonably valid. Some of these will appear in the next chapter, showing the legal basis on which Jesus obtained his authority as the Son of God and the Messiah.

CHAPTER SEVEN

JESUS' BIRTH AS THE SON OF GOD

THE WAY IT BEGAN

It was in the courts of United States of America that I learned legal concepts that helped me learn about Jesus. When I learned what a legal agent was, I thought of prophets and apostles, and I began to realize how important that concept was in antiquity. When I understood the significance of corporations, I thought of the legal body of Christ. The relationship between a principal and an agent taught me about the relationship among God, Jesus, and the apostles. When I learned how people could be born legally as well as physically, I remembered Jesus' command to Nicodemus, "You must be born again" (John 3:3-7). When I learned the way judges and juries function in modern courts, I realized why Jews and Christians have been anxious about the great judgment. The Scripture is filled with these legal concepts. When I learned the authority that was associated with various offices, I understood the official abilities of John the Baptist. This opened new doors for me that I will share with the reader in this chapter.

The earliest reference to Jesus in relationship to his ministry began when he was reported to be associated with John the Baptist. Like Aaron, Zadok, and Samuel, John was a priest. He was authorized to perform priestly duties, designed to purify people from all kinds of ritual uncleanness, called "defilement." His liturgical acts had legal consequences. When he declared that the liturgy through which any Jew went made him or her ritually clean, no one questioned the claim. In antiquity, liturgical forms were employed as contracts much more often than today. Maine said of liturgical forms,

> No pledge is enforced if a single form be omitted or misplaced, but, on the other hand, if the forms can be shown to have been accurately proceeded with, it is of no avail to plead that the promise was made under duress or deception.[1]

Jews who had committed crimes serious enough to be punished by courts through any kind of sacrifice or fine and had not paid the fine, were guilty of an offense, which was called "iniquity." It was a debt to God, which meant in a theocratic society that they owed a debt to the state. Priests, like John, had authority to deal with these debts. John could say what the debtors were required to do to compensate for their misdeeds and then, when he was satisfied, he could baptize them, and the crimes were legally cancelled. John was active, getting as many fines paid and as many debts cancelled as possible, so that the nation could be without any unpunished crime. He held public and private instruction classes, teaching people what each must do to have his or her

---

[1] S. Maine, *Ancient Law* (London, c1901, 17th), pp. 172-73 (U.S.A.: Dorset, c1986). For example if a scribe prepared a divorce document and witnesses signed it, and it was brought to the husband, it would not be valid unless the husband told the scribe, "Write," and the witnesses, "Sign" (mGit 7:2).

l their obligations cancelled. He also had the
rform rituals through which certain people
l.

are physically born only once. That is when
them into this world to start life. Legally,
ı be born again whenever he or she makes
vhereby she or he begins a new existence
d birth could involve marriage, adoption,
:ond birth could also happen through the
v office.
ıals could be performed by which an ordinary
ıgain and become a king. In some countries
n. In ancient Israel this ceremony was called
anointing. In this ceremony, an authorized priest would pour olive
oil over the citizen's head. This was one of the rituals John was
authorized to perform. There is no explicit report in the Gospels
stating that Jesus was anointed, but there are enough implications
to suggest that it was done. The evidence to support this claim
will be considered under some of the following headings.

1) There are precedents in the Scripture for secret anointings
   of kings.
2) When kings were anointed they received the spirit.
3) Anointed kings were those who could speak with
   authority.
4) At the River Jordan John performed a liturgy with Jesus.
5) As a result of this ceremony Jesus received the Spirit and
   spoke with authority.
6) Afterward Jesus was called by royal names that were applied
   only to messiahs or kings, such as "messiah (or Christ)," "Lord,"
   "king," "Son of God," "Son of David," and "Son of man."
7) John the Baptist obviously anointed Jesus in secret at the
   River Jordan.
8) Jesus lived in a political atmosphere in which it was necessary
   for political movements to be organized and maintained in
   secret.

SECRET ANOINTINGS

Long before Saul was known as a national leader, the priest, Samuel, anointed him when the two were alone in the city, declaring that *Yehowah* had anointed him as leader (*nah-geéd*) over his inheritance (1Sam 10:1).[1] In the same way that a father left his inheritance to his sons – and a double portion to his oldest son, his chosen one (*buh-kóhr*), so the Lord left his inheritance to his chosen people – and a double portion to the king, who became the *buh-kór* of God, even though, like David, he was Jessie's youngest son. This means that Samuel had acted as the Lord's legal agent who could speak and act for God. When Samuel anointed Saul, legally, it was God who anointed Saul. God was the principal, and the priest, Samuel, was his legal agent. As God's priest he was authorized to anoint someone in God's name, and he did. Later, after Samuel had lost confidence in Saul, he reportedly went to the home of David's father and anointed David in the midst of his brothers before David had participated in any national leadership (1Sam 16:13). Later both Saul and David functioned as kings of Israel, but Samuel, David, and Saul knew that Saul and David were destined to become kings much earlier. If the priest, John the Baptist, had anointed Jesus, Jews would have understood the significance of this secret event.

THE SPIRIT AND AUTHORITY

After Samuel anointed Saul the Spirit of God came upon him (1Sam 10:10). The same thing happened to David. As soon as Samuel poured oil upon his head, the Spirit of Yehowah came to David. At the same time the Spirit of Yehowah[2] departed from Saul

---

1 The Greek translation has " . . . as ruler over his people, over Israel" (1Kgdms 10:1).

2 This is the correct pronunciation of the Tetragrammaton. See Buchanan, "Some Unfinished Business with the Dead Sea Scrolls," *Revue de Qumran* 49-52 13 (1988), *Mémorial Jean Carmignac*, ed. F. Garcia Martínez et E. Peuch (Paris, 1988), pp. 411-20.

(1Sam 16:13-14). There seems to have been a close relationship between legal authority and the possession of the Spirit. Before Saul's time the Spirit of the Lord had taken possession of Gideon (Judges 6:2), Jephthah (Judges 11:9), and Samson (Judges 14:19; 15:14), and they all became tribal leaders. When Moses found the administration of the Israelites too much for him alone, he appointed 70 elders, and the Lord took some of the spirit that was on Moses and placed it on them so that they might share the burden. With the spirit came the legal responsibility and authority of leadership (Num 11:17, 25). Before Elijah was taken away into heaven Elisha asked him for a double portion of his spirit. Elijah had already chosen Elisha to be his successor as the prophet of Israel, but Elisha wanted more legal authority and power than Elijah had known (2Kings 2:9). When Elijah's staff of 50 employees saw that Elijah had died and that the spirit of Elijah rested on Elisha, they realized that Elisha was the new prophet, replacing Elijah, and they became his subjects (2Kings 2:15). With the spirit came the legal authority. That which biblical ancients called spiritual power, modern westerners would call legal authority. Even outside the biblical record an anonymous Norman said that at the moment the king was consecrated, the spirit "leaped" into this king and he became another man (*alias vir*).[1] This was a legal leap and a legal transformation. He was legally born again. When Paul was away from Corinth, through a written message he came to the Corinthians in the spirit. Through that spirit he gave the Corinthians legal authority to expel one of their members from the church (1Cor 5:1-5). Being with the Corinthians in spirit meant his legal presence was there even though he was physically absent. In Acts those who were baptized and received the Holy Spirit became legal members of the Christian community. When Jesus breathed the Holy Spirit on the twelve disciples they became apostles or legal agents of the Lord (John 20:22-23). These legal

---

[1]   E. H. Kantorowicz, *The King's Two Bodies* (Princeton: Princeton U. Press, 1957), p. 47.

transformations that took place were generally accompanied by some kind of legal ritual or ceremony, like anointing with oil, laying on of hands, foot washing, baptism with water, changing garments, or being consecrated into some office.[1] With all of these relationships between authority and reception of the Spirit, several of which are related to national leadership, we might suspect that anointing is implied when Jesus received the Spirit at the same time he was called God's son, a normal name for a king (Matt 3:16-17; Mark 1:10; Luke 3:21-22; John 1:32-34). After Jesus' so-called baptism, he was called one who was "full of the Holy Spirit." This probably meant that he had the authority of God's legal agent (Luke 4:1).

Implication is a legal function that is widely received. If, for instance, A male baby is both baptized and circumcised on the eighth day as a regular ritual, and it is said that he has been circumcised. Rabbis decreed that it is also implied that he has been baptized. Since judges and kings of Israel received the spirit and became leaders when they were anointed, and Jesus received the spirit and spoke with authority, it is implied that John the Baptist anointed him at the river Jordan, even though that is never said in any of the gospels. The political situation was such that it was not safe for Jews to say Jesus was anointed, but all Jews knew that, because it was implied. Only the Romans were kept ignorant of that fact.

Jesus is reported to have read Isa 61:1-2 before the congregation at Nazareth. When he quoted, **The Spirit of the Lord is upon me, which has anointed me to preach good news** . . . he said, "Today this Scripture is fulfilled in your ears" (Luke 4:17-21). He was claiming to have been anointed and to be the Messiah upon whom the Lord had placed his Spirit. The good news that he was anointed to preach was the same expression that Second Isaiah proclaimed: the kingdom was

---

[1]   See Further Buchanan, *Biblical Insights from Ancient and Modern Civil Law* (Lewiston: Edwin Mellen Press, c1992), pp. 16-17.

soon to be restored to the chosen people. Those who heard noted that Jesus spoke with authority and power (Luke 4:36).[1] Of course, those who did not know Second Isaiah would not have learned much from the message. Peter reportedly said that God had anointed Jesus with the Holy Spirit and power (Acts 10:38). Neither of these testimonies says that Jesus was anointed to be king, but that is implied.

A Psalm, praising David, who was physically the last born of the family of Jesse, legally held that David had become the firstborn of God. After David became an adult who was militarily successful, God became his legal father and God made David his **"firstborn, the** highest **of the kings of the land"** (Ps 89:28). This is precisely that which happened to Jesus. As with Moses, Alexander the Great, and others for whom birth stories were written, the birth narratives in the gospels were written after Jesus had been anointed.

In the promise to Mary during her pregnancy before the birth of Jesus, the angel supposedly said that the son Mary would bear would be called Son of the Most High and Son of God; he would inherit the throne of David; he would rule over the house of Jacob, which would be his kingdom (Luke 1:32-37). For all of this to happen the Holy Spirit would have to come upon him when he would be anointed king over Israel. That is implied. The text did not say that Jesus was the Son of the Most High at the same time that he was born to Mary. The promise was that the Holy Spirit would come upon him and he would *become* God's Son when he would inherit the throne of David and become king. That would not happen until he was anointed. He was physically born as Mary's son; he was legally born again, after he had become an adult, as God's Son. He was physically the son of Mary and Joseph, from the ancestry of David. He was legally adopted to become God's son. It did not happen in the reverse order as many scholars assume. He was not born the Son of God and adopted by Joseph

---

1   Buchanan, *Insights*, p. 131.

so that he could be the adopted son of David.[1] This is what Paul meant when he said of Jesus that he was

1) descended from David according to the flesh and
2) designated Son of God in power, according to the spirit of holiness (Rom 1:3-4).

On the basis of Luke 3:21-22 and Pss 2 and 110, the Odes of Solomon picture a dove landing on Jesus' head, and from there it began to sing. The message it sang frightened all who heard its voice. When it let down its wings creeping things died in their holes (Odes of Sol 24).[2] According to the Psalmist, at an enthronement ritual when a Jewish citizen was being established as king on the holy hill of Zion, the Lord declared to this adult Jew, "You are my son; *today* I have given you birth" (Ps 2:6-7). Legally there was no gestation period. The author of the Odes of Solomon, like the author of Luke 3:21-22, was expecting Jesus to act like the kings involved in Pss 2 and 110.

The Psalmist did not mention that the king involved was either anointed or received the Spirit, but that was implied, just as Jesus' anointing was implied when he received the Spirit and was called God's son. These items happened together with the same legal ceremony: Whenever one of these was mentioned, the rest were implied. The Gospel of John does not even mention the physical birth of Jesus. He described only his second birth at the River

---

1 It is also not true, as Y. Levin, "Jesus, 'Son of God' and 'Son of David': The 'Adoption' of Jesus into the Davidic Line," *JSNT* 28.4 (2006):433, holds "The writers of Matthew and Luke were apparently farther removed from Jewish tradition." The same kind of legal adoption took place when Solomon was anointed. It was practiced in monasticism and proselytism when every new member was legally born again and accepted into the family corporation.

2 See further S. Gero, "The Spirit as a Dove at the Baptism of Jesus," *NovTest* 18 (1976):17-35.

Jordan with John the Baptist. The gospel writer did not even call that a baptism. He said Jesus became the Light, and all of the rest was implied.

Paul said that Jesus was the son of David according to the flesh, but he was the Son of God according to the Spirit of holiness (Rom 1:3-4). This is what the Christian creed means when it says that Jesus is both Son of God and son of man, meaning, of course, son of a man and a woman. This was a distinction made between being a son physically and being a son legally (spiritually). A man was born as a physical son of his physical parents, but he could become a legal son through a legal ceremony. This is what happened when kings were crowned or anointed.

ROYAL AUTHORITY

The Sermon on the Mount closes with the observation that Jesus "taught them [the crowds] as one having authority, and not as their scribes" (Matt 7:29). The scribes were lawyers, legal agents, who spoke and acted in the name of someone else. In conflict with Jesus, the scribes were the lawyers of the Pharisees. Jesus, as king, spoke and acted with his royal authority being responsible only to God, his principal. That is clear from the Gospel of John where Jesus is reported as having said that he was not acting or speaking his own words or doing his own will, but the will of the Father who sent him. Legally, he was God. He had been anointed and was God's son. When the high priests and the Pharisees asked by what authority he did the things he did, Jesus did not tell them that he was the authorized Messiah. Instead he answered them with a coded question, asking by what authority John the Baptist did the things he did (Matt 21:23-25; Luke 20:2-4). If they thought John was a valid priest, then his baptisms or his anointings would also be valid. Jesus' authority depended on the validity of the ritual John performed on him. Baptism would not have given Jesus any authority as a royal leader. The Pharisees probably knew what this ceremony was, even though he was not openly called "king" until he appeared publicly and entered Jerusalem as king (Matt 21:5).

The Pharisees were alarmed about the effectiveness of Jesus' program. They were currently in leadership positions in the nation, and they liked their authority and status. They cross-examined Jesus about the source of his authority and the people he had assembled as associates. This would not have worried them if they did not think he had any claim to governmental authority. He was likely to become king, and they were not being given chief seats in his kingdom. He spoke of the first being last and the last, first (Matt 20:16). They feared for their positions in first place and the character of his rule. They evidently understood that his so-called baptism was more than a mere baptism.

THE TITLES OF JESUS

Jesus was called the son of David, the Son of God, the Christ, i.e., Messiah, king, and Son of man. These are all names given to Jewish kings. He was crucified as "king of the Jews" (Matt 27:37), the same title Josephus gave to David, Jeconiah, Alexander Janneus, and Antigonus. The term "Son of God" is a well-known title for a king.[1] Alexander the Great was called "the son of Zeus"; the Egyptian pharaoh was called "the son of Re." Solomon was known as God's son when he sat on Yehowah's throne ruling Yehowah's kingdom from Jerusalem (1Chron 28:5-7; 2 Sam 7:14). According to Nathan, God promised David that God would make David's kingdom secure, establishing David's son as king after him, and that God would be the father of David's son and that David's son would become God's son (2Sam 7:4-17). God's son, of course,

---

[1] It did not originate in the Jewish-Christian church, as W. Kramer, *Christ, Lord, Son of God* (London, 1963), p. 111, claimed. Kramer also misunderstood the role of a legal agent when he said God was the agent in Gal 4:4-5. God was the principal who sent the apostle or agent; Jesus was the agent who was sent (pp. 112-13).

was Solomon,[1] and these legal sonships were all legal fictions. A legal fiction is something that takes place legally, rather than physically. It is called a "fiction," because it cannot be seen and proved by human eyes, but it is real in court terms. A legal or adopted son has the same legal authority in court as a physically born son.

Jewish kings were also called "anointed ones" or the messiahs, which in Greek is "the Christ," because the ritual by which they legally became kings was an anointing ceremony (1Sam 2:10, 35; 12:3, 5; 16:6; 24:6, 10; 26:9, 11, 23; 2Sam 1:14, 16, 21; 19:21; 22:51, and frequently). Fourth Ezra called God's son "the Messiah" (4Ezra 7:28). Although Jesus asked his apostles not to call him the anointed one while they were trying to avoid suspicion of the Romans (Matt 16:16-20), his apostles recognized him as the Messiah, and after his death he was openly called the anointed one. Paul did not say, "*Jesus* died for our crimes"; he said, "*Christ* died for our crimes in accordance with the Scriptures" (1Cor 15:3) It was Jesus' legal office that could effect the legal offenses of the community. He also sometimes mentioned Jesus the Messiah (Rom 3:22, 24). First Peter referred to *Christ* who had suffered – not *Jesus* (1Peter 2:21). This would not have happened if Jesus had not been known as the anointed one before his death. The person, Jesus, would not have had the same importance that he had if he had not also been the legal Christ.

The title "son of man" could mean just "human being" in some contexts, but it had a special significance in Judaism. To Jews and Christians it was a code name for a particular leader. In

---

1   J. J. Collins, "A Pre-Christian 'Son of God' among the Dead Sea Scrolls," *BR* 9 (1993):36, said, "The figure who is called the Son of God is the representative or agent, *of the people* [emphasis added] of God." If ancient Israel had elected its kings by ballot, this would have been so, but since they were established either by inheritance or conquest, they were considered representatives of God.

the victorious visionary trial in Dan 7, the defendant called "the horn" was Antiochus Epiphanes, who died in Persia in 164 .B.C. He was given the death sentence in that drama of a heavenly trial (Dan 7:11). The plaintiff was called "one like a son of man," to whom the divine judge awarded the dominion, the glory, and the kingdom (Dan 7:14).

This happened the same year that Antiochus died and Judas the Maccabee won the famous Battle of Beth-horon and returned to have the temple cleansed. Judas was the "son of man" involved. Judas' mythological name in the drama was "son of man," just as Antiochus' mythological name was "the horn." To say that these were mythological names means that these were the names of characters in a play, the way Hamlet was the name of a character in one of Shakespeare's plays. In Greek concepts the myth was the highest form of communication. When it was not possible to get a point across using poetry, prose, music, or art, it could be cast into the form of a play to be performed in a theater. The myth was fiction only in the way that "The Scarlet Letter," "The Tale of Two Cities," or "Les Miserables" are fiction. Like Daniel 7 these stories dramatize a real situation in history that the readers can easily understand, and they probably communicate the human situation through drama better than any true historical report can tell.

Daniel 7 mythologized the divine judgment that took place in heaven when the temple in Zion was cleansed before the first celebration of Hanukkah. That was when the tide of the war turned, and Jews began to gain control of the kingdom David and Solomon ruled. It was probably read before a patriotic audience at Zion on the first Hanukkah after the defeat of the Syrians at Beth-horon.

Dan 7 is clearly a mythical description, or a description in drama, of the historical period up to and involving Hanukkah. One of the Dead Sea fragments is a commentary on Dan 7. In that commentary the character, which Dan 7:13 called "Son of man," the author of 4Q246 2:1 called "Son of God," "Son of the Most

High," and also "king."[1] Rabbis identified the Son of Man with the Messiah and also the Son of David (bSan 98a). When Jesus asked who the Son of man was, Peter said he was the Christ, the son of the God of life (Matt 16:14-17). The Christ was the one who had been anointed to be king; Son of God is a legal office held by a king. The Son of man is a code name for the new Judas the Maccabee (Dan 7), who functioned as national leader after the Battle of Beth-horon, and was accepted as if he were king, even though that name was not officially given.

Since Jesus was called by all of these titles that were associated with anointed kings it is reasonable to assume that he had also been anointed the way other kings were, and at that time he received the Spirit the way other kings did. Although there are texts that say he was anointed, they did not specifically say that he was anointed *king*. Since he acted like a leader who had been anointed, had the authority of one who had been anointed, received the Spirit the way kings who had been anointed did, and he was even called the anointed one, and after his death was openly referred to as the anointed one, the king of the Jews, why does the text not say

---

1   Another fragment (4Q448) offered a prayer to God for 1) the king, 2) the congregation of God's people Israel wherever they lived, and 3) God's kingdom (*mahm-lēkh-tuh-khāh*) (4Q448.B, 8). There is no way of misunderstanding what God's kingdom was in this case, because the king was named. It was King Jonathan (*yoh-nah-thahn hah-mēh-lehk*) (4Q448.B, 2; C, 8); i.e., Alexander Janneus, who ruled Palestine from 103 to 78 BC. Like the titles, Son of God, Son of man, Messiah, Son of the Most High, the Kingdom of God or the Kingdom of Heaven, God's kingdom is a political title, one that was recognized as a religious title for the Promised Land when it was free from foreign rule. This is the logical conclusion reached by "the correlation of various epithets and titles" that Collins advocates (Collins, *Scepter*, p. 60). See further Buchanan, "4Q246 and the Political Titles of Jesus," *The Qumran Chronicle* 4 (1994):77-80.

that he was anointed by John the Baptist at the time he received the Spirit? The answer lies in the political situation of his day.

THE POLITICAL ATMOSPHERE

Jesus lived and ministered in a land ruled by Rome against the will of the Jewish inhabitants of the country. In the first century Rome held the same position in Palestine that Israel holds today, and Jews then were subjected to some of the same kind of treatment Palestinians receive today. Jews had to plan any resistance subversively, in secret. Every time there was open resistance it was suppressed by the Roman military forces. Four Jewish military leaders who were aspiring to become kings were killed after the death of Herod the Great. Roman troops were widely distributed to suppress all potential insurrections.

Those who worked to liberate Palestine from Rome had to work underground and speak in coded language which only Jews who knew the Scripture and Jewish tradition could understand. Rome knew what a Son of God, king, or messiah meant, politically, so Jesus referred to himself as the Son of man, which sounded innocent enough for anyone who did not know Daniel and remember the Maccabean Revolt. He also warned his apostles not to call him the Messiah publicly (Matt 16:20). Instead of saying that John anointed Jesus to be the new king, they referred to his baptism, when he received the Spirit, spoke with authority, and was called God's son. The claim that he had been anointed was not said openly, but it was clearly implied.

After his important meeting with John the Baptist and his later assumption of authority, Romans might have wondered what happened between Jesus and John. Herod had John killed, because Romans thought he was leading an insurrection. This put Jesus under Roman suspicion. Did John anoint Jesus? Jews assured Romans that they did not have to worry. Jesus had been baptized there, just as many others had been. This should be nothing that would alarm the Romans, but for those who understood, John was typologically the Elijah who was predestined to precede the anointed Messiah. He was the messenger of whom Malachi prophesied that God would send him ahead to prepare the way for the Messiah (Mal 3:1; Matt 11:10-14).

JESUS AS TEACHER AND RABBI

Rabbis in Jesus' day were experts in law. They were judges who were expected to know both the law and the precedents that should be applied in judging legal cases. When they taught, they taught law students who were enrolled in what was then the equivalent of law schools, today. Jesus was called both rabbi and teacher, and anyone who will read the teachings recorded will acknowledge that he was highly skilled both in law and in teaching. His teaching methods were very similar to those of Diogenes. But he was more than just a teacher and a rabbi. He was a statesman, fully committed to doing God's will as a responsible Son of God. He had been wisely selected for his office. He was different from other rabbis and teachers, however, because he could also speak with authority. He was the Son of God, the Messiah. He had been anointed and received the spirit.

THE ROYAL DRAMAS OF JESUS

After Jesus had been legally born as the Messiah of Israel, his believers were convinced that he had been chosen by God to be the Messiah from the beginning of the world to become the ruler of Israel. This was a normal supposition for greatness. Jeremiah and Paul both thought they had been created for their missions from the foundation of the world. Two of the great dramatists of that day expressed their faith in dramas of his birth and early childhood. This had to be done subtly, in a land ruled by a foreign power, so that nationalistic Jews would get the message, but Roman leaders would not understand. These dramatists told stories that would reveal clues Romans would miss. One, called Matthew, told a story that began with Jesus' birth

Many great kings were eulogized by dramas of their births. The Pharaoh of Egypt was the son of Re, and Alexander the Great was declared to be the son of Zeus after he had conquered his kingdoms. When Olympia, Alexander's mother, heard of this declaration, she said, "Will that young man never stop accusing me to Hera?" Olympia, of course, knew that Zeus' wife, Hera, had not been consulted in this declaration. His legal birth was not contingent upon the details of his physical birth, but Alexander's eulogizers dramatized his birth to affirm his divine status. They did this by implying that he had divine genes. This drama told about the way Esculapius, the divine snake, crawled into Olympia's bed at her conception and impregnated Olympia. This was not a scientifically photographed account of his birth, but it dramatized his political power.

The stage was set for Matthew's drama by giving a summary of the family corporation of Abraham from its origin with Abraham until Joseph, son of Jacob, son of Isaac, son of Abraham. The drama began with an antitype of the old Joseph as Jesus' father. Jesus' mother was introduced as a virgin who had become pregnant miraculously, just as Olympia had done, without intercourse with Joseph. This was not a scientific account; it was an honorary title, a declaration of faith, just as Philo had done when he declared that Isaac was virgin born. If Abraham had never had intercourse with Sarah, why would she have complained that she could not become pregnant? Philo did not ask that kind of question. He was simply affirming his belief that Isaac was a great man, who had become the chief of the Abraham corporation. That gave him a divine status, according to Philo. Philo's drama was a historical fiction, told politically and poetically rather than scientifically. Philo was an apologist and not a scientist. So was the apologist Matthew. It was not until Jesus was recognized as the anointed Messiah that people claimed that Mary was a virgin before his birth. First he was born as a human being to Mary; next he was legally born as an adult and became the Son of God. After that Jesus was dramatized as one born of a virgin. It is not a valid practice to force modern western meanings into ancient words. We are obligated to read enough ancient literature to learn what meanings the ancients gave to ancient words and concepts. That does not prevent us from Christmas celebrations. The original dramas were intended for theatrical reenactment, but the celebration is not contingent upon the belief in the scientific virginity of Mary when that was not the belief of the early church.

When Jesus was born he was destined in advance to be the fulfillment of the prophecy of Isaiah, according to this dramatist. He was to be the new Immanuel, and his name would be called Jesus. This drama was written to show Jews that Jesus was the new Messiah without disclosing this pretense to the Romans. Instead of declaring openly that Jesus was the Messiah, the dramatist presented him as the fulfillment of Isaiah's prophecy applied to the king of Israel. Jews would quickly have understood the point and realized that this was a subversive message to tell them Jesus was the new messianic king. Another clue would have been the presence of angels to communicate with Joseph. A third clue would have been to tell of his birth at the same place where the great King David had been born. The introduction of great wise men from the East to worship Jesus the way they would recognize the reign of a great new king of another country was another clue.

This was done, again, to fulfill the divine prophecy of the great prophet, Isaiah. The death of the infants in Bethlehem by the wicked king, Herod, was designed to remind Jews of the ways Israelite infants had suffered deaths at the hands of the Egyptian king. It also reminded them of the insecurity of their own political situation. At a time when the greatest scientists known were the astrologists, the star appeared to remind the Jews of Jesus' great status. These great scholars brought expensive gifts to lay at the feet of Jesus.

Another secret message was disclosed when an angel appeared to tell Joseph that he must flee to Egypt, just as the ancient Joseph had done a thousand years earlier. The narrative of the death of the children associated with Herod related Jewish anxiety with Herod to the anxiety of the Israelites with Pharaoh in Egypt years before. The encouragement of this story reminded Jews that the Israelites had escaped from the earlier king of Egypt, and it implied that they also would escape from Rome at the hand of the new son of Joseph.

Rachel had earlier wept for the deaths of the children of Israel before the captivity into Babylon, and current mothers wept for their children who suffered at the hands of Herod. The Jews who were taken captive to Babylon were later allowed to return and resettle their land at Palestine. It suggested to the current generation that they too could expect deliverance. The old Joseph had brought salvation to the children of Jacob, and the new Joseph delivered the new Son of God from Egypt to the Promised Land.

This was all part of the dramatist's implications, without ever telling the Romans that they had a new subversive leader in their midst. The author did not write this drama to be circulated to the Romans. After the Bar Cochba Revolt was completed, Romans planted spies among Christians and Jews to check to see if they were teaching any subversive material. Both Jews and Christians had to revise their canons to remove all materials the Romans thought were suspicious, but they missed the implications of the birth dramas. These birth stories were part of the secret literature for the chosen people. Another dramatist with a similar purpose told a different story to a different assembly of Jews, perhaps in the diaspora of the Jews away from the Promised Land.

Luke was aware of the fact that John the Baptist was also a messiah, destined to be the high priest in the new kingdom. Therefore his birth must also have been miraculous. Like Abraham and Sarah, John's parents, Zechariah and Elizabeth, lived to their old age without being able to have children. Then came the miraculous change. Zechariah was a priest, and on the Day of Atonement, while he was in the temple, the angel, Gabriel, appeared to him and announced that Elizabeth would give birth to a son. That priest was so startled by the news that he was speechless until the time of John's birth. This happened in the days of Herod, king of Judah.

After Elizabeth had been pregnant for five months, the angel, Gabriel, appeared also to Mary, a virgin who was engaged to Joseph, but had never had intercourse with him. Nonetheless, Gabriel told Mary that her son would become the Son of the Most High, meaning that he would become king. He would sit on the throne of David and rule over the house of Jacob in the age to come. Mary and Elizabeth were relatives. While Mary was visiting Elizabeth she recited a poem of exultation, similar to the one Hannah recited after the announcement of her pregnancy before the birth of Samuel. When John was born, his father regained his speech and prophesied that this child was a promise that God had visited and redeemed his people, and that this child would go before the Lord to prepare his ways, just as he later did, fulfilling the role of Elijah.

All of this happened in the days of Herod the King. The great King Herod died in 4 B.C. The author must have intended Herod Archaelaus, who ruled from 4 B.C. to A.D. 6, because Jesus was not reported as born until the taxation of Caesar Augustus (6/7 A.D.), after Archaelaus had been deposed. The author of this drama probably did not intend to say that Mary had a 10-year pregnancy.

According to this drama, all of this began in Galilee, but since Jesus was born in Bethlehem, there had to be a journey from Galilee to Bethlehem, where Jesus was born in a stable. This was not unusual, because a woman and her child were both defiled at birth, so most children were born either in stables or in separate sections of a house, so as not to defile others. It would not have been proper for a child to have been born in a hotel. It was some later editor, who did not know of these rules, who added the explanation, "Because there was no room at the inn" (Luke 2:7).

Instead of wise men from the East, there was a large number of heavenly angels who came to local shepherds singing,

> Glory to God in the heights (heaven), and on the land,
> peace for the people of his favor [the chosen people]
> (Luke 2:14).

Both of these dramas were the kinds of stories that were composed after the event. After Jesus had become the Son of God, legally, most Jews secretly recognized him as the Messiah who would bring liberty from the Romans to the Jews of Palestine. Although Luke reported that Jesus was circumcised on the eighth day and was given the usual Bar Mitzvah ceremony that most Jewish boys experienced, the dramatist bypassed details of his growth until he became "about thirty years of age." Luke really did not know much about Jesus' early years. He conjectured his circumcision and Bar Mitzvah, as well as his appearance as a national leader at about the age of thirty. According to a Dead Sea document a Jewish king had to be at least thirty and no older than fifty when he began to rule (CDC 14:9). Luke said Jesus was about thirty. The Gospel of John said he was not yet fifty. This means that neither gospel writer knew the age of Jesus, except that he qualified for leadership.

Very few great national leaders are known during their childhood days, unless they were born princes. Most Americans do not know much about the birth and childhood days of earlier presidents of United States of America, even though most of this can be learned in libraries. People become interested in leaders after they have demonstrated their leadership. That is when Jesus was born again legally as the Son of God. It is after that that the story of Jesus really began, so far as our record shows. That is also the part of his life that earlier chapters in this book have introduced.

SUMMARY

From the chreias and parables, Jesus was pictured as a man in a hurry. He had been anointed to a very serious office, and he was determined to fulfill it responsibly. His skill as a teacher, statesman, and logician is obvious. The ethical demands he made on himself and his apostles were extensive. He moved rapidly and judiciously. He could not take out time to mourn for John the Baptist, even though he respected him very highly. Nonetheless, he was never in a hurry with God. Jesus recognized his role as God's apostle. The Gospel of John mentions 40 times that Jesus acted and spoke only on the authority of the one who sent him. He did not act on his own authority. God was in charge. Jesus was not free to act independently as if he were the principal. While his apostles were eager to get something started, Jesus had patience as he waited for signs from heaven. That will be evident in the next chapter.

CHAPTER EIGHT

WAITING FOR GOD

ENTRY INTO JERUSALEM

After his program had been underway long enough and well enough established for Jesus to plan to declare openly that he was the Messiah, he prepared to enter Jerusalem. As in other situations, Jesus tried to follow the Scripture for the direction of his activities. At Passover time he was waiting for God to give him directions for acting. Zechariah prophesied of the Messiah:

> Say to the daughter of Zion,
>> Look! Your king comes to you,
> meek and seated upon a donkey,
>> upon a colt the foal of a donkey (Zech 9:9).

When Jesus entered Jerusalem, riding upon a donkey, the crowd knew what this meant. So did the Pharisees, who feared the Romans would find out, because of the noise the crowd made as they shouted and threw their garments and palm leaves on the ground over which his donkey would walk (Matt 21:1-11).

Following the order given in Matthew, Jesus went at once to the temple, which he promptly cleansed, turning over the tables of the money changers (Matt 21:12-13). There are some practical problems with this report. The temple was the national treasury and the best fortress in the land, except for Herod's fortress "Antonia," which was less than 600 feet north of the temple area, fully equipped with at least a legion (ca. 6,000) of soldiers and arms permanently stationed. The notion that any person could enter this well-fortified area, upset a few tables, give orders, and leave without any military response seems unreasonable. There are two alternate possibilities.

1) It never happened. This was all conjectured on the basis that the Messiah would do all the things earlier kings had done. Hezekiah cleansed the temple and Judas the Maccabee cleansed the temple. The Messiah must have cleansed the temple. Like other ancients of the Middle East, Jews believed that time moved in cycles. It never came to an end. A week came to an end, but another week began immediately after. The same was true of months, years, seasons, Jubilee years, and eras. At certain times of each year there was a feast. That which happened before would happen again. Prophets counted on this and predicted the future on the basis of current events. In the Near East the weather was reasonably predictable. There was a rainy season and a season when it did not rain. Seasons were predictable. Days of the week were predictable. They always happened in the same sequence. Activities were somewhat predictable. The events of the Sabbath would be different from the events of common days. From this they conjectured that the activities of the eras could also be predicted. That effort was far from accurate, but it was attempted. Historians filled in details of spaces in the cycles by conjecturing them on the basis of events in earlier cycles. All the author had to do was fill in the details.

2) The other possibility is that the event was much bigger than it is reported. Jesus came in with troops and took over the temple area, its treasury, and its fortress by military force. If that had happened, it is very unlikely that he would simply have walked away afterward, and left the scene, as he is reported to have done. He would have held this fortress, once he had it under control. If he had already engaged in military action, there seems to be no reason why he would have been looking for a further sign from Heaven telling him how to act.

A Sign from Heaven. The Pharisees had asked Jesus for a sign from Heaven to show them that he was the Messiah. He refused. He was confident that he was the Messiah, but he needed signs from Heaven himself to tell him how to act at strategic times. He was God's legal agent, and he was careful not to act without God's direction. His principal way to learn God's will was to read God's message in the Scripture. In the Scripture there were only two texts that told what was reckoned as righteousness:

1) One was about Abraham for his faith. He believed God, and it was reckoned to him as righteousness (Gen 15:6).
2) The second was about Phineas. When Israel was confronted with a great plague and many Israelites were dying. Phineas thought it happened because Israelites had associated with the Midianites. Then an Israelite, Zimri, brought a new Midianite wife into his tent. While they were having intercourse, Phineas took a spear, jabbed it through both of them, and killed them. The Psalmist, reporting the action, said,

> Phineas arose and judged [the case],
>> and the plague was stopped,
>>> and it was reckoned to him as righteousness
>>> (Ps 106:30-31).

The passive voice in the third line of this statement was used to avoid saying the name of God. It means, however, that God reckoned Phineas' action as righteous. Later Jews identified Phineas' action, typologically, with that of Joshua and the Maccabean rebellion. The Maccabean revolt was conducted in the name of "our forefather, Phineas." Both of these rebellions were successful in acquiring the land. That proved to Jews that God approved killing foreigners and Jews who mingled with foreigners.

The Babylonian exile was different. At that time Jews did not engage in military activity. They observed the Scripture carefully, suffered for the crimes they had committed, and they believed that the Lord would fulfill the promises made to Abraham. They also negotiated with Cyrus. Cyrus was a master of military intelligence, and he succeeded in taking both Media and Babylon with a minimum of bloodshed, depending on spies inside enemy territory. In Babylon it was the Jews who acted as spies and guided his troops, and in repayment Cyrus allowed the Jews to return to the Promised Land without any Jewish or Persian bloodshed. Jews learned and profited from Cyrus' techniques. Jesus was evidently familiar with them.

In NT times both of these techniques were being tried. Both were live options for Jesus, who trusted the word of God in the Scriptures. Jesus was required to fulfill God's commands. This limited him to the Scripture as a method to learn God's word. After the death of John the Baptist, Jesus seems to have struggled to learn which of these options was God's will. The temptation story tells how Jesus struggled with Satan to learn whether or not he should lead a war. The same was true with the prayer at Gethsemane. These stories may not be factual events, but they reflect the disciples' realization that Jesus struggled at these two points in his career, and with these two choices available to him. When Jesus predicted that Herod's defiled temple would be destroyed, the disciples asked,

> When will these things happen? And what will be the sign of your public appearance and the end of the [evil] age (Matt 24:3)?

Jesus did not tell them specifically, because he was looking for a sign from Heaven, himself, to tell him how he should act at this time. Was this the time when he should lead a war, or should he continue to negotiate and plan further with Jews in Rome and Parthia to see if another Babylonian miracle could happen? Was it the action of Abraham or Phineas that was required at this time?

He was apparently prepared for either direction, if he could only get a sign from Heaven. He depended on the Scripture to give him the necessary clue. He expected to find it in Ezek 47. Ezekiel prophesied that in the age to come, water would flow out from under the temple which was above the Spring of Siloam, and it would flow down the Kidron Valley and the streambed that led past Wadi Qumran to the Dead Sea, where it would sweeten the water of the Dead Sea, so that there would be fish in that sea, all the way from Ain Gedi to Ain Eglaim (Ain Feshka).

This was not a fantastic dream. The water from the Spring of Siloam actually follows the course Ezekiel expected. At the end of the streambed that leads through Wadi Qumran are the ruins of Qumran and also a large spring, today called Ain Feshka with a nearby pool to catch water from the spring. Today the Dead Sea in this area is almost dry, but in 1957 and 1967 when I was there, I saw small fish in the pool near the spring with water flowing from the spring into the Dead Sea, and there were fish in the Dead Sea as far as the fresh water from the spring would sustain them. Ezekiel visualized much more water flowing down this wadi than ever flows today, even during rainy season. He also pictured fruit trees in the Kidron Valley near the river producing fruit every month of the year. This means there would never be a season without fresh fruit in the Kidron Valley

This was the sign Jesus needed. If he could only find ripe figs in the Kidron Valley, out of normal season, then he would know the new age had begun and God would bless the action he might take at that time. The report is as follows

Early the [next] morning after he had gone into the city, he was hungry, and he saw a fig tree along the way. He

> came to it, and he found nothing on it but leaves. Then
> he said to it, "No longer will any fruit come from you in
> the age [to come]" (Matt 21:18-19).

This unit is clearly a chreia. Jesus is identified through the context; the situation that prompted him to speak is given; his quotation is given; and the entire unit is very brief. This is coherent with the 24 other chreias given in earlier chapters, so this is very likely a quotation from the historical Jesus.

That which Jews of NT times expected to take place at the introduction of the new age was not the normal but the miraculous. The text said that Jesus looked for figs when he was hungry (Matt 21:18). He may actually have been hungry, but that was not the main reason he wanted ripe figs to appear on that tree just before Passover. This was a strategic sign that would determine his future activity.

When Jesus found no fruit he was understandably disappointed, so he cursed the fig tree. Since it did not produce fruit of the new age at that time, Jesus asked that it not be one of the trees blessed with the ability to bear fruit out of normal season "in the age [to come]" (Matt 21:19). That was the curse. According to the chreia, Jesus did not ask that the tree dry up. That was a later addition, employed by a later scribe who misunderstood the curse and misinterpreted it to prove that Jesus' curses were effective.

The insights Jesus gained from this knowledge determined that he would not begin action against Rome at that time. He would wait for a sign sometime in the future. He was not primarily a military rebel. He had been preparing for either method. He had agents sent out prepared for any eventuality, depending upon his guidance from God. He was only willing to act under God's direction. Like Abraham he would live by faith. When the Passover meal was served, and the disciples learned of his decision, Peter denied him, and Judas betrayed him. They thought of him as a saboteur. They had favored the alternative plan, but the Passover was still held.

Messianic Definitions. From the time of Herod the Great (d. 4 B.C.) there were messianic uprisings in Judah. At Herod's death, for example, while Herod's son, Archaelaus, was in Rome, getting permission from Caesar to rule the country, three messianic pretenders led rebellions. Judas, the son of Ezekias, was a rebel leader whom Herod the Great had subdued many years earlier. Another, named Simon, took the crown and led many troops. Both of these were apparently either Hasmoneans or of Davidic stock, because a third pretender, Athrongaeus, was distinguished from the others as not being from any royal family. These three aroused such a militant force that Josephus said all Judea was the scene of guerrilla warfare. (War 2:55-65). The Roman general, Varus, entered the picture, subdued the rebellion, crucified 2,000 of them and sent the leaders to Caesar for judgment. Caesar pardoned all except those of royal blood, which probably means that he killed all of the messianic pretenders (War 2.75-79), although Josephus did not specify what happened to individual leaders.

During the war of A.D. 66-70, three more messiahs appeared – Eleazar, John, and Simon (War 5:210). During a pause in the Roman attack on Jerusalem, while Vespasian was conducting the civil war in Rome, all three pretending messiahs fought against each other in the City of David to learn which would be the king when the Romans were finally destroyed. During that time John evidently had himself anointed and held a messianic banquet in the temple where the sacred oil and wine were kept, using up all of the oil and wine (War 5:562-565). After three and a half years of warfare, John and Simon finally surrendered (War 6:433-34). Simon emerged from his hiding place probably from the tunnel that still exists west of the Spring of Siloam. That tunnel begins at the top of the shaft that brought water from the spring and comes out in the very place where the temple had been before it was destroyed, but there was a drought near the end of the war, and even the Spring of Siloam dried up, leaving the tunnel dry for Simon's escape. This is further confirmation for the correct location of the temple. Simon was dressed in white with a purple mantle, showing his royal status (War 7:28-31). Since he was forced to surrender, he wanted to surrender as a king. John spent the rest of his life in prison, and Simon was led in victory parade before being killed. Eleazar and his group of sicarii (*see-káh-ree-ee*, dagger bearers) finally faced death at the last military stand against the Romans at Masada (War 7:337-367).

If Jesus had been only a military messiah, he would have led a battle on Passover eve. With thousands of Roman soldiers prepared for war in the fortress of Antonia, less than 600 feet from the temple, Jesus and his followers would probably have faced the same disaster that military messiahs faced. Jesus, however, was an excellent student of Scripture and a superior statesman. He knew there were two biblical bases for righteousness. His way of checking which one to employ was to see if there were figs in the Kidron Valley out of season as Ezekiel promised would be the case in the age to come. When there were not, Jesus accepted the alternative method. Knowing that his life was threatened, he then proceeded to authorize his apostles to become the new corporation of Christ and parties to the new contract.

Passover Plans. Before Passover, Jesus sent two disciples to Zion to a place near the Spring of Siloam, or possibly the Pool of Siloam. He told them to wait there until they saw a man carrying water. When that happened, they should follow him to his residence, and there make plans for Passover (Mark 14:12-16). Since women carried nearly all of the water in the Near East, the man carrying water was an exception. He had to be a monk, and his residence could not have been far away, because he had to carry water on his head in a pottery jar. The residence was probably right there at Zion, the City of David, a small town. Today all that is left of the city is a little more than 10 acres behind the Spring of Siloam. In earlier times, however, it was much larger. When the disciples met the water-carrying man at the spring and followed him, they did not arrive at a normal family residence with wife and children, but they met the masculine manager of the building (Mark 14:14) who was equipped and prepared to provide hospitality for a group of thirteen qualified monks.

Jews had believed for a long time that the Messiah would come and appear at Passover time and that he would reestablish God's contract with his people. A new contract was demanded because God had annulled the contract made with Moses when he sent the people out of his house and burned the temple. The Passover gathering of Jesus with his apostles was the time the Messiah Jesus appeared, and he renewed the contract.

The rules for divorce in the Scripture were that a man would have to obtain a written document of divorce, put it in the hand of his wife and send her out of his house, the way Abraham sent Hagar out of his house (Deut 24:1). When the temples (God's houses) of Jerusalem and Gerizim were burned, the Israelites and Jews were sent into Assyria and Babylon, respectively. Hosea and Jeremiah declared that God had divorced his people. Jeremiah said that God had sent his people out of his house, and that it was implied that he also gave them a document of divorce. He also promised, however, that after God's people had paid double for all of their crimes that God would return them to the Promised Land and give them a new contract. That is what the Messiah was expected to do as God's legal agent, acting in his behalf.

Second Isaiah, however, raised the legal question. The law required two parts to the divorce. Jews and Israelites have received only one part. Where is the divorce document? If it does not exist, there is no divorce. Jews were divided on this issue. Some accepted Jeremiah's counsel and others insisted Second Isaiah was correct (Isa 50:1). Jesus belonged to the group that believed a new contract was necessary, and he came to the Passover prepared to initiate a new contract. This was to be performed through the liturgy of seisin. Blackstone described an old English liturgy for transferring property, called "livery of seisin" (*seé-sin*):

> And then the feoffor [seller], if it be of land, doth deliver
> to the feoffee [buyer], all other persons being out of the
> ground, a clod or turf, or a twig or bough there growing,
> with words to this effect: "I deliver these to you in the
> name of seisin of all the lands and tenements contained

> in this deed." But if it be of a house, the feoffor [seller] must take the ring or latch of the door, the house being quite empty, and deliver it to the feoffee [buyer] in the same form; and then the feoffee [buyer] must enter alone, and shut-to the door, and then open it, and let in the others.[1]

English jurists do not know how this ceremony originated. They know only that it is very old. The livery of seisin did not originate with the English in the Middle Ages. It was practiced 3,000 years ago in Palestine. It is as old as the ceremony through which Boaz confronted the next of kin to Naomi. That relative had the right of first refusal for buying Naomi's land and marrying Ruth. When the next of kin agreed to surrender this right, he took off his own sandal and gave it to Boaz and said, "Acquire it for yourself" (Ruth 4:8). This transferred his rights of purchase to Boaz (Ruth 4:1-9) just as efficiently and completely as property was transferred in England by handing the new owner a clod of turf or a twig from the property. This was done legally, in the company of witnesses. The same was true when David and Jonathan agreed that David would succeed Saul as king. Jonathan gave David his robe, his armor, his sword, his bow, and his belt (1Sam 18:3-4). These were all seisins to confirm the contract. With these seisins the legal clothing that had belonged to Jonathan was transferred to David, just as the legal authority of Elijah was transferred to Elisha through Elijah's mantle. The use of seisins to form contracts was already a common practice in Bible lands and with biblical people before the time of Jesus.

Following this ordinary practice, when Jesus began the Passover meal with his apostles, he took ordinary Passover bread and said, "This is my body" (Matt 26:26). He did not say, "This is my flesh." It was not his flesh. Physically, this bread was not Jesus' physical

---

[1]   Blackstone, *Commentaries on the Laws of England* (Chicago: Callaghan and Co, 1884, 3d ed. rev) II, p. 314.

body, either, but through the proper legal ceremony, as his seisin, it could become legally his legal body, his corporation, and it evidently did. In NT times, as today, corporations were formed by legal action. These were given the name of "bodies" (*corpora*) because they could function legally as existent bodies. They could be sued, fined, and taxed, and they could represent themselves in court. Of course, these were all legal fictions, but they were very significant in court. A corporation by definition is immortal and continues even though all of the members of the corporation change. The corporation never dies. Corporations were legally born through ceremonies and contracts,[1] just as people were legally born again through ceremonies and contracts.

Once Jesus had formed a legal corporation of his apostles (legal agents), and the Passover meal was coming to a close, he took the ordinary Passover wine and used it as another seisin to form a contract with his newly organized legal corporation. As God's legal agent the Messiah was authorized to act and speak in the name of God, in his behalf, and at his responsibility. If Jesus made a contract with the apostles that would be the new contract Jeremiah promised that God would make with the new community. Jesus then

> took the cup and after he had given thanks, he gave [it] to them, saying, "Drink from it, all of you, for this is my **blood of the contract which** is being poured out in behalf of **the many** for **the forgiveness of sins**" (Matt 26:27).

That cup was not filled with blood. It was only a seisin of blood. The contract Moses made with God was one in which he slaughtered a beast, took the blood and sprinkled half of it over the altar of God and half of it over the people. He called this blood, "The blood

---

[1]   E. H. Kantorowicz, *The King's Two Bodies* (Princeton: Princeton U., 1957), pp. 12, 501.

of the contract." Since Moses used blood of beasts, Jesus used a seisin of his own "blood of the contract." That was not actually Jesus' blood, either. It was the fruit of the vine, but it was the legal medium necessary to make a contract with Jesus' corporation, the body of Christ. The cup contained the seisin of Jesus' own blood, because it formed the corporation which was legally his own body. Because of this liturgy the legal blood of Christ flowed though the body of Christ, and the church was formed. All of this happened before the crucifixion. It was not blood, and the later communion service was not a cannibalistic drinking of human blood. This was performed in a legal contract ceremony.

The establishment of this corporation was the formation of the church. The church would have existed after this even if Jesus had never been crucified. Jesus was a very learned leader and statesman. Before his crucifixion he developed a group of the best leaders in Palestine, and he raised enough money to make this group financially sound. Then he organized it into a legal corporation, which was the body of Christ. Just a few years after the crucifixion, Paul told Christians, "We who are many are one body in Christ" (Rom 12:5). He told the Corinthians, "You are the body of Christ, and individually members"(1Cor 12:27). Since this is Christ's body, Christ's corporation, "he is the head of the body, the church" (Col 1:18). Anyone who is in this body is legally "in Christ." This is not anything physical. It is legal. It is sometimes called "in Christ mysticism." This mysticism is really a legal presence. Jesus spoke of the Father being in him and he being in the Father, believers being in Christ and Christ being in them (John 14:10-11, 20).

The spirit is the legalizing factor, so that those who are in the spirit are in Christ; those who are baptized into Christ become legal members of the body of Christ and drink of one spirit. Legally, the principal is in the agent, and the agent is in the principal. The agent speaks and acts in the name of the principal, in behalf of the principal, and at the responsibility of the principal. Legally the agent is the principal, and anyone who has seen the agent has seen the principal (John 14:9). The ambassador is legally the king or president who sends him or her. Legally the attorney is the person or company he or she represents and is in him or her. That is not true physically. Physically, the principal is greater (John 14:28). Since a corporation is a legal body, agents of the corporation are the corporation. Jesus' apostles were his legal agents; he formed them into a corporation, the church. When Christians participate in the service of Holy Communion, they are typologically in the place where the apostles had been when they received the bread and the cup as seisins from the Lord's hand and become members of the corporation of Christ.

There were several other leaders who aspired to become kings in NT times, each one had large groups following him, but none of them left a surviving group of followers that continued after their deaths. All were killed, but we have no record that any of them left followers who were legal agents and incorporated (War 2:55-79). There were already churches in Asia Minor (modern Turkey) and Rome before Paul began his ministry there. That was so, because Jesus had already sent agents into the Roman Empire to extend his program. Jesus was different from other pretending messiahs. He organized a stable, legal corporation that was fiscally sound, and was in communication with the diaspora before his death, thus enabling the church to develop quickly in the Roman Empire with its movement.

In Jewish tradition, after the Passover meal, the service is allowed to continue as long as all the participants are awake. They can sing or pray. After the meal, Jesus is reported to have gone away to Gethsemane to pray by himself, leaving his apostles to stand guard as his security agents. Luke said he went about a stone's throw away (Luke 22:41). If he were this far away, how did the early church know what he said when he prayed? The early church would not have heard him pray, but it knew Jewish tradition. In time of deep trouble, the worshiper should ask first for deliverance, and then submit to the will of God. Jesus is reported to have done just that. The church was probably correct in its deduction.

When Jesus returned to the apostles the first time he found them sleeping, he was able to speak to them, so he went back and continued to pray. When he returned the second time the apostles were again asleep, but he was still able to talk to them. After a third time, he told them to continue sleeping (Matt 26:36-46). According to Jewish tradition, a person is not really sleeping if he or she can be addressed and still respond. This is only nodding. If the person cannot hear when addressed, that person is sound asleep, and the service must be discontinued.

When Jesus came to the fig tree in the Kidron Valley and did not find the ripe figs that Ezekiel 47 had promised would appear in the new age, he accepted this as a sign from heaven, and he decided at once not to follow Phineas, but to trust God to direct him, as Abraham had done. At the supper, the disciples expected him to begin an aggressive action against the Romans. He did not. Instead he told them that the project would take a little longer – but not more than one year. He would not drink again of the Passover cup until he drank it anew in the kingdom of God (Matt 26:29). That would be the following year at Passover. In between he would be waiting for directions from God. He was still asking for that direction at Gethsemane. He offered no resistance; he accepted the appearance of the Roman soldiers as if it were God's command, and he was willing to suffer and die, if that was God's will. He was a faithful legal agent of God, acting only in his name, in his interests, and at his responsibility.

Jesus' final obedience was not out of character. He was anointed to be king, like Solomon who rode on the royal mule to the tent of God at Gihon to be anointed (1Kings 1:28-40). Following the guidance of Zech 9:9, however, Jesus entered Jerusalem, riding on a donkey. Instead of parading his wealth like a king, and wearing royal garments, the way Simon did as he surrendered to the Romans (War 7:28-30), Jesus gave up all of his wealth and became a monk (2Cor 8:1-9). The Pauline document to the Philippians put this characteristic of Jesus into a confession, urging Christians to be like Jesus, who, as God's legal agent, was legally God. He was authorized to act and speak in God's name, in his behalf, and at his responsibility, but instead of flaunting his status, he humbled himself, took on himself the form of a servant. He joined a monastery (Philip 2:5-9).

Jesus had all of the administrative skills necessary to rule a kingdom, but he prepared for that kingdom by giving away all of his money and living like a monk. If he had led a military rebellion after the Last Supper he would have been only one more failed messiah, but he was organized also for program that developed like the one in Babylon. At first Paul was a follower of Phineas, and he began by persecuting Christians until he learned the significance of Jesus' decision to reject the example of Phineas. Then he too rejected the zeal of Phineas and promoted salvation by faith, following the examples of Abraham and Jesus. Jesus established churches in the Roman Empire and had agents functioning there. He organized his legal agents into a legal body of Christ that continued and developed evangelistically until it formed the Holy Roman Empire under the leadership of Constantine. The program did not stop there. This Body of Christ now exists in every nation in the world, thanks to Jesus' great skill as a statesman.

CONCLUSIONS

SCHOLARLY DEFAULT SETTINGS

For years biblical scholars have operated on mental default settings that severely limit the data they dare to examine. My mental computer is not limited by nineteenth century default settings. Like a hound dog chasing a beast that comes to a fence with a NO TRESPASSING sign I have no default setting to hold me back. I go right through these obstacles and analyze all the data I can obtain. Landowners have a right to put up signs prohibiting others from trespassing on their property, but the nineteenth century New Testament scholars who formulated the hypotheses that limit research, do not own the land.

Every Bible student is free to study all of the material that is available. Because I accept this freedom, I come to different conclusions from those of the inhibited scholars who always agree with the consensus. These NO TRESPASSING signs or restrictive default settings have been exposed and compressed in this little book so that others will not have to spend 50 years in research to learn the truth about Jesus. Those of you who have read this little book have realized that the more examples of chreias and parables you read the more convinced you became that these were valid historical units and that Jesus was an important statesman who has been accurately reported in the New Testament gospels. He was legitimately called the Messiah, King, Son of God, and Son of man. He was born, physically, from Joseph and Mary. His earthly father was Joseph, a descendant from the family of David, just as the Gospel of John reported, and he was born again, having come down from heaven legally (John 6:42), as the Son of God at the River Jordan when John the Baptist anointed him.

Biblical Possibilities for Righteousness. The Bible was the primary method Jesus had for learning God's will. The Bible recorded only two ways by which the Promised Land could be acquired. These were the two methods that were reckoned as righteousness in the Scripture.

1) following the righteousness of Phineas, through military war, such as the ones led by Joshua or Judas the Maccabee, or

2) through the faith of Abraham, directing international negotiations, such as the time Jews cooperated with Cyrus, helping him to conquer Babylon in a feast when all of the Babylonian leaders were drunk.

At that time Jews negotiated with Cyrus to return the Babylonian Jews to the Promised Land. These two choices have opposing techniques. With only these two options, Jesus had to plan carefully in order to be politically successful, on the one hand, and precisely obedient to the will of God on the other. This required the kind of statesmanship that only Jesus possessed. As the Messiah Jesus was not physically God; but he was God's legal agent. He was not leading his own show. Therefore, he was obligated to do the will of his principal, who was God. He had to study carefully to learn which choice God wanted for him.

It would not be easy to conquer a large empire like Rome that had the strongest military force in the world at that time. Jesus had to withhold his cabinet until the Jews in Rome were all trained and ready. It would take first class intelligence to get the "strong man" bound hand and foot. That could not be rushed.

Because both methods were included in the Scripture, Jesus was probably prepared to lead either movement, but only if he had God's approval. When he descended from the Mount of Olives and found no ripe figs out of season, he took that as a sign from God not to become a new Judas the Maccabee, even though, like Judas, he had been called the "Son of man." He never led troops the way other messianic pretenders, like Judas the Galilean, Zadok the Pharisee, John, Eleazar, Athrongaeus, or Simon did. Instead he led his cabinet in preparing for any eventuality. His choice of Abraham by faith rather than Phineas by zeal later persuaded Paul to give up his zeal of Phineas and become a leader in the Christian corporation. Jesus taught his apostles to pray,

> "Lead us not to the test," which would have meant, "Save us from a military war."
>
> "But deliver us from the evil one," meaning, "Rescue us from Rome."

Jesus understood that God's kingdom could not appear openly so long as the political situation continued as it had been. A change was required. The only question was, "How would this be brought about?" Would it come by means of a war, like the Maccabean Revolt and the conquest of Joshua or could it come about the way it happened with the Jews in Babylon, through repentance and international negotiations. Jesus taught his apostles to repent and forgive, because the kingdom could not come until all of the debt of crime had been removed. He probably also had extensive plans to weaken Rome from within.

The overwhelming historical evidence available shows that Jesus was a remarkable statesman. He developed his underground government and cabinet in the most difficult of times and situations. He was himself a wealthy, intelligent, and well-educated monk. He not only recruited the very wealthiest and most competent leaders in Palestine, but he trained them, authorized them, and commissioned them to recruit still more leaders in Jesus' behalf. To have been able to train such competent men, Jesus had to be a very intelligent and skillful teacher. Jesus required complete commitment of his apostles. Like Jesus they had to give up all of their wealth, their businesses, their property, and their families. Jesus was never the peasant Jewish Cynic that Crossan painted him. Crossan seems not to have read the parables to learn from them the people Jesus addressed. The "nobodies" of the world would not qualify as cabinet members for a kingdom.[1] Crossan also appears to have deduced his picture of Jesus from nineteenth century life in America, where people could move from the log house to the White House in one generation. In the strict class system in the ancient Near East peasants did not have audiences with wealthy political leaders. To think that a peasant could have persuaded very wealthy businessmen to give up all of their possessions and accept a peasant as their leader is absurd.

The Dual Mission. Jesus apparently had two missions. One was to the local nation of Palestine. This was coded as the twelve tribes to which he sent the twelve apostles (Matt 10:6-23). The other was to the diaspora, coded as the seventy nations. The seventy returned with joy, reporting their success. Jesus responded by saying, "I saw Satan falling like lightning from heaven" (Luke 10:17). A centurion came to Jesus asking that his daughter be healed. He was obviously a Jew, however, because he knew it would be improper for Jesus to come under the same roof where there might be a corpse. There were thousands of Jews in the Roman army in Jesus' day. The centurion was one of these. He was also obviously someone who lived outside the Promised Land, because Jesus contrasted his faith with that of local citizens. He said further,

---

[1]   J. D. Crossan, *The Historical Jesus: The Life of a Mediterranean Jewish Peasant* (San Francisco: Harper San Francisco, 1991), p. 421.

> Many will come from the east and west (Isa 49:12) and sit
> at table with Abraham, Isaac, and Jacob in the kingdom
> of heaven, while the sons of the kingdom will be thrown
> into outer darkness (Matt 8:12).

Jesus was saying that the promise and prophecy of Second Isaiah would be fulfilled. The diaspora Jews would return, and when they did, they would crowd out the local Jews, just as the Babylonian Jews did when they returned with Ezra and Nehemiah. There were Jews in Syria when Judas the Maccabee was fighting the Syrians in war; there were Jews in Parthia when the Parthians overthrew Herod and placed the Hasmonean, Antigonus, as king on the throne in Jerusalem. It is quite likely that Jesus had agents in Rome supporting his program. At a time, no later than A.D. 40 (2Cor 11:32-12:2; Gal 1:18-2:1), Paul was already engaged in his mission to the Diaspora. By that time there were already Christian churches in Asia Minor and Rome. This seems to mean that Jesus had a spider web organization already at work in the Roman Empire before his crucifixion. This was very important to the future of Christianity. When Vespasian and Titus overthrew nearly every town and city in Palestine, completely destroying the City of David, the Jews and Christians who survived and kept their faith alive were almost all in the Diaspora.

Before his crucifixion, Jesus gathered his apostles for the Passover meal at the City of David where he performed the liturgy necessary to organize the apostles, legally, into a corporation with which he also renewed the contract between the Lord and his people. Like other corporations, the body of Christ never died. It has continued to this day.

Jesus' Two Bodies and the Resurrection.

1) A physical body that could be born of a woman, get sick, and die, and
2) a corporate, legal, body that lives forever. Jesus' foresight made it possible for the church to come into existence and

for Christians to continue the mission of Christ both in the City of David and throughout the Roman Empire.

Immediately after the crucifixion the apostles were understandably disappointed. Some of them went back to fishing. Very soon, however, they realized that they must continue the mission to which they were appointed. The king has two bodies, and when the king's physical body dies, his office is immediately transferred to his successor, and the corporate nation continues. That happened with Jesus. When he was crucified the corporate body of Christ continued. Evidently it was Peter who continued as chieftain of the body of Christ. It took a while for the apostles to remember their inherited offices and their legal responsibilities. This realization is reported in terms of Jesus' appearance to them either on the road to Emmaus (Luke 24:13-53) or while they were fishing in the Sea of Galilee (John 21:3-25). From experiences like these the apostles realized that they were still parts of Christ's corporation under commission to function as the Body of Christ. This corporation, which seemed dead, was revived. As this happened the body of Christ was raised from its death. Paul seemed to think that this was the resurrection of the dead. He said with respect to the resurrection that the body that had been raised was not the physical body that had been crucified. How did this happen? There was a transformation in the resurrection:

> ICor 13:42-44That which is sown is perishable. That which is raised is imperishable. It is sown in dishonor; it is raised in glory. It is sown in weakness; it is raised in power, it is sown a physical body. It is raised a spiritual (i.e., a legal) body.

This is consistent with Paul's great dissertation on the flesh and the spirit. He contrasted the law of the spirit of life with the law of crime and death (Rom 8:2). There were some who walked, thought, dwelled, and were obligated either to the spirit or to the flesh. Those who functioned in the spirit were those who were in

Christ Jesus (Rom 8:1-10).[1] True security is in the spiritual body and not in the body of flesh.

When Jesus was crucified, his physical body died, but the legal body, the spiritual body, the corporation Jesus formed at the Last Supper, was called into existence and became alive and active. Some members of the body of Christ had met Paul, somewhere near Damascus, and convinced him of this resurrection. Paul had never met Jesus in the flesh, but the risen body of Christ confronted him. Paul said of Jesus that he was

> Rom 1:3-4descended from David according to the flesh, but designated Son of God in power according the Spirit of holiness by his resurrection from the dead

Some of the most recent scholarly views of the resurrection appear in a collection of essays written by five different scholars. They evaluated the literature and the tradition. They analyzed the ways in which the term, "resurrection," could be used metaphorically, but none of them upheld a historical basis for the physical resurrection of Christ.[2] Jews as late as the Crusades expected messiahs who would appear, redeem Israel, and raise the dead. Many messiahs did arise and lead military movements, but there is no report that any of the expected messiahs actually raised corpses. When Herod said Jesus was John the Baptist raised from the dead, he meant that Jesus was an anti-type of John the Baptist. He was another John-like figure, and Herod worried that he was a national threat, just as John had been. There is no data that would prove to a historian

---

1   For the relationship of the spirit and law in adoption terms, see B. Holdsworth, "The Other Intercessor: The Holy Spirit as Familia-Petitioner for the Father's Felius-Familia," *Andrews University Seminary Studies* 42.2 (2004):325-346.
2   James H. Charlesworth, C. D. Elledge, J. L. Crenshaw, H. Boers, and W. W. Willis, *Resurrection: The Origin and Future of a Biblical Doctrine* (London: T. & T. Clark, 2006).

that either John the Baptist or Jesus was raised as a physical, historical person that was once a physical corpse. That does not mean that Christians cannot believe in the physical resurrection. The physical resurrection of Jesus has often been affirmed but not historically demonstrated. It seems not to have been held by Paul or the early church fathers. It has been testified in Scripture, so it may have happened, but even if it did, it is not the most important resurrection of Jesus on record.

Early Jews and Christians did not think physical death was something to be greatly feared, but they worried about the possibility that they might lose their souls, be expelled from the community, never to return. This was the death from the community where they had found the religious and legal life, which defined their existence. They believed that there would be life after physical death, where they could again belong to the good life in Christ. Belief in the resurrection meant that they could be restored to their religious existence where alone life was possible. The earliest followers of Christ did not only affirm the legal or spiritual resurrection of the body of Christ, but they became the earliest members of the body of Christ that was raised after the crucifixion, that has survived, and which continues to exist. As Jesus' legal agents it was only through them that Jesus could continue to speak. It was through them that his word became flesh.

If Jesus had not formed the legal body of Christ at the Last Supper, even his death would not have been beneficial for Christians today. His death would have been only a tragedy like that of Socrates who drank the hemlock. But Jesus was a great statesman who designed, organized, and established the body of Christ, both fiscally and legally, that could continue even after his crucifixion. Like other legal corporations, the body of Christ is immortal. All of the members of the body can be changed, but the corporation itself never dies. Today Christians realize that and are reminded, as United Methodists are upon admission, that "The church is of God and will be preserved until the end of time, for the due administration of his word and ordinances, the edification of believers, and the conversion of the world. All – of every age and station – stand in need of the means of grace which it alone provides." When Jesus was anointed, the word became flesh and dwelled among us, full of grace and truth. When he formed the body of Christ he made that means of grace possible for all Christians that followed after him. Christians today are the body of Christ that has received the grace that was promised and we are ourselves the spiritual body of Christ that has been raised.

There were thousands of Jews in the Roman Empire during the time when the body of Christ was coming into existence and developing, and it developed rapidly. Only 300 years after the crucifixion there were enough well organized Christians in Europe to be able to negotiate with Constantine and establish the Holy Roman Empire. The earliest church historian, Eusebius, like the apostle Paul, Jesus, and John the Baptist (Matt 11:1-6), understood the resurrection legally, and he interpreted the victory of Constantine as the fulfillment of Jesus' ministry (HE 9:9, 4-5; 10:4, 12) – the new exodus (Exod 15:4-5), the revival of the dead bones after the Babylonian Captivity (Ezek 37), and the resurrection of the dead. Eusebius said that before Constantine, Christians were not only half dead (*hay-meeth-náy-taws*) but "foul and stinking in their tombs, but he raised us up" (HE 10:12). He understood that, not only Jesus, but Eusebius himself was among those who had been raised from the dead.

Other messiahs of the first century all died, and with them their legal (spiritual) bodies also died. After the death of Jesus, the body of Christ came to life, and early Christians, like Paul and Eusebius were excited about it. They could have joined modern Christians in singing, "Up from the grave he arose!" without being concerned about the physical body of Jesus. It took more than physical death to put an end to the body of Christ, and so Christians continue to celebrate Easter and be glad to claim their membership in the great body of Christ.

One of the popular current views among New Testament scholars is that our information about Jesus comes to us because of the "impression" or "impact" that he left among people, generally.

Community groups talked about this and possibly asked people like Mary Magdalene to tell them what they knew – just as if Mary Magdalene would have known more about Jesus than the apostles. People in these groups spoke about Jesus orally, they say, because there were no textbooks. These scholars say that some stories from general oral conversations were then later written down and preserved by various and sundry unknown reporters, and they probably became modified considerably in communication, but that is what has been preserved in the New Testament. It is true that Jesus made a great impression on people, but it was more than the subject of popular gossip. He made a great impression on his apostles who received their information directly from Jesus, either orally or in writing. Those rich men were so greatly impressed that they gave up all of their possessions to Jesus' movement, and became monks. This was not all done orally. It was done in writing, which we still have in the New Testament. It was written much earlier than most scholars realize.

Text Books and Teaching Methods. The twenty-first century scholars who conjecture that there were no text books in Jesus' day have failed to read the textbooks of antiquity that still exist. Greek Rhetoricians composed some of these, and students were required to read the writings of their teachers as early as the fourth century B.C. They were required to memorize parts of them and construct chreias from them. Archaeologists have unearthed school buildings with benches for students and written experiences of students in schools as early as 4,000 B.C.[1] Jewish boys were taught to read and write for their Bar Mitzwah exams.

Those who have read this book realize that the impression Jesus made was much greater and earlier than modern scholars suppose. While Jesus was training them, apostles wrote quotations and impressions down in the form of chreias to remind themselves of more extensive literary materials, which they already knew.

---

[1]   Hans Bauman, *In the Land of Ur*, pp. 95-99.

Jesus probably wrote down many parables himself and gave them to the apostles to use in their promotional programs. It was because the apostles had written lists of these parables that the parables and chreias have been saved and survived until they were gathered together into gospel form. The beautiful parables of Jesus were not extemporary compositions that grew up in gossip groups and were written down by some of the few members of the groups who could read and write. An excellent literary artist expertly designed the parables for the purposes intended. From these parables the purposes of their composition can be understood.

The written materials became available to the apostles, first of all, while they were still students of Jesus, before they were sent out on missions. The parables were most likely written by Jesus, himself, and provided to his apostles in written form. The chreias and parables were not recovered from the preaching of the apostles. They were sources the apostles used in their preaching. The impressions grew as parables and chreias were shared by the apostles, both in oral and written form, as they continued their work of leading the corporation of Christ. All of the apostles were sent out with the same lists, so that the message could be consistent and as coherent as they still are. The early church had its origin among the intelligent, well educated, upper class Jews of Palestine and the Roman Empire. It was not a grass roots organization that emerged from the discussions of illiterate common people. The apostles of Jesus were men for whom reading and writing was a normal part of life. They had all passed their Bar Mitzwah exams years before.

If Jesus had not been the skilled, highly intelligent, legally trained statesman that he was, there would not have been the competent cabinet to continue the development of the legal body of Christ that emerged. If our gospels depended only on the general impressions of various community groups, as James Dunn supposes, the effect of Jesus' Messiahship would probably have been no more successful than that of other messiahs who led movements during the same century.

Jesus was not a "loner." Because he recruited wealthy CEOs and demanded that they give all of their money to the monastery, the corporation Jesus formed was financially sound and able to finance the mission. Because he selected only the best leaders to be his apostles and organized them into a legal corporation, these competent and committed men were prepared, equipped, and legally organized to continue his program – even after the crucifixion. If the legal body of Christ had not been raised after the crucifixion, we would never have heard of Paul. It was from members of the risen body of Christ that Paul became convinced of the resurrection and all that which Jesus designed. If Jesus had limited his mission to the Land of Palestine, the church may never have survived the wars of A.D. 66-70 and 132-135. It was because Jesus chose not to lead a military rebellion that his followers were not engaged in the Bar Cochba Revolt, even though they were persecuted for their non-resistance. They were prepared to live by the faith of Abraham and to exist in the Roman Empire as normal citizens. Early Christians, like Paul, learned from this judicious statesman, whose faith was unfailing, the commitment and methodology that led to success. It was because of Jesus' skill in statesmanship that the church could become well established in the Roman Empire where it could continue to grow until it became strong enough to command Constantine's attention, carrying out the mission Jesus initially designed and directed. Echoes of his faith and wisdom have continued through the centuries.

PERSONAL REFLECTIONS

Hound Dog Researching. It has been more than 50 years since this hound dog researcher set out on the trail to learn about the historical Jesus. It has certainly been a worthwhile venture. There were many historical insights hidden in ancient literature just waiting to be discovered. Many insights had been hidden under NO TRESPASSING signs installed by nineteenth century scholars, with default settings to keep them from ever appearing. These NO TRESPASSING signs came in the form of hypotheses, most of which had been formulated in the nineteenth century. The NO TRESPASSING signs insisted that scholars all realize that the word "end" always meant the end of the world or of time, even though the context does not imply that. They also forbad anyone from thinking that any of the political titles and terms had any political meaning.

Benefits. This study began in the parish where I was challenged by questions asked by members of the church of which I was the pastor. The questions asked not only helped my parishioners. They also helped me. I understood that they were important, so I took these questions to the seminary and the graduate school. They put me to work for more than half a century, and the questions asked about Jesus have rescued me from two traps into which other scholars have fallen:

1) Skepticism, and
2) unfounded fantasy.

Jesus was given such political titles as the Messiah, King, and Son of God. Nevertheless, scholars have not wanted to admit that Jesus was in any way related to politics or government when he spoke about a kingdom. To avoid admitting the obvious, scholars have resorted to hypotheses, rhetoric, psychology, and the composition of myths. Starting with the hypothesis that Mark was the earliest gospel, scholars have rhetorically dismissed the other gospels as additions of the later church in which we could have no confidence. Since Mark is more of a summary gospel than a historical document, there is not much from this gospel that we can learn about Jesus. Most of the chreias and parables are in Matthew and Luke. Therefore, by following the Markan lead, as Albert Schweitzer declared, Jesus comes to us as one unknown – and some scholars prefer it that way. They do not want to admit that any of the political references to a king and a kingdom have anything to do with a real king and kingdom. With only the information that Mark provides, scholars can be free to conjecture a twenty-first century character that leads every movement the individual scholars approve. The result, however, is not the Jesus of history.

I do not accept that methodology. That is why I began this research. By finding ways to check the historical reliability of the gospels, I have learned that there is a lot that can be learned about Jesus, and it reveals a great leader who was a skilled statesman and a very intelligent legal scholar with high ethical principles. By studying ancient drama and legal concepts, I learned how Jesus could be born of a human mother and born again as a Son of God, how there could be a legal trinity, a dramatic virgin birth, and a meaningful resurrection. All of this is part of our religion that we can celebrate. Early Christians who understood the culture

and the concepts knew what it meant. It has been confusing t
Christians who thought only in scientific western terms or in terms
of black magic. But once we learn the ancient concepts, it makes
sense also to us. With all of the data available, skepticism is not
reasonable. Magic is not necessary, and grace is accessible. These
years of investigation have delivered me from unnecessary doubt
and skepticism and provided me a great sense of appreciation.

Salvation and Study. I have also been rescued from the fantasy
of unquestioning faith as well as the unreasonable projection of
a fictional Jesus who was like a glorified fairy godmother who
could wave a wand and change pumpkins into chariots or like the
superman in the comic strips that could fly though the air like a
bird or appear as a normal human being, whichever he chose. The
facts I have discovered show that Jesus was not a demi-god who
had infallible judgment, who knew everything without studying,
who never made a mistake, never suffered or was anxious, who was
fully human but had no human limitations, and was also physically,
fully God. I am not confronted with irrational inconsistencies.

The Jesus I have come to know does not fit all western ideas of
perfection. He was not born into poverty. He was not a myth, nor
a great labor leader, nor a champion of women's rights. He did not
promote democracy. He was an exceptionally competent political
leader in his own age and spoke the language of his people. He
spoke to people of his own day and not directly to our day. We
receive his message only through the agency of the church that
has given us a faithful representation.

By researching the data without accepting rhetorical limits I
have learned that the church can recognize obvious insights and
accept the truth. It requires a firmer faith, a greater trust, and
better sense to dare to question than to apply rhetorical blinders,
hypotheses, and default settings to hide the facts. The further
question that all of this poses is, "Once we think of Jesus as a
remarkable human being, what do we do with this knowledge? Can
we benefit from his teachings and goals without being limited to
them?" Within the basic assumptions and limitations, which Jesus

ɔm his society and tradition, it would be difficult to find
... his ability, dedication, motivation, ethics, or judgment.

Reality and Ethics. In the western world, however, after 2,000
years of scientific advancement, Christian laymen and women
still ask more questions: Are Christians required to accept the
same limitations as those imposed on first century Christians? Is
it disrespectful to Jesus to acknowledge that twenty-first century
Christians might have learned some things in 2,000 years that
were not known in Jesus' day? Is it wrong to think that Jesus was
right when he said his legal agents would do greater things than
he had done? He apparently expected that to happen. Great
leaders normally organize corporations to extend their own
influence beyond their own abilities. How great would insurance,
fast food, computer, hardware, or lumber companies be without
corporations, legal agents, and franchises?

During my lifetime farmers studied almanacs to anticipate weather
conditions and plan their agricultural activities. These were not very
reliable. They would have been more reliable in the Near East where
half of the year is always rainy and half of the year is always dry than
in the Mid-western USA where the seasons vary greatly. Nevertheless
almanacs were used in the Mid-west, because there was not much
else available. The people who composed almanacs did the best they
could with the limited data available. Now, however, we have the
benefit of satellites, and we hear weather predictions on the news
regularly. Weather prophets are amazingly accurate! They not only
tell us whether it is going to rain, snow, or be sunny, but they even
tell us within a few degrees what the next day's temperature will be.
Very few people rely on almanacs any more.

Those who no longer anticipate weather conditions on the
basis of an almanac might question the wisdom of still following
a projected calendar of predestined historical events as they were
conjectured and assumed in Jesus' day without the benefit of
satellites. The techniques employed for predictions in Jesus' day
were similar to the ones used by the authors of weather almanacs,
and they were often mistaken in their own days. For example, in

A. D. 66, Jews reasoned that their relationship with Rome at that time was very similar to the relationship between Jews and Syrians in about 68 B. C., when Judas the Maccabee began a guerrilla war against the Syrians that lasted 3½ years before Judas won a famous battle and returned to Jerusalem with a great deal of Syrian military equipment and cleansed the temple at Zion. That was a victorious war, and it was a predestined history that was part of a determined plan. It fit in to a special time cycle that rotated systematically. According to their almanac, it seemed to first century A.D. Jews that they were then in the very place in the predestined cycle of time as the Maccabees had been when they began the revolt against the Syrians, in the second century B.C.

Since they wanted the same result that Judas the Maccabee obtained, all they had to do was to tie into the wheel of destiny and ride it out for 3½ years and they were certain to obtain freedom from Rome, just as Judas had obtained freedom from Syria. This was the clue from their cyclical "almanac." So they started the war that lasted 3½ years. They fought bitterly for 3½ years, but after they were forced to surrender unconditionally to the Romans, they reasoned that since they were not successful after 3½ years, they had somehow misread the signs. But they did not believe that their almanac could be wrong, so in A.D. 132, they tried it again, and Bar Cochba led an all-out war against Rome again. After 3½ years they again concluded that they had misread the signs. You might think they would stop relying on that cyclical almanac, but they continued believing that it was infallible. Between then and 1940 there were 75 more identifiable Jewish military messianic rebellions, somewhere in the world, and each time some leader declared that the signs were right, and they would have to lead another war against Rome. Each event resulted in failure.

Do you remember Hal Lindsey[1]? After 1967, he declared that according to his almanac, the world would come to an end by 1974.

---

[1]   H. Lindsey with C. C. Carlson, *The Late Great Planet Earth* (Grand Rapids: Zondervan, 1971).

On TV he said that by 1974 he would be recognized either as a prophet or a fool. So? What have we learned? These facts prompt some rather practical questions: After all of these experiences, is it reasonable to think the system works? Is that almanac a reliable guide to national action and the conduct of "holy" wars? The almanac Jews and early Christians used to predict future history was not intended to apply to western culture 2,000 years later. It was understood for NT times and for Palestinian geography. It failed even in those times. Why would anyone think it could be used to apply to the 21st century? Failure seems to be no deterrent. More than a hundred years ago Johannes Weiss confronted the failure by changing the goals. Instead of national victory, he started the clock ticking for the end of the world, with the old almanac still in place.

Would Christians still be satisfied with a kingdom as a form of government? Is a purified temple or undefiled monastery the only place where God can be present? We owe a lot to the monks who have preserved the Scriptures over the centuries and designed the earliest legal communities. It was the monks that broke away from paternalistic administration and taught us how to organize movements without familial limitations, with presidents, secretaries, and treasurers. Nevertheless, we might question the ancient monastic assumption that God can be present only in a monastery or temple.

Phineas theology was based on a logical fallacy. The Psalmist reasoned that just because the disease that was afflicting the Israelites ran itself out sometime after Phineas had killed the Israelite, Zimri and his foreign wife, that this murderous act of Phineas caused the disease to stop. This is called *post hoc, propter hoc* logic. That means that everything that happens before something else is the cause of the following event. That has been recognized as a logical falacy for centuries. For example if a person washed his or her car in the morning and it rained in the afternoon, the car washing did not cause the rain – even though it happened before the rain. Suppose you drove your car over a nail in the road and got a flat tire. Did the nail cause the flat? Yes, but suppose you brushed your teeth that morning before you got the flat. Did brushing your teeth cause the flat tire? No! That is the faulty logic of the Psalmist who evaluated the act of Phineas, and Jesus recognized that. The psalmist thought that this act of Phineas was that which God reckoned as righteousness even though it was in direct conflict with Abraham's act of faith that was reckoned as righteousness. When the Apostle Paul learned of the new body of Christ that Jesus established, he gave up his Phineas theology of salvation by zeal and accepted the example both of Abraham and Jesus of salvation by faith. In the name of Phineas, Christians have led the Crusades, the Spanish inquisitions, and the conquests of Mexico and Peru. Following Phineas, European Christians reasoned that the only good American Indian was a dead American Indian. Like Zimri's wife, the American Indian was not a Christian, so he or she deserved to die. That is prejudiced logic that is faulty. Other sons of Abraham, namely Jews and Muslims, have also forgotten Abraham's example and have followed Phineas to take over lands owned by others and to kill those who were not members of their clan. Is it necessary for Jews, Christians, and Muslims to contradict the conclusions of Jesus and Paul in order to continue to follow Phineas?

How important is the isolation and segregation of monasticism? Is nationalism the highest ideal? What about the apartheid doctrine of election that Phineas encouraged? Did God create all of the world's population and choose to love only a few who happen to belong to the right family, race, or nation? Is it possible for anything that is biblical, traditional, Jewish, Christian, and Muslim still to be bad and need reformation? It is important for Jews, Muslims, and Christians to struggle for ethical answers to these and other questions rather than just wait until reasonable answers happen accidentally. It would be still better if all of the legal children of Abraham were to discuss them together.

It is possible to hold to a tradition, appreciate it, and even celebrate it without clinging to every detail of the tradition. A good example of that is the relationship that has existed for years between England and Scotland. They have fought in military battles for years. The tribal Scots all had tribal colors, which they wore to declare their loyalty to their tribes. These were the equivalent of waving anti-English flags, and the English did not like it. When the English overpowered the Scots they forbad them to wear these loyalty colors, and the Scots resented that very much. They kept their colors in hiding. When finally they were allowed to wear the colors again openly, they devoted a special day in May each year to come to their churches and dedicate their colors on the altar of the church as a sign of the great religious feeling they had for these anti-English colors and the independence they declared. This was called the "Kirkin of the Tartans."

Around Washington, D.C. there are so many proud Scots who want to celebrate the Kirkin of the Tartans that there is no other church that will hold them except in the Anglican Cathedral, so this is where the celebration takes place. It is still a great expression of Scottish loyalty and pride, but the anti-English military conflict is over. The English allow their greatest church in America to help the Scots celebrate this meaningful expression of faith that was once an expression of hostility. The Scots come to the Anglican Cathedral, parading their tartans, playing their bagpipes and bass drums, and laying their colors on the altar of the Anglican cathedral. There is no sign that it will ever stop, but no one expects a guerrilla war to break out on that day. That is a wonderful way for deeply divided groups to change and still maintain their history and tradition. Sometime in the distant future Jews, Christians, and Muslims may also live in peace together, reserving all of our holy war theology to pageantry and celebration. By then we will have learned the foolishness of following Phineas.

The kinds of questions that laymen and women used to ask me when I was a pastor are still legitimate. They are not to be feared but encouraged. Many times there are answers for questions, but not always. There is more to life in this world than we can ever ask or think. There will always be a mystery to religion. As new facts are learned and cultural changes appear it is almost necessary and ethical for religion to make appropriate changes as well, holding still to all that is good, including ancient celebrations.

The physical resurrection of Jesus is not all there is to Easter, and the physical virgin birth of Jesus is not all there is to Christmas. It is not a federal crime or anything that requires punishment of any kind for a person to believe in the physical virginity of Mary before Jesus' birth or the physical resurrection of Jesus, but the early church did not emphasize the physical dimensions of these doctrines. Therefore, it is important for the church to remember also the legal birth of Jesus and the legal resurrection of the body of Christ.

Jesus is still important to the church, and there is much more historical data about Jesus that is available for examination than has been recognized, and much of this deserves the highest admiration and praise. Nevertheless there are many things that modern Christians do and teach that never occurred to Jesus, because he did not confront those problems or situations. If these are ethical and upright, there is no reason Christians should not continue to do them, but not in Jesus' name. Jesus did not invent computers or flush toilets. It is not legitimate historical analysis to project onto Jesus all of the questions we ask today or to claim that our conclusions were also his, just because we like them and think our arguments would succeed better if they were attributed to Jesus.

We should study history as carefully and as accurately as we can – not just so that we should confine ourselves to the limitations of ancient science or ancient moral judgments. Based on his knowledge of his Jewish tradition, Jesus opened some new paths, and he expected his disciples to continue. Jesus expected the church to project his legal body and to do greater things than he did (John 14:12). The teachings of Jesus should motivate us to understand the goals and motivations of Jesus and inspire us to similar goals and commitments as we confront ethical problems that were unknown in Jesus' day.

The answers found here open up still more opportunities for questions. I discovered some of the answers while researching the life of Jesus. I learned what the ancients meant by the concepts they used that had been confusing to us. When these meanings were understood, their statements make sense. There will always be more valid questions for the person with an analytical mind who has enough faith to test the available data and enough good sense to trust his or her own judgment. The church can benefit from all the available insights.

The trail that I followed was both interesting and important. The discovery that I made was still more important than the trail. There is now no question that the real Jesus of history existed. It is no longer fair to consider the gospels the biased compositions of later writers who obtained their materials and training from oral gossip groups and wrote and published them to promote their own views. The character of the Jesus discovered at the end of the trail is outstanding. His sayings are faithfully preserved in the gospels, and the gospels themselves were composed and edited by skillful literary writers who preserved the teachings of Jesus and the reports about Jesus much more reliably than modern scholars have recognized. The more critically the gospels are analyzed the better they are found to be. The more we know about Jesus the more reason we have for admiration and praise.

APPENDIX

PROBLEMS WITH HISTORICAL JESUS RESEARCH

Schweitzer, Kähler, and Brown. Some of the problems I confronted fifty years ago are still with us today. For example, Dan Brown's new book, *The Da Vinci Code*[1] challenged many beliefs of American Christians, and James Tabor's, *The Dynasty of Jesus* followed it. This has left many Christians wondering who and what the historical Jesus really was. People are asking, "Will the real Jesus please stand up?" This is not a new problem. More than a century ago, Martin Kähler was one of the first theologians to question the possibility of using the gospels as sources for the scientific biography of Jesus. He concluded that the authors who wrote the liberal lives of Jesus had failed. Fourteen years later Albert Schweitzer surveyed the liberal lives of Jesus throughout the eighteenth and nineteenth centuries, planning to write a book on the historical Jesus. Following Kähler, he concluded that it was impossible to write such a book. Instead

---

[1]   D. Brown, *The Da Vinci Code* (New York: Doubleday, 2003).

he wrote a book telling about his project. The English translation of that book is called *The Quest of the Historical Jesus*. It has been widely read, and many people remember some words of his final paragraph: "He comes to us as one unknown, without a name."[1] The reason we cannot know about the historical Jesus, Schweitzer said, was two fold:

1) Christians are so highly committed to some particular notion about Jesus that they cannot enter the quest objectively,[2] and

2) It is impossible to separate the teachings of Jesus from the additions of the later church.

Because we could not learn about the historical Jesus, Schweitzer turned the readers' attention to eschatology. He held that our only alternative to skepticism was eschatology. Following Johannes Weiss he held that the goal of Jesus was not historical at all but looked to the end of this world and time. This has been complemented by Darby's "the rapture," which still claims the beliefs of many Christians.

Dibelius and Bultmann. About 25 years after Schweitzer's book was published two German scholars, Martin Dibelius,[3] and Rudolf Bultmann,[4] tried to solve Schweitzer's historical problem from

[1] A. Schweitzer, *The Quest of the Historical Jesus*, tr. W. Montgomery, Susan Cupitt, and John Bowden (Minneapolis: Fortress Press, 2001), p.487.

[2] M. Grant, *Jesus: An Historian's Review of the Gospels* (New York: Charles Scribner's Sons, c1977), p. 200, noted that critics still claim that it is impossible for Christians to be objective. Martin Kähler wrestled with this problem even before Schweitzer. M. Kähler, *The So-Called Historical Jesus and the Historic Christ*, tr. C. E. Braaten (Philadelphia: Fortress Press, c1954).

[3] M. Dibelius, *From Tradition to Gospel*, tr. B. L. Woolf (London, 1934).

[4] R. Bultmann, *Die Geschichte der synoptischen Tradition* (Göttingen, 1931).

a literary point of view. They studied the gospels to determine which kind of literary forms would be the most likely ones to record the teachings of Jesus. They both looked to small units. Bultmann thought the earliest form was the *apothegm* (Greek *apopthegmata*), known by the early Greeks that might have been used by Jesus, and not by the early church but the *apothegm* was not a very distinctive form. It was a story of almost any length and character. How could *apothegms* be used to determine the teachings of Jesus from any other materials? Bultmann, himself, doubted that *apothegms* were really sayings of the historical Jesus. Most of them were legendary and of Hellenistic origin, in Bultmann's opinion. In fact he said there was nothing certain about the life of Jesus in the gospel reports except the crucifixion. Discouraged with his results Bultmann gave up this research and turned to existential philosophy.

Dibelius conjectured the *paradigm* as a small unit, which he distinguished from the *novel*, which was more extensive.[1] He thought these units developed out of preaching and teaching and were used as texts for preaching. Except for the passion narratives, which Dibelius thought were the very earliest of the reported words of Jesus, the paradigms were the second earliest teachings of Jesus on record. They were not quoted words of Jesus, but words that came from the oral preaching about Jesus.[2] Dibelius conjectured these from small statements found in the Gospel of Mark that contained pronouncements of Jesus. Taylor called these "pronouncement stories." Dibelius identified eight of these in Mark (Mark 2:1 ff., 18 ff., 23 ff.; 3:1 ff., 20 ff.; 10:13 ff.; 12:13 ff., 14:3),

---

[1]   M. Dibelius, *From Tradition to Gospel.* Tr. B. L. Woolf (London, 1934).

[2]   J. Dunn has modified Dibelius' conjecture. Instead of the oral preaching, Dunn argued that there were discussion groups in the early church that talked about Jesus from time to time, and that the earliest expressions of Jesus emerged from these oral groups that later formulated Jesus' words into writing. Dunn expressed this conjecture at an SNTS meeting in Germany, 2002.

and since he believed Mark was the earliest gospel, he searched only this gospel, assuming that all of the teachings recorded in Matthew and Luke were composed by the later church. Dibelius knew about the literary form, "chreia", but he did not understand its definition or limitations. He thought it could be either brief or extensive. Units that he gave as examples from Xenophon were not chreias.

It is not surprising that these two scholars could not identify better the literary forms used in the NT that were found and defined by the Greek rhetoricians. Chreias existed and are clearly defined. But today they are available in very technical classical Greek documents that are difficult to understand.[1] Neither Bultmann nor Dibelius worked through these Greek books of grammar. Their efforts did not last very long.

After these two scholars there was a steady progressive movement away from literary and critical aspects of the gospels to the gospels' theological importance. Instead of textbooks on the introduction to the literature of the First Testament and the New Testament, college and theological seminary professors taught from textbooks on biblical theology. The anti-Jewish movement in Europe before and during the Second World War had strengthened this movement. Christian scholars used psychological and philosophical methods of avoiding early Christian and Jewish history.

The New Questers. There has been a slow movement back to historical interest in Jesus because of the Dead Sea Scrolls that have

---

[1]   I. Spengel, *Rhetores Graeci* (Leipzig, 1856) 3 vols.; H. Rabe, *Rhetores Graeci* (Leipzig, 1926); C. Walz, *Rhetores Graeci* (Stuttgart, 1834-36. Even if you look up every technical word in the unabridged Liddell and Scott's, *Greek-English Lexicon*, it is still difficult to determine the distinctive meanings in their given contexts. I worked at this for 12 years before I was comfortable with the messages intended. That is probably the reason Bultmann and Dibelius did not use these forms more carefully.

been found before there had been any possibility of later editing. In Europe, Ernest Käsemann, C. H. Dodd,[1] and Herbert Braun,[2] tried to revive the quest. In America some of the best known of these were James Robinson,[3] Norman Perrin,[4] Michael Grant,[5] and Robert Funk,[6] but Schweitzer's problem has not yet been solved. Käsemann said,

> Our Gospels believed, in all good faith, that they possessed a tradition about the earthly Lord, which was reliable over wide stretches of its content. Historical criticism has shattered this good faith as far as we ourselves are concerned. We can no longer assume the general reliability of the Synoptic tradition about Jesus. Worse still, we cannot improve the situation merely by making corrections in the tradition in the light of historical criticism.[7]

Käsemann also said that Christianity "is not minded to allow myth to take the place of history nor a heavenly being to take the place of the Man from Nazareth."[8] The problem is not, just as Käsemann thought, that historical criticism has destroyed the basis for faith. It is that criticism has not gone far enough to validate the gospels. That which the new questers did not even attempt was also not

1   C. H. Dodd, *The Founder of Christianity* (New York: Macmillan, 1970).

2   H. Braun, *Jesus: Der Man aus Nazareth und seine Zeit* (Stuttgart: Kreuz, 1969).

3   J. Robinson, A *New Quest of the Historical Jesus* (Naperville, Ill.: Allenson, 1959).

4   N. Perrin, *Rediscovering the Teaching of Jesus* (New York, 1967).

5   M. Grant, *Jesus*.

6   R. Funk, *The Acts of Jesus* (San Francsco: Harper San Francisco 1998).

7   E. Käsemann, "Reopening the Quest," ed. G. W. Dawes, *The Historical Jesus Quest* (Louisville: Westminster John Knox Press, 2000), pp. 299-300.

8   Käsemann, "Reopening," p. 290

done by Dibelius and Bultmann. That was to discover how to distinguish the teachings of Jesus from the additions of the later church. Both Dibelius and Bultmann knew there were Greek literary forms, such as the chreia, but they did not know their definitions or their limitations. The interest in Jesus has continued, but the critical literary development has been minimal, so we are still left with the skepticism Käsemann expressed.

The computer in the library at Wesley Theological Seminar contains a list of 5,484 items related to Jesus. This indicates that people are still interested in Jesus. Anyone who checks all of these titles, however, will find very few that deal with critical literary or historical problems. There are a few, like David Flusser,[1] W. D. Davies,[2] Geze Vermes,[3] and Richard A. Horsley,[4] who reported on Jesus historically, just the way they would have treated the writings about such ancient figures as Plato, Aristotle, Julius Caesar, or Rabbi Johanan ben Zakkai, without solving the problem claimed by scholars who argue that most of the gospel material was added by the later church and was therefore invalid. These did not wrestle with the question that Kähler proposed and Schweitzer asked. Many consensus scholars would dismiss these works, for their failure to recognize them as later interpretations of Jesus, on the one hand, or, like Kähler, on the other hand, for their failure to be committed to the true doctrine before beginning research. Johnson studied the results of the new questers extensively and called some of their efforts "madness."

He said,

> At some point, the question must be asked whether an epistemological monism has not in fact distorted the very

---

[1]   D. Flusser, *Jesus*, tr. R. Walls (New York: Herder and Herder, 1969).

[2]   *The Sermon on the Mount* (Cambridge: Cambridge U. Press, 1966).

[3]   G. Vermes, *Jesus the Jew* (London: Collins, 1973).

[4]   R. A. Horsley, "Abandoning the Unhistorical Quest for an Apolitical Jesus," J. D. G. Dunn, and S. McKnight, *The Historical Jesus in Recent Research* (Winona Lake: Eisenbrauns, 2005), pp. 288-301.

concept of history by insisting on discovering history where it cannot be found. Does the multiplication of contradictory hypotheses – each apparently with an infinite shelf life – suggest that this branch of scholarship really has no hard criteria at all with which to test theories?[1]

The term "history" has been so loosely used among the new questers that Aulén did not use the term in relationship to Jesus. Instead of the historical Jesus, Aulén used the expression, the "earthly Jesus."[2] Johnson further objected to the new questers' tendency to separate the gospels from other NT books, which are thought to predate the gospels. Johnson held that the gospels were themselves legitimate sources, and taken as a whole present a pattern of Jesus that is reasonable and consistent.[3]

James Dunn obviously wanted to get back to the flesh and blood Jesus. He first claimed that there was no distinction between the Jesus of history and the faith of Christ. He said, "The first forms of the Jesus tradition were indeed the expression of faith."[4] All the historical data began with faith. Then he emphasized the impression that Jesus made on people, which is true. He also emphasized the fact that people in Jesus' day spoke orally and had good memories. He said,

> Once again the point is that the tradition was *living tradition* [italics his], celebrated in the communal gatherings of the earliest churches. There was no concern to recall all the exact words of Jesus; in many cases the

1   L. M. Johnson, *The Real Jesus* (San Francisco: Harper San Francisco, c1996), p. 101.
2   G. Aulén, *Jesus in Contemporary Historical Research* (Philadelphia: Fortress Press, 1976), p. 15.
3   Johnson, *The Real Jesus*, pp. 151-158.
4   J. D. G. Dunn, *A New Perspective on Jesus* (Grand Rapids: Baker Academic, 2005), p.25.

precise circumstances in which the teaching was given
were irrelevant to its continuing value.[1]

Dunn said, "First-century Palestine certainly was an oral rather than
a literary culture." He acknowledged, "that royal officials, priests,
scribes, and Pharisees would have been made up of the majority
portion of the small literary minority." Then he said further," We
have to assume, therefore, that the great majority of Jesus' first
disciples would have been functionally illiterate. That Jesus himself
was literate cannot simply be assumed."[2]

One of the problems with the theories about the oral tradition is
that people who could read made the only written record we have
of the things that went on. They did not tell any of the detailed
claims Dunn made about the many church gatherings in which
the imaginary people talked about Jesus. How can Dunn know
that all of that happened?

One of the advantages of the oral tradition and all other
assumptions that none of the teachings of Jesus was original is
that it implies that the church that invented all of these teachings
was unreliable. By putting a great distance between Jesus and the
recorded teachings, the scholar is free to pick and choose the
teachings of Jesus, willy-nilly, to match the subjective ideas of the
western scholar. Those that do not match can be detailed as later,
inaccurate additions of the later church.

Dunn's detailed reconstruction of the oral tradition is nothing
new. It is simply more precise and specific in its fabrication. Sixty
years ago this was a widely accepted position. For example, in
1942 John Knox wrote,

These words of Jesus were not first written, and, even
when they were committed to writing, it was the

---

[1] J. D. G. Dunn, *Jesus Remembered* (Grand Rapids: Eerdmans Publishing
Co., c2003), p. 238.

[2] Dunn, *A New Perspective*, p. 36.

words themselves which had authority rather than the documents in which they were contained. But as time passed and memory faded and as the oral tradition became more diffused and unreliable, documents became more and more important, and it was inevitable that eventually they would be thought of as having something of the same value as the words of Jesus themselves.[1]

Like Dunn, Knox thought the gospels began orally, but the great oral modification came after they had been written down but were not used. Christians later turned to the written documents because the oral tradition was unreliable. Dunn did not think that there was a written tradition until after there had been a long period of oral modification.[2]

There is an amazing amount of literature that has been preserved from the Mediterranean area to have emerged from a culture where people could not read and write. It is true that people talked orally in Jesus' day, just as they do today, and they sometimes remembered what was said, but it was obviously not *only* an oral culture, and that which is preserved of the past is *only* the literate record. Some people could also read and write, and they wrote some things down to help them remember.

Dunn could affirm that the gospels were sources that were valid. They contained teachings of Jesus that had been preserved by the oral memory in their approximate form, but he could not show

---

[1] J. Knox, *Marcion and the New Testament* (Chicago: U. of Chicago Press, C1942), P. 27.

[2] Dunn, *A New Perspective*, p. 24. After Dunn's huge book, *Jesus Remembered* (Grand Rapids: Eerdmans, c2003), appeared, B. Gerhardsson, "The Secret of the Transmissions of the Unwritten Jesus Tradition," *NTS* 51 (2005):1-18, pointed out the many flaws in Dunn's conjecture.

1) that the gospels were not the products of the later church;
2) that the oral tradition was infallible; or
3) that the preserved material had not been influenced by oral or written development.

That which he did not have, but which he needed for his case, was a discovery of written sources that could be identified and tested for historical accuracy independent of the later gospels in which they had been preserved. The problems that Dunn left unsolved and the problems that Johnson discovered are valid. The challenge that is still left is one which this manuscript is accepting. There is valid history in the gospels themselves when it is properly recognized, and this history is not contingent for its validity on the distant memory of oral expressions of faith or the existence of any hypothetical document.

This appendix is only a summary of the many attempts of new questers. For an extensive analysis of this problem, see C. A. Evans, *Fabricating Jesus* (Downers Grove, Il.: IVP Books, c2006).

INDICES

WORDS

GEOGRAPHY

ANCIENT PERSONALITIES

MODERN SCHOLARS